RAMBLES ON THE EDGE

WENDY MAITLAND

Published by Dolman Scott in 2020

ISBN: 978-1-911412-94-6
iBooks: 978-1-911412-96-0
Kindle: 978-1-911412-95-3

Also by Wendy Maitland:
Rambles with my Family – Published in April 2017 (978-1-911412-44-1)
Rift Valley Rambles – Published in April 2018 (978-1-911412-65-6)

Published by Dolman Scott Ltd
www.dolmanscott.co.uk

Also by Wendy Maitland:

Rambles with my Family – Published in April 2017 (978-1-911412-44-1)

These are no ordinary rambles, and the family is no ordinary family. On the first page they trip innocently into a war zone and the story gathers pace as they flee from one hazard to the next. These perils don't end with the war as the family becomes nomadic, led by a headstrong, intrepid father who is restless and driven. As his family ever more hopefully clings to dreams of normality, the story is both funny and tragic but, always compelling.

"This is a completely delightful narrative, written in an easy and fluid style. It portrays a significant time in history and is totally engaging in its multiplicity of themes. The author expertly and honestly describes the complexity and influences of family dynamics and all that becomes normalised in the interactions. Throughout the narrative one is led to admire stoicism and realise the power of endurance in challenging circumstances. It was a huge disappointment to reach the last page and know that there would be no further opportunity to be enveloped in the life and times of this intriguing and unique family."

Rift Valley Rambles – Published in April 2018 (978-1-911412-65-6)

RIFT VALLEY RAMBLES continues the story told in Rambles with my Family as Wendy returns to Kenya at the age of twenty four, leaving behind the jumbled misfortunes of life at home as she sets out to find new purpose and direction in a country on the verge of independence from colonial rule. She arrives with hopes and plans that are quickly challenged as it remains a recurring feature in these rambles that nothing ever goes quite to plan. Setbacks impose themselves unpredictably alongside a shifting tide of history that in Africa has its own momentum and drama. The observation of these events with candid humour provides an antidote to misadventure, while all this takes place on a farm in the great wide, wild and glorious Rift Valley of Kenya during a time of political change and evolution.

"This is the long awaited second part following "Rambles with my family" by Wendy Maitland. Having read her first book I was desperate to know what happened next. It is an inspiring account depicting the life of a remarkable woman in Africa during the sixties. Like the first novel (which I highly recommend to read first) I was unable to put the book down (252 pages!). The author has the gift to draw you into a different place and time. Having read the difficult journey through her childhood in her first book I was amazed about her ability to forgive others and concentrate on the joys of life as a young married woman. Her own liberal and non-judgmental views give her account of events great credibility. If we all had a little bit of Wendy's honest and fine humoured character in us, the world would be a truly magical place."

To Charles
who from his head and his heart
gives the most generous of gifts

Introduction

This is the third book in a series based on the true story of my family as we became caught up in world events from the start of the Second World War to a roller-coaster of family dynamics as normal life failed to resume. In this concluding book the story moves from Kenya to Rhodesia where we arrive full of optimism with no inkling of future events. During the closing years of white rule there were many good and happy times to enjoy, until the ferocity of what became a terrifying war erupted with destabilising force and sent us on a new search for somewhere safe to live. As usual in these rambles, nothing goes entirely to plan, and there is both tragedy and comedy as the story unfolds.

Right at the top of the list of people to thank this time are those like you reading this introduction, so you are included among generous readers who wanted another book and encouraged me to go on with the story. Then there is Ros, and Louise too, for their corrections if I have got things wrong. Next there is my very kind friend Sue Daly who puts photos and text together and gets it all sent off, and before any of this can be done there is wonderful Vivien Lipski who edits and assists my ramblings: thank you Vivien, and all of you.

People who have appeared in previous stories turn up again in this one, so they are mentioned here to avoid confusion:

David	a family friend
Adam	my husband
Louise, Simon and Peter	our children
Fa and Muz (Craddock)	my parents
Babs	Fa's new wife
Andy	Muz's new love
Elaine and Ros	my sisters
Andrew (Spindle)	my brother
Les	Elaine's husband
Len	a previous admirer of Muz
Lanner	long lost love of mine
Alison and Cen (Hill)	Adam's parents
Fran	a family friend
Nakuru	the town in Kenya where I grew up
Glanjoro	the Hill family farm in Kenya

CONTENTS

Chapter 1

As soon as the decision to leave Kenya had been made, it was as if we had launched ourselves like surfers on an unstoppable wave rolling at speed towards a far shore that was only vaguely visible. There was very little time to get our move underway and my main concern had been for our much loved Kipsigis ayah Elizabeth, who was grief-stricken to be losing 'her' children (having no confidence that I was capable of looking after them myself), and finding a new family for her where she would be appreciated and well treated. She and David had established a link through mutual despair at our departure and he promised that he would take care of her until a new position was found.

He came to help me pack up, bringing tea boxes and piles of newspapers, telling me that army people are experts at packing and moving as that is what they do all the time. He was an immensely kind and reassuring person to have around, practical and methodical, while Adam disassociated himself from any actual hands-on involvement in the packing-up process, saying that he had better things to do. He was planning a route for us to drive through Tanzania and Mozambique to our new home in Rhodesia, carrying as much luggage as could fit inside and on top of our Cortina Estate. Adam's valiant 1956 Land Rover that had seen us through so many years of adventures and never let us down, very sadly had to be sold.

The Labradors, Roger and Ruin, were despatched to an animal transport company in Nairobi from where they would be flown by cargo plane to Salisbury. Our third dog, Beetle, had already gone to join the pack at

Glanjoro House, which was a good move for her as one of the Pointers was her mother.

We were almost ready to leave when Fa decided it was too risky for us to drive with a baby thousands of miles through the African bush, without medical facilities or any kind of civilised amenity along the way. All we could be sure of encountering, he said, were swarms of mosquitoes and tsetse flies and insisted that I should go by plane with the children while Adam took the car. There would be more space in the car for luggage that way too, he suggested.

David once again helped out and took me to the airport with the children and Elizabeth, resulting in a highly distressing scene as we said goodbye and Elizabeth refused to let go of Peter, clinging onto him and wailing so loudly that ground staff came to see if he was being kidnapped. By this time all of us were sobbing and David had to prise Peter from Elizabeth's arms, putting his own arm around her as he led her away through the airport, and I felt utterly bereft. For months and years afterwards, the person I missed more than anyone was Elizabeth. She was much more than a nanny: she had been a kind and motherly figure to me as well as the children, scolding me when I was forgetful or made silly mistakes, but most of all laughing with me and being perpetually cheerful and loving.

Friends told us the difference between Kenya and Rhodesia could be summed up as follows: 'Kenya is the Officers' Club and Rhodesia is the Sergeants' Mess.' I was curious about this distinction and wanted to see what was meant by it when we became part of this new society. European settlers in Kenya were mainly British, which they might have thought gave them an edge, while many Rhodesians were descendants of Dutch Afrikaner families who had trekked north from South Africa to escape the aftermath of the Boer War. The conditions they endured were so brutally harsh, they needed to be very tough to survive and had done so with pride in this new country.

Adam had accepted a dairy manager's job offer by post from a farm at Gwelo in the southern part of Rhodesia, without meeting the owners or seeing the farm in advance of our arrival. Up to this point our only contact with Rhodesia had been a brief excursion a few weeks earlier to have a quick look around. This had followed reports from friends already there who sent glowing accounts of the country's prosperity and lifestyle with, in particular, excellent schools, which for us was a pressing issue now that Louise had reached school age.

Kenya was our home and leaving was something we could never have contemplated before independence in 1963 brought uncertainty for those of us who, despite feeling we were Kenyans and having a deep allegiance to the country, were not indigenous Kenyans and that was a crucial difference. Adam had been born in Kenya and knew no other life apart from school in England, so it was more wrenching for him to leave, but Rhodesia was still Africa and offered a quality of life enhanced by an environment of surpassing beauty and diversity. The splendid mountains, thorn trees and golden savannahs of Kenya were there replaced by monumental granite outcrops rising from the russet colours of Mopani woodlands and plains: Africa in a different guise, but no less glorious.

Our nearest neighbours in Gwelo were Afrikaners, Letty and Henk, who spoke Afrikaans at home with their children, either Shona or Ndebele on the farm with the African workers, and English when they were with us. Swahili was unknown and everything felt very different and foreign, especially the climate: scorching hot just then at the height of the southern African summer and, later on, bitterly cold in winter.

We moved into the dairy manager's house with the possessions that Adam had managed to bring with him in the car, and waited for the dogs to arrive. We needed their company to help us feel like a normal family again. The animal transport service was an efficient organisation that handled all manner of live cargo for zoos as well as transporting domestic pets. Expert care from door to door was provided with veterinary supervision, at no little cost. Quarantine restrictions did not apply in this case and the dogs were delivered all the way to the farm, arriving in massive crates that looked solid enough to have transported lions, but were impressively clean with plenty of bedding. The dogs were in excellent health and spirits, leaping out to greet us ecstatically and race around sniffing all the new scents. Having them with us lifted morale all round.

Our house was quite superior by farm manager standards with a guest cottage and swimming pool in the garden, but best of all, a telephone. The owners of the farm were what Adam described as local cattle barons and lived in grand style, displaying their wealth in a way that successful farmers in Kenya never did. It was almost a point of honour among those who were better-off in Kenya settler communities that the more you had in the bank, the less you let it show, which in some cases meant very short rations for farm managers and other employees. Here in Gwelo our new bosses, Lawrence and Thelma Maclean, exhibited none of that modesty and were in addition devout Baptists who believed in Christian charity, heaping us with generous perks and hospitality. Adam had been surprised and delighted to find that he was in charge of a pedigree Friesian herd luxuriating in cultivated pastures, with a modern milking parlour and well-trained, reliable labour.

Simon, now three years old, went with him everywhere and was called 'Baas Stompie' by the African workers, amusing them as he scurried about on his short (*stompie*) legs. Peter was already walking at ten months and sometimes went along too, hand in hand or carried piggy-back by Simon who was his devoted carer. African children often carried babies on their backs, but Thelma Maclean disapproved of Simon doing the same. 'Going around like an African,' she complained, and insisted on engaging a nanny for us, explaining that it was important for us to have the right kind of nanny. 'We don't have *ayahs* here,' she said. 'That's for Indians.'

We had arrived in time for Christmas 1969 and I went to look for cards to buy in Gwelo town, twenty miles from the farm, after dropping Louise at primary school. She had settled into Class 1 enthusiastically, expecting that she would be reading and writing within days since being given new pencils and an exercise book.

Gwelo was a sizeable town on the main road running all the way from the capital city, Salisbury, to the Limpopo river marking the border with South Africa. It was a big step up for us from Nakuru's one street of hugger-mugger shops with very little choice or variety. Gwelo had department stores and restaurants along pavements lined with flowering trees that spread their bright petals like confetti underfoot. I could even buy a newspaper, a rare treat, at one of the stationery shops selling Christmas cards. Some of the cards showed the usual nativity scenes and among them were others that stood out with bold lettering. 'Those are the most popular ones,' the shop assistant said when she saw me looking at them. Printed across a snow scene there was a caption in large letters: 'KEEP CHRISTMAS WHITE.' I stared at the words, dismayed. That kind of message would not be tolerated by anyone in Kenya and I had not been expecting anything like that here.

The Christmas cards symbolised an attitude that we became increasingly aware of, particularly on outings with the children and our new nanny, Alice, when we stopped at roadside cafés as we used to in Kenya, all sitting at a table together having something to eat and drink on a hot day. The first time we did this in Rhodesia we were told: 'Blacks are allowed in here, but they are not allowed to sit at the same table with whites.' This made me feel very uncomfortable and out of place after the more congenial manners of Kenya.

Despite the Maclean's kindness and the many advantages of the farm, I was terribly homesick for Kenya and a way of life that I fitted into, while in Gwelo I felt displaced. I missed Fa, and Muz too, disappointed that neither of them seemed inclined to visit. There was nothing connecting us to the rest of the family and all my friends, except letters.

A surprise visitor did come during those early months, introducing himself as Sidney Franklin from East Grinstead in Sussex, explaining that he was a friend of Fay Craddock (Muz) and wanted to meet us. She had not mentioned anything about this friend and we were intrigued. He was our first visitor and was a charming cultured man, a widower, who it turned out had known Muz for some time so her silence was puzzling, especially as it became clear during his stay that his feelings for her were more than casual. We sensed that he was looking for approval and that this had been the purpose of his visit. It was an approach that seemed very sensible, but how could he not know about the lurking presence of hopeful Andy, standing first in line of prospective suitors?

'I'll have to go and check on Muz,' I told Adam, 'and see what's going on with Andy, and why she hasn't told us about Sidney who is precisely the kind of man she should go for – genuinely caring, with his feet on the ground; also very well off so he could give her security.'

'Ros says your mother is still stuck in a bog of depression, taking all sorts of pills to help her sleep and stay sane. She might not be in a frame of mind to be receiving suitors, whoever they are.'

'All the more reason for me to go and see what's going on. But I'll have to get a job to pay for fares, I know that. Anyway I need a job; I need to use my nursing, and keep my brain in gear.'

Getting registered with the Rhodesian Nursing Council was straightforward and in less than a month I was working as nurse/receptionist for a surgeon, Mr Comline, at his consulting rooms in the town. This fitted in with school runs for Louise, and the boys were safe on the farm with Alice and Adam.

Mr Comline was very exact in the way he worked, slightly austere but devoted to his patients and highly regarded. As well as all routine clinical nurse procedures, I did his book-keeping, sent out bills, typed his letters and enjoyed every day at the surgery. The work was satisfying as I understood how Mr Comline liked things to be done after years observing Fa who was similarly meticulous. Mr Comline appreciated what I did for him so it was a mutually agreeable situation, besides which my wages were mounting up week by week.

There was a small hotel in the same street where I went for lunch each day and the same table was always reserved for me, with two places. A demure woman called Marguerite occupied the second place since the head waiter had put her there on my first day, which I thought was a friendly gesture and that Marguerite was an unusually friendly girl. All through lunch, every day, men would stop at our table to chat and make dates with her. She noted down days and times in a diary that she kept beside her on the table, making me curious.

'You seem to have an awful lot of boyfriends,' I remarked after a few days.

'They're not boyfriends, they're clients,' she laughed.

'What sort of clients?'

'What do you think?'

I looked at her, confused by the contrast between her modest appearance and what she was suggesting.

'I would never have guessed.'

'It's why the waiter put us together, to make things look respectable. You sitting there in your uniform sharing a table with me. You don't mind, do you?'

'Of course not. I like you. And your clients are always very polite to me.'

'You've given them ideas. Some of them want me to put on a uniform like yours now, when they come round. But it's kids' stuff compared with some of the weird nonsense they ask for.'

'Such as?'

'Not nice. But the worst are the police. They think they're entitled to freebies. It's mostly when they're on night shift, getting bored. They come round any hour when I've closed up and gone to sleep, waking me up for what they think is their perks. Then they want to hang around smoking and drinking while I'm trying to get rid of them, telling them I don't do night work.'

Gwelo was a surprising place, full of Dutch Reformed Church repression alongside more relaxed elements like Marguerite's services openly on offer, and others that Adam discovered when he went to have a haircut. Finding what looked like a barber shop with a sign saying 'Gentlemen's Hair Parlour,' he went inside and was directed to a booth in a line of similar booths occupied by men. This looked ordinary enough until he noticed that all the hairdressers were topless girls, wearing nothing but the briefest of mini-skirts.

'I didn't want to look as if I'd been caught off guard, so I had to pretend this was normal, sitting there with breasts bouncing around my face as scissors were applied to my hair,' Adam told me when he came home. 'You know how I detest mammary hyperplasia. It's bad enough in cows, but in humans, it's obscene.'

'You seem to have survived the ordeal, and you've had some proper styling for a change, instead of army scalping. What did it cost?'

'I can't even remember how many dollars I shelled out in the end. All I could think of was how to escape before getting suffocated.'

At weekends our swimming pool was popular with neighbours and friends. We enjoyed having *braais* (BBQs) and everyone contributed, bringing baskets and boxes of food and beer. The Afrikaner families brought *boerewors* sausage and enormous steaks as well as, for dessert, a type of doughnut that was a completely new discovery for us in the area of gastronomic thrills. These exquisite pastries were called *koeksisters*: made in the shape of plaits and deep-fried before being submerged in chilled syrup to come out golden and oozing. I had never encountered these before coming to Rhodesia, and there was another superb national favourite – piri-piri chicken, which appeared on all restaurant menus and was a staple of household menus too. *Braais* were an art form in Rhodesia and purists dug a pit or trench which was filled with burning logs under a metal grille, where the men of the party gathered with long forks to supervise the sizzling and turning of the meat. We had one of these *braai* pits in our garden and used it for parties despite my fear that a child might fall onto the burning embers. Our neighbours couldn't understand such squeamishness and said even the dogs knew better.

The pool was another wide-open menace, again laughed at by others, most of whom had their own unfenced pools and believed all objects, including children, were equipped with natural buoyancy. At one of our Saturday parties, watching children jump in and out of the pool with a great deal of noise and bobbing about in the water, it looked safe enough from where I was sitting with other mothers, drinking and chatting. Louise ran up at one point saying something that I couldn't hear through the clamour and thought couldn't be very important, until she started pulling urgently at my arm to get attention, when I caught the words: 'There's a baby in the bottom of the pool.' She pointed to a small shape lying on the pool floor, only faintly visible among the ripples. One of the older children, alerted by the sudden panic, dived down and retrieved the baby, lifting it up and bringing it to the side. Amazingly, as soon as it was out of the water it spluttered and cried, appearing none the worse for nearly drowning, but this incident showed how easy it was to miss a child slipping in unobserved despite so many watchers, and made me permanently wary of pools.

Peter had his first birthday at the farm with a tea party and cake with one candle, over which Simon hovered closely to blow it out for him should he hesitate. All the children who came were wearing their best clothes, under instruction from Thelma Maclean, I was told, to whom appearances mattered almost as much as Godliness. Peter had an infant-size safari suit for the occasion, following male fashion since all Rhodesian men wore safari suits: casual ones with shorts for every day, and smarter ones with long trousers for the office. School uniform for boys was a khaki suit of the same style with shorts, a very practical arrangement. Peter looked cute in his tiny outfit and was a charmer, always smiling and cheerful. His petite size was constantly remarked on as most other children his age were twice his weight and height, while he remained physically dainty with big dark eyes and long lashes that he was prone to blink beguilingly. I was impatient for Muz to meet him while he was still at this endearing age and it was not long after his party that I had enough money saved for fares, so I was able to gather up the children and take them to England. Direct flights from Salisbury to London were banned under sanctions and we had to fly to Johannesburg to catch a connection from there. Adam was nervous about letting us go, fearing the separation and how it might unsettle us even further. Rhodesia didn't feel like home. Despite its many advantages, we still felt like foreigners.

When I arrived with the children at Muz's house with its very English name, Forest Lodge, and there she was, waiting at the door in her apron, it felt wonderfully warm and welcoming after relays of very long cramped journeys by plane and train. The children thought it rather novel to have a gran as well as a grandma, and Louise was especially glad to see her Gran as she had missed grandma Alison along with so many other loved and familiar people left behind in Kenya. When Ros arrived for the weekend that was another excitement as she and Louise were already close, almost like sisters instead of aunt and niece. They actually resembled each other in looks as well as temperament, and even the way Louise walked reminded me of Ros at a similar age. Ros and Peter were meeting for the first time, and then there was Spindle who arrived to great fanfare from the children, his face radiant as he watched them playing with some of his old toys brought out for the occasion. Unable to resist joining in, he lay down on the floor with them, his long legs splayed out as they all tumbled about and Spindle became a happy child again, released from the constraints of hospital life, or home life, trying to conform to adult expectations.

Peter had lately grown into a habit of fastening himself onto one of my legs like a small monkey clinging to a tree branch for safety and comfort. All the recent travelling and unaccustomed activity seemed to have unnerved him. If I was wearing a skirt he would hide underneath, much to the amusement of Spindle who thought it comic that Peter was using my skirt as a tent. Having Peter clamped to my leg was limiting in a household with no domestic help and innumerable chores to be done, so Muz borrowed a play-pen from a neighbour and Peter was put behind bars. Spindle and the others played zoo games with him, roaring through the bars as he stood there trapped, while they jumped up and down and ran around the room pretending to be animals. This made him screech until the noise level erupted sufficiently to disturb Muz in the next room listening to serious music on the radio.

She decided that Louise was old enough to start ballet lessons at the Bush Davies School where she worked as its musical director, and we all went along to watch her first steps in the beginners' class as she entered self-consciously equipped with a pair of pink satin dancing shoes. Boys were not allowed into the house unless they were pupils, so Spindle was put in charge of Simon and Peter who were to wait outside in the garden, while the rest of us went in to watch the class. Miss Bush was a martinet who tolerated no interruptions and drilled her pupils with a steely eye and voice, tapping fiercely and frequently on top of the piano (at which Muz sat), to correct any dancing error or inattention.

It became evident quite quickly that Louise was never going to be a graceful light-footed dancer, and I didn't want her to be traumatised by Miss Bush's sharp criticisms. On this first day, long before the class ended, there was a sudden furious tapping on the piano lid by Miss Bush as she stared transfixed at figures with staring faces pressed against the windows of the room, looking in from outside.

'There are some horrid urchins observing us!' she cried, as if there might have been a hundred of them instead of just three ragged boys peering in. I ran outside and quickly pulled them away before Miss Bush could investigate, leaving Muz to bring Louise home. After that experience none of us dared go back, except Muz, who remarked that she hoped Miss Bush would never find out that the urchins were her own son and grandchildren.

Muz was in better spirits than I expected from Ros's reports and my arrival with the children clearly lifted her, but the real reason for her renewed optimism was a blossoming romance with childhood sweetheart Andy. I didn't have to wait long to meet him as it soon became obvious that he was a fixture in Muz's life, purring up the drive in his Austin Princess car, reverently rubbing a duster over it before he lumbered into the house. He plainly resented my presence and pointedly ignored me each time he arrived. Muz would hurry to greet him at the door, fumbling to remove her apron before being clutched by him in a clumsy embrace.

'My lovely little bit of feminine pulchritude waiting for me. Delicious Fay – I'm here again,' he would exclaim eagerly as Muz allowed herself to be seized in this blundering way. Ros and I thought it was horribly creepy and that there was something distinctly repellent about Andy altogether.

When I suggested to Muz that Sidney Franklin was a much more suitable prospect for her, she rejected it with a wave of the hand. 'He's much too old for me,' she said dismissively.

'He's not that old,' I argued, 'and he's done much more with his life than Andy who has spent his life doodling.

'Don't be silly. He had an important job as a draughtsman. It was a reserved occupation during the war, so he wasn't allowed to be called up because he was needed at home as part of the war effort.'

'It's hard to imagine Andy making an effort in any capacity let alone any extra exertions due to there being a war on. He's a nonentity – even Mary his sister says so.'

'I don't know why you're so down on him,' Muz replied defensively. 'He has a very loving nature. He is the only person who has ever helped me with Andrew, driving me to and from the hospital, taking an interest.'

'Sidney is very concerned about Andrew too, and wants to help. He has contacts that could get him released from hospital into sheltered accommodation, with support to lead a much more normal life.'

'Yes, I know about that, but I doubt Andrew would qualify. Sidney has all kinds of contacts in the health and education world. He is one of the governors of Christ's Hospital school and provides bursaries from his own money. He's a very generous man and a good friend, but Andy is the man of my heart since your father has gone.'

It seemed there was nothing more to be said now that Sidney was written off along with war hero Len (a previous suitor), and we were left with lumpy Andy. The looming prospect of a more formal partnership between him and Muz provoked me to increasingly desperate attempts at confronting her with the realities of such a scrounger becoming a permanent attachment. 'How can you put up with Andy being so lazy that he refuses to walk anywhere? He never does more than amble a few steps from his car to the nearest armchair. We are a walking family, it's in our DNA. It's what we do at every opportunity. We never sit about. You used to despise people like that.'

'It's because of his accident years ago. He never completely recovered his energy.'

'It's nothing to do with any accident,' I said scornfully. 'You said yourself he used to sit on his mother's lap even as a young man, just sitting there, lolling about.'

'Well, it was charming at the time, and now he likes me to sit on his lap, which is charming too. But not in front of you, of course, since you are so disapproving of our lovemaking.'

That observation put an end to any further conversation on the subject as any mention of lovemaking in association with Andy was too much to bear.

East Grinstead was in an area of glorious walking country that included Ashdown Forest where we took the children on mellow afternoons, Peter in a pushchair while Louise and Simon ran ahead. If Andy came too he would drive us there and then sit in the car reading a book while we walked. Ros likes to tell the story about one of these walks when I was wheeling Peter in the pushchair, deep in conversation with Muz, while Ros and Spindle walked behind. Peter stood up in the chair, pointing to a bird he had spotted, trying to draw my attention to it, but lost his balance and fell out of the chair onto the path in front. 'You never even noticed,' Ros reminds me on those occasions when family misdeeds are being revisited. 'You just ran him over with the empty pushchair and carried on completely oblivious, yakking away to Muz. When you eventually noticed, and stopped to pick him up, he didn't even whimper or make any fuss at all, obviously used to that kind of negligence.'

It was just as well that none of us were soft-centred when we went to stay with Adam's aunts at Howleigh and the children were introduced to their legendary beach picnics. These carried on all year regardless of weather, so that in winter we would be crouched on the shingle like survivors from a shipwreck, huddled together with wet dogs, lashed by an arctic wind. None of this deterred the aunts who rallied us with forced cheerfulness and sandy sandwiches that the dogs snatched from our hands. 'Here, have a b-boiled egg instead, the d-dogs don't like those,' Aunt Diana would stammer through frozen lips. 'It's slightly b-bracing today.'

Back at their house, keeping warm offered a different set of problems in the absence of central heating or provision for such unaccustomed requirements as drying nappies. 'Granny mustn't catch sight of them,' the aunts warned me, 'so you'll have to hang them on the rail above the Aga after she's gone to bed.' Granny had never been exposed to the sight of a nappy. There had always been nannies and nursemaids to deal with such things for her own children and she would find it offensive to observe, even accidentally, any such article on display now at this stage of her life. Regardless of these and other eccentric prohibitions, we all loved being at Howleigh where the aunts fondly prepared such a varied programme of events for us that it was impossible to be bored or unhappy.

On other visits, in summer it would be long hot days at the county show or village fetes, in between picnics in meadows where we lounged on tartan rugs, buzzed by wasps. Evenings were spent in a twitter playing cards or getting out the sherry glasses for neighbours coming round; the glasses sticky with lip and finger marks from the previous time used, with only a dip-wash afterwards by the aunts before being put away ready for the next round. Howleigh's tiny scullery did not allow for hygienic washing up in a stone sink at knee-height designed for dainty Victorian kitchen maids, and now visited as briefly as possible by the aunts.

'We can't seem to get village girls to come up the hill and oblige any more,' Granny complained, unable to comprehend that those village girls who used to slave in the kitchen for a pittance were long gone. Somerset village girls now went to university or took the bus to Taunton where they worked in smart offices or shops, while Howleigh stayed mothballed in a time-zone where innovations such as a washing machine or electric kettle were thought by Granny to be dangerously modern.

Muz however had a marvellous invention called a twin-tub that was wheeled out on washdays when hoses were attached to the sink to provide a water supply and draining outlet. One tub did the washing while the other was a spin dryer, working together in a combined operation that I found captivating despite the close supervision required. There was a tendency for the machine to lose control at maximum revs when the wash-tub went into rock-and-roll mode, slopping soapy water onto the linoleum floor, while the spin-tub tottered and lurched to a roar of increasing vibrations. At this point there would be a shout from Louise in the sitting room next door where she and the others were watching *Magic Roundabout* on TV: 'We can't hear anything, Mummy. You're making too much noise.'

We were settling into a contented routine at Forest Lodge and I wanted to enjoy it for as long as possible but the children were starting to ask: 'When are we going home? When are we going to see Daddy?', making it clear they were missing him. The time away was having a different effect on me as the energising environment of southern England began to evoke a sense of belonging and continuity. In the early mornings I opened my bedroom window as wide as it would go and leaned out to take big breaths of air that were stingingly fresh and cool, making me feel supremely alive. The break from Africa was giving me a sense of renewal, re-connecting with Englishness and the reassurance of a shared history and heritage that I had not fully comprehended or appreciated before. I didn't want the children to be unaware of this identity themselves, and was conscious of an increasing unease about the situation in Rhodesia as the children imbibed the spirit of Ian Smith and all that he stood for. Adam went along with the ideology for the sake of good relations with others we had to live with, and his vision of our future was whole-heartedly Rhodesian. Whatever my own feelings, I had to go back there and make the future work for all of us.

I was standing at the open window one morning when Muz called me. 'There's a telegram for you.' I thought it might be Adam asking about a return date. But it wasn't. It was from Agadir in Morocco with just one sentence pasted on the paper form:

SURVIVED EPIC ACROSS SAHARA ARRIVE BLIGHTY 2 WEEKS MUST SEE YOU DAVID.

I showed it to Muz, who was hovering anxiously. Telegrams arriving unexpectedly were alarm bells for anyone who had been through the war. 'Who's David?' she asked suspiciously. 'Why is it so important for him to see you?'

'He and his wife were friends of ours in Nakuru and David in particular helped a great deal with our move, helping me pack up, and looking after Elizabeth. No doubt he has news of her and other things to tell me about.' But I knew the invitation held more than casual interest, especially if he was on his own. I went upstairs with the telegram in my hand and stood at the open window again, looking out until I was shivering both with the cold air and unexpected anticipation. David had told me about a plan to drive across the Sahara with army friends when he was posted back to re-join his regiment, but there had been no expectation that I might be in England myself when he arrived.

On fine days when Muz wasn't working, we often went on picnics and the children's favourite place was the end of the runway at Gatwick airport where they could watch planes landing and taking off. What they watched out for most eagerly was a Cessna that looked like Grandpa's plane, keeping alive the hope that any Cessna arriving might be his. Gatwick airport in 1970 was hardly more than a runway with sheds at one end where passengers assembled in an atmosphere of no great formality. A nursing friend who had trained with me at the Royal Free Hospital, now lived nearby under the flight path in a rambling house where she had settled in bohemian disorder, absentmindedly gathering babies and children around her. Four of these were her own, and three were stepchildren who came with someone else's husband whom she had collected along the way. On visits to her, my own three were absorbed into this blithe household, running wild in the paradise of their tangled garden abandoned to the incessant roar of planes overhead. For a family of plane spotters like ourselves this was nothing but joy, and I loved the old house that had evolved during three distinct architectural periods.

Its centrepiece was a modest but exquisite Tudor house crowned with a fanciful crenelated roof, standing between a Georgian wing on one side and a Victorian wing on the other. Each section had its own staircase where all ten children (when we were there) raced up and down, swinging from the banisters like lemurs.

It was into this tumult of family life that David arrived, unshaven, sunburnt and dog-tired, hours after driving off the Dover ferry, having arranged to meet us there. This was to spare Muz the dilemma (had he appeared at Forest Lodge) of deciding where he fitted on her moral spectrum of suitable friends for me to be associating with. There were no scruples in the minds of the children who were so pleased to see David that they all wanted to sit on his lap at the same time. Louise perched herself there proprietorially, reaching up to rub the bristles on his face while being flirtatious in a way that looked overly impudent at her age. If anyone was going to flirt with him it would be me, I thought peevishly, not my six-year-old daughter. Several days followed in a carefree state of unstructured time as clocks and watches were ignored and mealtimes occurred randomly. A great many bottles of wine were emptied as we sat around the enormous kitchen table, chatting and idling until tugged by the children to go and look at something they had built or knocked over during mad games. Too soon David had to leave, to go and visit his mother in Somerset, and we returned to Forest Lodge knowing time was short before tickets back home had to be booked.

Muz was scandalised at the state of the children's clothes waiting for her twin-tub when we returned. 'Whatever can you have been doing to accumulate so much dirt, and all these grass stains? Your friend must have let the children run riot by the look of them,' she grumbled, while allowing the precious machine to be wheeled out on a day that wasn't washday. We were sorting through the grubby pile of clothes when the phone rang and Muz went to answer it. 'It's for you,' she called from the hall where the phone lived on a small table next to the front door. 'It's a man. He didn't say who he was.' That will be David, I thought. But it wasn't. Incredibly it was Lanner, his voice unmistakable as he said, 'I heard you were over here, visiting your mother.'

'Yes,' I managed to reply after a moment of stunned hesitation.

'I'm on leave, staying with my parents, not too far from where you are. I thought of driving over one day,' he suggested casually. My voice seemed to have dried up with the shock of hearing him instead of David, and I needed to collect myself. 'What about your wife?' I asked after a pause.

'She's not here. I came on my own with the children.'

There was silence as I took this in. What was he saying? Had he and his wife split up? Why did he want to see me?

'Are you still there?' He sounded surprised.

'Yes. But you can't come over, I'm just about to leave. I'm living in Rhodesia now,' I added lamely as if whole continents stretched between us instead of a few miles of English countryside.

'It would be a pity to miss a chance to meet again since last time was so awkward and offered no opportunity for any meaningful conversation. Especially with no shortage of subjects for discussion,' he added enigmatically.

'It's just not a good time,' I answered quickly, feeling trapped, and annoyed with Lanner for thinking he could walk back into my life so abruptly after the years of anguish he had caused me.

'I would like to see you again,' he persisted.

'Why?'

'In case there have been past misunderstandings.'

'We are both in different places now, looking ahead, not looking back.'

'Sometimes looking back offers perspective, and can be a good thing, helping to understand the past.'

'Looking back is what people do when they're lost,' I said, directing the remark at him, and noticing a slight sadness in his voice as he replied. 'I can see you will not be persuaded, but I hope, one day, fate will look upon us more kindly and provide another opportunity for speaking.'

'Yes, possibly,' I said, feeling relieved that we could end on good terms. 'It does seem as if fate conspires to engineer some strange encounters for us.' He laughed in the chuckling way which was familiar and dangerously engaging, so that I had to hold onto myself to say goodbye and put the phone down. I was shaking as I did so, but glad to have avoided the complications that any meeting inevitably would have caused.

Muz wanted to know who it was, and when I told her and how the conversation had ended, she was irritated. 'You could easily have let him come here. It would not have been disloyal to Adam. In any case I would have liked to see Lanner again. He was in love with you, you know.'

'No, he wasn't,' I said fiercely. 'He cut me off with no explanation or the slightest twinge of conscience, just like Tom did with Elaine.'

'Elaine is still friendly with Tom. She doesn't hold it against him, even though he married someone else. It's the Christian thing to do.'

'Not all of us in this family are very good at doing the Christian thing,' I reminded her, thinking of Fa, but not saying so.

Muz switched the subject to Ros. 'I hope Ros is going to be all right with her new friend, sharing a flat with him and that other couple at Earl's Court.' I knew what she was thinking: that she hoped they all had their own bedrooms and there was nothing improper going on. When Ros had been on a caravan holiday with a previous boyfriend, Muz had fretted about the lack of privacy in such cramped quarters. 'Where will Ros get dressed?' she fussed. 'There isn't even a normal bathroom in the caravan for her to get changed, or put on her nightdress at night.' I thought it best to avoid enlightening her that Ros was unlikely to be wearing a nightdress while she and her boyfriend occupied the one and only caravan bed each night.

Ros was still working at Bart's Hospital in the medical art department where they were developing a teaching aid for medical students which was innovative at the time. It offered desks with video screens displaying a menu of clinical subjects, accompanied by illustrations and films of surgical and other procedures. Her 'new friend', as Muz called him, was Gary Pritchard, a Fine Arts graduate like herself. He was Welsh, from a mining family in the valleys, an only child, talented and ambitious. He had won a scholarship to the Royal College of Art in London and from there joined BBC Television as a set designer and was a good foil for Ros, scooping her out of the dark corners of Craddock muddle with a hearty attitude that he applied to all aspects of life. He was a generous and flamboyant character who exhibited quantities of Welsh charm along with a lilting Welsh accent, so that even Muz allowed herself to be teased and complimented when Gary was visiting. But for Andy he had nothing but scorn. 'A total waster,' was Gary's comment on the hapless Andy.

David phoned or wrote from his mother's house, and if Muz answered the phone he smoothed her suspicions with a Sandhurst drawl put on to disarm her. 'Your army friend is a perfect gentleman,' she commented after one call. 'He has lovely manners. He didn't ask straight away to talk to you, but asked me about myself and we chatted for quite a long time. What a nice man. Why don't you ask him over?'

'He's too far away, and there isn't time,' I told her. But I missed him and so did the children. They had become attached from an early age when happy hours were spent with him and his children in Kenya while his wife was often away. He was an inspired inventor of games for them, such as constructing mini-assault courses with water features and rope bridges, combining energetic activity with mad frolics and dogs joining in. But he was just as happy to sit down with the rest of us for a few hands of cards, a glass always within reach.

I had to acknowledge the intense affinity that had grown up between us, emphasised by this latest encounter, while also acknowledging that it could be no more than a momentary distraction from our own entirely separate commitments. His wife wanted to stay in Nairobi where the gracious life of expats suited her, while David was determined that his son and daughter should join him in England and have an English education. His focus was on them and his career path in the British Army, intentionally putting aside other considerations while not wanting to put me aside altogether, but I had my own focus and it remained far from England. Such a rare type of person is hard to let go, I thought, and Louise echoed these thoughts when she said: 'I wish David could come to Rhodesia with us. He's my friend as well as yours, you know.'

The aunts were insistent on a last visit to Howleigh and I was glad afterwards that there would be no more complicated train journeys with luggage and small children after the latest experience, when we had to change trains several times to reach Taunton. On one of these legs the train was packed tight like the Delhi Express as I squeezed in, carrying Peter, pushchair, suitcase and bags, with Louise and Simon clinging to my coat, terrified that they might get swept away in the crush. Once safely on board I thrust Peter onto the lap of a surprised woman sitting in a crowded carriage while

I went to search for spare seats. She looked greatly relieved when I returned to retrieve him, and he looked even more relieved, as he could never be quite sure when he might find himself forgotten during the uncertainties that accompanied our nomadic life. When we all spilled out at Taunton it was a further relief to find the aunts waiting on the platform, ready to fold their arms around us and make us feel safe again.

It was a brief visit followed by sad farewells when we had to leave all too soon, the aunts coming to help us onto the train as they brought along assorted carrier bags full of presents for Adam and his parents, that had not been wrapped. These objects kept falling out of the bags as I tried to keep all my pieces of luggage together. The presents included a pair of stirrups with leathers (bound to come in useful, the aunts said), knitted socks, pots of Marmite and Gentleman's Relish, garlic grown in the garden, long rubber waders that had belonged to their father Percy, and homemade marmalade. All of these had to be jammed into suitcases a few days later when we left to go home, facing another tortuous journey.

This time I was changing planes with six pieces of luggage and three small people whose heads I had to keep counting to make sure none had gone missing. When we reached Cairo airport it was a vast milling multitude of people camping out like refugees; whole families with bedding spread out and barely an inch of space between them. I needed to find lavatories and a nappy-changing space for Peter, hoping there would at least be running water for a wash. When I located the reeking conveniences and put Peter down on the filthy floor to change him, it felt like being in a war zone and I was thankful beyond measure that our next stop would be Johannesburg.

The previous day, leaving this time from Heathrow instead of Gatwick, David in a final gesture of kindness had booked rooms at a hotel near the airport for us, and had come to help with all the details of departure and make sure we got off in good order. That evening, putting the children to bed, they asked, 'Are we leaving David behind again?' As ever, children's remarks can be keenly perceptive, and our departure the next morning was no less emotional than a year before at Nairobi when we left for Rhodesia with every one of us in tears, including David. He was left behind again, to return to his regiment and single life in England, his own children still far away, while my future had to be in Rhodesia, making things work for us.

Chapter 2

Adam had driven down to Johannesburg to meet us and was standing at the arrival gate with a nervous smile and big bouquet of red roses. That was a tender moment as the children ran to him and we all stood clutching each other in a huddle among our motley assortment of bags and baggage. We had a long drive ahead, but Adam had booked comfortable places to stay along the several hundred mile route, going north through the Transvaal to the Limpopo border and home.

None of the Transvaal shopkeepers or hotel people we met on the way seemed able or willing to speak English on the long dusty trail, until at last we reached a beautifully cool and refreshing mountain retreat called Louis Trichardt, on the South African side of the border. We spent the night there gratefully, looking forward to a hot bath, stiff drink and good dinner, after putting the children to bed. Locating the hotel bar I went in with Adam for that urgent gin and tonic, to be told that ladies were not allowed to drink with men and there was a cocktail bar where I could have a drink with other 'ladies'. This was a surprising restriction: like an apartheid against women, in an otherwise friendly hotel. In the cocktail bar I took the opportunity to introduce myself to those women who had no objection to speaking English, and find out what they thought about the rule. 'It's *lekker* (great) getting away from the men,' they laughed. 'We don't want them with their guns and rugby bullshit. Keep them out!' Apartheid was on the other foot here it seemed.

Gwelo was another three hundred miles north from the border driving via Bulawayo where we spent the next night and then, when we were nearly home, Adam delivered a piece of news that was deeply unsettling. 'I didn't want to tell you while we were enjoying ourselves, and I didn't want to depress you when you had only just arrived,' he began in the same ominous tone that Fa used when about to deliver a torpedo into the conversation. If any kind of disaster was about to be announced I wanted to hear it fast and straight. 'Yes?'

'The Macleans suddenly decided they want their son to take over the dairy, so I haven't got a job any more, which means we're on the move again. It's a bit of bind, but luckily they have fixed me up with a friend of theirs who is a director of the Dairy Board and has a big herd at Hartley. I've been waiting for you to get back so we can pack up and do the move.' He was trying to sound matter of fact and break it gently, but it was bad news coming so unexpectedly and so soon after arriving back. I took a deep breath and steadied myself, trying to see this as a new opportunity instead of a setback.

'It's a step up for you, darling, working for a big dairy chief, and the Macleans must have recommended you highly to have got you the job.' I wanted to sound up-beat, and it worked as Adam replied enthusiastically, 'Yes, sweetheart, you're right, it's a leg-up in the dairy world, and comes with more pay as well.'

Repacking tea boxes with all the possessions we had brought from Kenya hardly more than a year before, I thought of Muz repeatedly doing the same. Perpetually moving, taking down and folding curtains to put into boxes along with her Singer as I was now doing with my own sewing machine. I didn't want it to become a symbol of curtain-making for an everlasting series of different-sized windows, and remembered promising myself during the early days at Glanjoro that my own family would never be subjected to the same upheavals. Now, here we were on the road again, with another change of school for Louise. But Hartley, a small farming town further north on the road to Salisbury, was more our sort of place I consoled myself, more like Nakuru, and we would make a proper home there.

'Remember to pack the dogs' beds, and their bowls when we go,' Louise reminded me. 'If they've got their own things with their own smell on them, they won't mind being in a new place. And when we get there, remember you promised we can have cats, one for each of us. I'm already thinking of names. And you said we can have chickens too, for laying eggs. Mum – are you listening?'

The district of Hartley with its rich agricultural land lay almost in the dead centre of the country where the main arterial road from the capital, Salisbury, ran south to the border, bisecting the town. For shopkeepers and cafés the passing trade was a bonus. The town itself was very much smaller than Gwelo, having just one main street of shops serving a farming community that radiated from this rural hub into pastoral countryside, where the climate was considerably less harsh than further south. This is where we arrived with our boxes and dogs and furniture at the start of 1971. I had not seen either the farm or the house where we would live before moving and it had been a scramble to relocate ourselves, since Adam had been given only a month's notice and this was almost at an end by the time I got back from England. He had been to see the new farm, Rogate, and the manager's house which he described as hardly luxurious but adequate. What he failed to mention was that the house wasn't really a house at all but a converted grain shed, standing all by itself in the middle of a bean field. It was a large field, which I noted was just as well since on one side traffic thundered past on the main Salisbury road after leaving the town speed limits. We were five miles from the town, so that shops and school were conveniently close – similar to the situation we had left behind in Nakuru – a positive feature that could be used to make us feel more at home I decided.

Any other plus factors to be found in this latest move were hard to identify. The house itself was so dismal in every possible way that it surpassed even Fa's worst excesses during the periods of his crazed purchases and building schemes. I consoled myself in thinking about the laughs I could have when describing it to Ros, and how outraged she would be that I was reliving the travesties of our childhood. Adam tried to be encouraging about the house. 'At least it has three bedrooms so Louise can have her own instead of sharing with the boys, and there are neighbours quite close on the next-door farm with a daughter the same age as Louise, so they will be going to Hartley School together and you can share school runs.'

I contemplated these assets while introducing Louise to her own private bedroom, and when she pointed out that the window had no glass, only chicken wire stretched across the open space, I reminded her that Grandpa and Grandma's dining room window at Glanjoro was the same and she hadn't complained about that. 'Well, I wasn't sleeping in the dining room, and rain never came in that window, but here it will come right onto my bed. And mozzies will come in too. Look, you can already see where there have been puddles on the floor. Look, Mum, you must show Dad.'

'We'll screen the window somehow, don't worry about that, just be glad to have your own room.'

There was no time to think about screens or anything else at that stage while unloading our furniture and boxes into the house before any rain did arrive. The rainy season had started and we were lucky that the furniture van had been able to ford a small river that looked a bit too close to the house for safety if it overflowed. I wondered if that factor had been a reason for abandoning the use of the building as a grain shed. The dogs, freed from the back of the car where they had been piled in with suitcases, ran around getting in the way, so the first unpacking was to bring out their bowls, and a kettle to make tea for ourselves and the removal men.

Our furniture was a sparse collection of essentials hastily assembled when we first arrived in Gwelo and now looked even more dreary as the assorted pieces became dispersed among rooms, but I was glad to see that we did have electricity and a telephone.

Simon stood outside dangling Peter's pot by its handle in one hand, while the other hand held Peter's reassuringly as, side by side, they looked up at the sky where dark clouds were rolling in. 'When we went in Grandpa's plane it could go really high,' Simon was telling Peter earnestly, 'and it could go inside clouds, but only white ones, not black ones like these. Grandpa said they were too bumpy and the plane had to go round them.' Peter listened but said nothing in reply. At two years old he was not yet talking, having no need to while Simon anticipated every need and looked after him so attentively that I began to think it might lead to arrested development. Simon himself was only four, but had already become a commanding presence with assumed responsibilities that included taking charge of Peter and the pot. This was carried around like a trophy to be flourished at any moment of indication. Peter had just one word of speech: 'Wa-wa,' his name for Simon. Instant attention would follow whenever Peter spoke this word. It was endearing in a way, but not if normal speech became permanently delayed. In addition he was still very small for his age, but Muz pointed out that her family were all petite and small-boned, including her father, and this went with handsome features she assured me.

I longed for her to visit, or Fa, or Ros; especially Ros who was a great ally in converting any setback into a cause for merriment and parody. We had found this was a good way of defusing all kinds of stresses and weirdness as we grew up clinging onto our madly spinning family carousel. The laughter remedy probably saved us from joining poor Spindle in mental oblivion.

There was little chance of Muz visiting, as she explained she could not contemplate coming without Andy, but that he had no inclination to accompany her and risk encountering savage animals and deadly African diseases. Instead they were enjoying frequent forays into the civilised and charming territory of France to explore its great motorways, with Andy hugging the highroad like Mr Toad. Once he was behind the wheel in the redoubtable Austin Princess he was unstoppable. 'Now that your father has got his divorce,' Muz wrote, 'I am free to marry again, and it will no doubt help to ease any guilt he might feel in having abandoned me if I am safely married off to someone else. Andy continues to press proposals of marriage at every opportunity and I can see no reason to go on refusing, despite Mary's opposition. I don't love him in the sense of being in love, but he incessantly declares his love for me most sincerely, and we have a loving friendship. At my age I can't really ask for more, so I will accept him the next time he asks.'

There was nothing I could do about this, so I tried to be glad that she had found a solution to her loneliness, hoping that somehow it would turn out all right despite Mary's warning.

Our new employer, Eric Hornby, was well known in Rhodesian farming circles with a Friesian herd of 380 milking cows on several thousand acres of prime land that produced a variety of crops, including cotton. The rich flat fields were ideal for crops or cattle raising, but did not provide a very arresting landscape. Looking out from our house in the bean field there were no scenic landmarks and most of the trees had been cleared. A few of these had been left to indicate a boundary between us and the smallholding of Thornby Farm next door, where Eric's sister Hazel lived very frugally with her husband and five children. They ran a small market garden and farm store that struggled to generate an income, in contrast to Eric's prosperous acres. Hazel and I became good friends as we combined what resources we had to help each other in these mutually barren circumstances.

There were compensations as life was peaceful and well-ordered in terms of government services like health, security and administration. We could not have imagined, just then, that our unremarkable district of Hartley would find itself in the front line of a brutal war within seven years, and that poor Hazel's family would be decimated.

For now, our first day at Rogate was ominous in its own way as the glowering rain clouds that Simon and Peter had been watching from outside soon burst in a violent storm. A deluge fell onto the house and surrounding bean field while we were still moving in. Adam had just unrolled carpets and rugs to disguise the effect of concrete floors, and Louise was arranging her bedroom having made her bed and unpacked toys and clothes, when the storm erupted. There was no time to cover her chicken-wire window against incoming rain when she shouted, 'My bed is getting soaked, and the carpet is floating away.' It wasn't just her bedside rug that had become waterborne; all the others, newly laid, were bobbing about in a tide of muddy water surging in under the front and back doors. The construction of the building had not included obvious essentials to avoid this problem. Were we expected to bring duck-boards with us I wondered in this new situation which was several notches down from the Maclean's superior housing. All we could do was wait for the rain to stop, which it usually does abruptly in Africa, and then get to work with brooms and mops.

Milking times were at 3.30 am, 10 am and 3 pm. This intensive routine was designed for maximum milk production, but was punishing for the dairy workers, and for the cows as they got worn out and had shorter lives than when they were milked twice a day. After each milking there was the cooling process to supervise, sick animals to treat, cows lined up for AI, cows calving, outside herds of followers (young animals) for checking, bulls to be visited in their pens and calves in theirs, and then a good deal of office work. Adam would come home for breakfast at 9 am, and later for lunch, then not until 7.30 pm when the boys were in bed, but Louise was allowed to stay up to say goodnight to him. It was a demanding life, but there is a particular type of satisfaction in dairy farming that is difficult to explain to anyone who has not lived it. Cows have personalities and even in a big herd there are misfits and rebels: the canny ones looking to see how they can beat the system; others that are gently affectionate and charming; the younger ones who are curious and friendly, their noses outstretched enquiringly. The warm smell of these animals is comforting; the soft neck and flank of a cow at close quarters with the feel and scent of its body and that of hay or fresh grass has a soothing intimacy. Cows are vegetarians so their pats are nothing more obnoxious than chewed and digested plants. The relationship which develops between man, woman and beast in the steamy environment of milk production is a close and committed one. It can border on addiction, I used to think, as Adam's dedication to this relentless routine had its frustrating times, such as weekends and Christmas in addition to the long working hours each day. He was supposed to have regular days off, but these were often spent catching up on office work. If it was an addiction then there was little hope that he might consider a change, I thought.

The children took all this as normal since they had known no other life, and the boys quickly made friends among the children of African workers on the farm, where they roamed free and came home looking as dirty and ragged as any other scamps met along the way. It would have shocked Muz, so I consoled myself that she had not come to view our fall from grace. Louise did not join the boys, preferring the friendship of Hazel's daughters whom she joined at Hartley School and settled there without a qualm. It was a popular school, famed for its academic and sporting excellence, so this helped us to feel better about the various shortcomings in our situation. Rugby was almost a religion in Rhodesia and training for boys started at age five in the first form, which made Simon very impatient to start school and go off with Louise each morning. Meeting other parents was my own passport to making new friends and now that we were living close to a town, I thought the Anglican church might offer some opportunities for socialising.

On my first visit I took the children who had been scrubbed and put into decent clothes, but not decent enough for us to be ushered into pews near the front where the children could see what was going on. Ladies in hats and gloves showed us where we should sit, but when I noticed that the back rows were filled with Africans I decided to go and sit with them. 'No, you can't go there,' the hat ladies said. 'You can't sit with blacks,' and went on to insist that I accept the pew offered. Later, when communion was served, I saw that the Africans waited until everyone else had been served before they left their seats and came up to receive communion themselves. When I asked about this I was told that whites could not drink from the communion cup after blacks, so whites went first. This made me decide to make a point of joining the Africans for communion next time. This is the church of Christ where we are all one body, I thought. What is going on here?

Despite this form of apartheid practised at the church I wanted to persevere because the hat ladies were all passionate cooks who gave phenomenal tea parties organised by a large bouncy woman called Elsa. She might easily have been a model for Beryl Cook postcards if she had not ended up in the obscurity of Hartley, where her tiny short-sighted husband worked for the local cotton ginnery. Elsa had a refreshing view of Christianity in which any occasion that encouraged the eating of vast quantities of food could be counted as an a blessing received from above. 'I don't have to worry about dieting,' Elsa explained, 'because I say a prayer with each meal asking Jesus to take away the calories.' I looked at her generous bulk overflowing the chair as she reached for another slice of cake. 'Does it work?' I asked, making the question sound innocent. 'Of course it does – if you have faith,' Elsa said. 'Maybe not straight away. You have to be patient. Jesus works in mysterious ways. It's a promise from the Bible.'

Another of these prodigious tea parties was given by a church member whose husband was a senior manager at the ginnery, with the kind of salary that allowed his wife to indulge her tastes in home décor. At the party I was admiring her new curtains, which clearly had not come from the local textile factory, when she said she would be glad to tell me how to find the best ones as her method never failed. I was curious to hear it, and she went on: 'When I'm in a curtain shop in Salisbury looking at all the designs on display, I ask God to choose.'

'How does he do that?' I asked, riveted.

'I walk slowly along the rolls of fabric and when one catches my eye, I take that as a sign and say a prayer. It is the most amazing thing – God always chooses the best ones however expensive they are.'

Such a novel way of choosing curtains left me with much to contemplate as I surveyed the drab assortment in my new home and how I might involve God in locating better ones. When it was my turn to host one of the tea parties, I invited Eric's wife to join us. She had never visited the converted shed where we lived and neither had any of the other church women, so I decided this was a good opportunity to show them the kind of accommodation that Eric thought suitable for his farm manager and family to live in. When the first guests arrived, surprised to find themselves in a bean field where tea was to be served in a shack, they were clearly taken aback, and when Eric's wife arrived there were enough disapproving murmurs and remarks made that guaranteed the degree of embarrassment I had intended. She was not an uncaring person and apologised, explaining that she and Eric were planning to move to Salisbury and we would have their house when this happened.

I was impatient to tell Adam this unexpected good news and thought he would welcome it, but when I told him, he had his own entirely surprising announcement to make. 'I've decided to give up dairy,' he said. 'It's a mug's game. No sort of life for any of us. I want to have a complete change, no longer sculling about on frigging dairy farms where I'm working half the night as well as the day. I've always liked the idea of being a city slicker, wearing a suit, going to work with a briefcase instead of a rubber glove. Leading a civilised life, earning proper money. What do you think?'

We were just beginning to settle to life in Hartley and this was a complete turnaround, but I didn't want him to burn himself out with dairy work if there was a good alternative.

'What sort of city-slicker job could you get without any of the qualifications or background they would be looking for?'

'I've already heard of something from one of the sales reps who comes round all the time. It's with Bowmaker, which is a finance company based in Salisbury. They need a cattle specialist to head up their beef-stock department. It would mean travelling around the country, appraising herds and negotiating loans. Right up my alley.'

'Living in Salisbury?'

'Yes. Then you'll be happy because you can get a job as well. Several hospitals to choose from, or doctors' surgeries. It's a golden opportunity. I've already written to Bowmaker and they're going to give me an interview. I didn't want to tell you until there was something more definite to go on.'

'Well,' I paused, caught unawares. 'It's a bit sudden. You could have given me some advance warning of this latest change of plan. But I won't mind having a proper house instead of living in a field with all these beans, I can tell you. It isn't so good for Louise, though, having another change of school.'

'The schools in Salisbury are far superior to any out in the countryside. It will be a great move. I'm confident about Bowmaker. The rep has put in a good word for me.'

It didn't take long for a reply. The letter from Bowmaker gave details of the position and invited Adam to meet them. It all happened very quickly when he drove the eighty miles to Salisbury on his next day off for the interview, and came back the same day, elated.

'It went even better than expected,' he said as he took off his shoes and socks to walk barefoot on the cool floor after a hot day in the city, and went to the drinks cupboard to pour each of us a gin and tonic. Settling himself into an armchair, he said, 'I hit it off straight away with the boss who seems an easy-going sort of chap. As soon as we'd got the formalities out of the way he took me for lunch at Meikles which was very civilised of him. I can see how city life is going to suit us.'

'What about the pay?'

'That's still under discussion, but will be a lot better than what I'm getting here. On my next day off we can go and look at houses to rent. Let's drink to a whole new life, my love. City life!'

Adam's new boss suggested we should go to the government housing agency for one of their subsidised houses, which sounded to me like council housing reserved for impoverished tenants. This would not be improving our lifestyle in the way Adam had described, but anything would be better than the bean house. It was a considerable surprise, then, to find that we were offered a rather grand house which had lately been an ambassador's residence. When UDI was declared a number of ambassadors were recalled to their own countries, leaving their big houses unoccupied, so these needed suitable tenants to look after them. The one offered to us was close to a good school in a select neighbourhood of leafy streets and trim gardens, where big shiny cars stood in gravelled drives – a very different community from the one we were leaving behind. As if this was not enough of a leg-up in terms of social elevation, the house stood in its own grounds with a walled garden, for privacy as well as security we were told. The entrance gate opened onto a short driveway with parking for several cars beside an imposing house where a flight of steps led to a porch embellished with pillars – allowing no entry for rainwater, I noted.

There was a woman caretaker currently in residence making sure the house was kept safe until tenants moved in, the agent told us, but she was not at home on the day that he showed us round. Beyond the front door, the house was a rambling pile of a place with a central courtyard almost like a cloister with numerous rooms around it, while the kitchen was located discreetly at the back among a warren of sculleries and pantries, There was even a butler's pantry and a meat larder with its own cooling system. Going from one extreme to the other, I wondered how I would cope with all this. But the drawing room was a clincher: forty foot in length with a fireplace at each end and, crucially, a television set which was a fixture so I knew the children would be instantly won over. The walled garden would please them too, with a spacious play area and even a swing and climbing ropes. At its centre a mature avocado tree had grown so tall that it was higher than the house and heavy with fruit. I imagined the parties we could have in the big drawing room with guests spilling into the garden, and friends from country areas would come to stay when shopping in Salisbury, just as others had done when we lived in Kenya conveniently close to a town.

Adam was impatient to start his new job and the children were excited about the move, especially Simon who would be starting school the next term. I was excited too, but sad to leave Hazel and her family as well as the many new friends we had made in Hartley. The hat ladies had blossomed in friendship once they discovered that my tea parties met their standards, with my cakes and sandwiches almost as good as theirs. Elsa was famed for her salad sandwiches and no one else was allowed to copy them, but everyone had their own specialities rolled out on each occasion. Mine were paté sandwiches with a good slug of brandy mixed in, giving me a sense of triumph when those ladies who were ultra-orthodox Christian teetotallers took big bites and exclaimed on the excellence of the paté.

Moving house is seldom a soothing experience and flood water had damaged our furniture and carpets to such an extent that very few of these were worth keeping, so there was minimal packing up this time. We would be virtually camping in the big Salisbury house until we could re-equip ourselves more usefully from a second-hand shop or auction. The caretaker at the house was due to move out with her dogs the day before we moved in, and said she would leave the keys with the agent.

After an early start from Hartley with an easy drive to Salisbury, we called at the agent's office to collect the keys, but he said the caretaker was waiting for us at the house so we should go straight there. When we arrived with our van and the car filled with children and dogs, we found the caretaker inside, sitting at the kitchen table surrounded by empty boxes and her own dogs, showing no sign of any imminent move. Having expected a middle-aged caretaker, a government employee perhaps, I was startled to see instead a young woman who introduced herself without getting up from the table. 'I'm lovely Lulu,' she announced with a mocking smile and provocative wriggle that completely demolished any illusions I might have had about the kind of person I imagined meeting. I looked in wonder at her curvy body and complexion the colour of golden syrup, suddenly finding myself lost for words. She was wearing silk pyjamas of a similar colour that clung to her figure, and I noticed Adam's eyes widening.

'I've been a bit held up,' she went on, 'but I'll be gone by tomorrow and meanwhile you can bring all your stuff in and make yourselves at home. I'm cooking mealie-meal for my dogs,' she said, getting up to stir a pot on the stove.'

We stood uncertainly watching her and the dogs that stared back at us menacingly. We needed to let our dogs out of the car where they had been confined during the entire journey, jammed in with the children and pieces of luggage, so we asked if she would keep her dogs inside while ours were allowed out. She turned from the mealie pot in alarm, 'I didn't know you were bringing dogs. No one said you were bringing dogs.' She sounded affronted, as if we were guests in her house instead of the new tenants, and that it was highly inconvenient for us to be there at all, but she offered to put her dogs on chains outside.

As soon as our dogs were let out, Lulu's dogs went into a frenzy, barking hysterically and straining at their chains, enraged to have other dogs invading their territory. Ours, seeing that hers were tied up, felt empowered to bark back at them with such fury it led to uproar and we had to take them for a walk to get them out of the way. The children, as glad as the dogs to be released from the car, came too, all of us feeling relieved to escape the frantic scene, but shaken to find ourselves in this unexpected situation.

'What are we going to do about the dogs?' Louise asked as soon as we were out of the gate.

'It isn't the dogs we need to worry about so much as finding that our new house is still occupied, so we can't move in properly until that woman Lulu moves out,' Adam said, sounding thoroughly rattled.

'She did say we could move our stuff inside, and there are enough bedrooms for all of us to sleep there tonight, and then tomorrow she'll be gone,' I said, wanting to sound practical and reassuring.

'What about Roger and Ruin with all those horrible dogs?' Louise persisted.

'The dogs can stay on their chains and we'll tie ours up on the veranda on the other side of the house. We'll put their beds there. They won't be able to see Lulu's dogs, and hers won't be able to see ours. Then tomorrow they'll be gone.'

'Can I choose a room for Peter and me?' Simon asked, excited at the prospect that we would be moving in after all.

'Yes, of course. There are lots of bedrooms. The agent wasn't even sure how many there are, so the first thing you can do is count them, and make sure you find out where the bathrooms are.'

That first night was the kind of camping experience which all of us were used to, except that when we started exploring the bedrooms we found that several of them were occupied by Lulu's relatives who were unaware of any plan to move. At supper, all of them gathered to sit around a refectory table in the dining room and everyone brought their own food. I had ours in a cool bag ready for the evening when I thought we would be celebrating our first supper in the new house, so we had something for ourselves, including a bottle of wine, which was immediately seized and passed round. The children had no qualms about the unexpected dining arrangements, thinking it was all rather jolly, but my own concern grew as I looked around, thinking that we had inadvertently joined a commune. Lulu gave no impression that any move was planned for either the next day or perhaps ever, despite the presence of packing cases in the kitchen. She invited Adam to sit next to her at the table where, I noticed, she leaned her silky curves towards him and he became quite animated in response, showing none of his usual distaste for mammary hyperplasia.

Afterwards, when he and I had retreated to the empty bedroom into which our double bed had been decanted and now stood looking forlorn among scattered suitcases, I confronted him, feeling too tired and stressed to be tactful. 'We've got to get rid of Lulu and her motley family. Please don't get friendly with her, encouraging her to think we can all live happily together.'

'Please, darling, all I need just now is peace and quiet for starting my new job, without any bust-ups on the home front. Lulu has given her word that they are leaving tomorrow. You can see all the proof you need with her packing cases everywhere. It's just that one of her brothers has nowhere else to go, so he might have to stay for a bit.'

'What do you mean – her brother?' I asked in alarm. 'Have you agreed to that?'

'Yes, but it's only temporary. He's blind and they haven't got anywhere else for him yet. Someone comes in every day to look after him. He won't be any trouble. You can sort out the house tomorrow after Lulu and the rest of them have left. Just try to keep things sweet. You're good at that. I'm relying on you, sweetheart. I need to be at the office early to get briefed and pick up a company car so we can have independent transport. Now we're paying rent we have to get my job underway smartish. It's still "*kazi kwanza*" (work first). Nothing has changed where that is concerned.' I was too tired to think of a riposte to that mantra, and preferred to remember a verse we had sung as children at Nakuru School when facing yet another wearisome task, driven like mules by the teachers: '*Take your pack and trek, forever, take your pack and trek.*' So there we were, lifting our packs again, but all I wanted at that moment was a cool bed and deep sleep.

Adam wanted an early breakfast, and all the others were still in their rooms when I went to the kitchen next morning to make toast and coffee from supplies unpacked from our own boxes. It was a relief to have the kitchen to ourselves and the children still asleep while I was impatient to check on Roger and Ruin and take them for a walk out of sight of Lulu's dogs. When I got back from the walk, there were two vans in the drive and packers had arrived, so that was a welcome sight. Lulu herself was still in her room, asleep I was told, because she worked nights at a strip club. After hearing that I was ready for almost anything.

Louise and Simon were impatient later to go and buy school uniforms, and see the school itself, which was only minutes away. We took the dogs with us, exploring such civilised amenities as a botanical park and avenues lined with jacaranda and flamboyant trees. 'Can we have bikes?' the children wanted to know, seeing other children riding past. 'Peter will have to start on a tricycle because his legs are too short for a bike,' Louise pointed out.

Back at the house, boxes were being loaded into the vans, Lulu was still in bed, and I went to fill water bowls for the dogs, get drinks for the children and make a cup of tea for myself. In the kitchen I was just in time to rescue my kettle, teapot, mugs and other crockery from being packed up with Lulu's things. She was not there supervising the packers or any other activity, and family members were drifting about in a daze. I asked about the blind brother and was told that he never came out of his room, but the helper would be there with him.

'Where is Lulu moving to?' I asked, 'and all of you? Where are you going to live now?'

'Lulu is going back to her husband, and we are going to our farm at Mazoe.'

It was a confusing picture and the best I could do was make sure that no more household goods of ours were packed up with Lulu's by mistake, while trying to keep things calm and controlled during the process of getting her and the others moved out. When Lulu had finished sleeping she didn't hang about, and without a goodbye went off to her husband's house with the van and the dogs, where she was refused entry. It appeared that he had changed his mind about having her back, but I was beginning to suspect that all her promises were a sham. The only consolation when she returned was that her husband had kept the dogs. I didn't want Adam to be confronted with any domestic turmoil after his first day at work, so I had a drink ready for him with a welcoming kiss and his own armchair when he got back, tired but pleased to show off his new company car, and pleased with his new job.

Lulu's boxes came back with her, but during her absence I had unpacked our own things into empty cupboards and drawers so there was no room for any of hers if she tried to unpack. I told her that she must find somewhere else immediately, having no patience now that I suspected her of prevaricating. If there was a problem then I would ask the housing agent for an eviction order, I said. At the mention of the housing agent she became conciliatory. 'I can't go to the farm where the others have gone, because of my job,' she said.

'What about your brother?'

'He doesn't like the farm.'

'You will have to take him with you wherever you go. He can't stay here with us.'

'My friends will help out. I can get a flat. I just need to get on the phone to fix something.' The phone was in the hall and she padded off towards it, still wearing the silk pyjamas which seemed to be her daytime wear.

The house had resident staff who occupied what was referred to as servants' quarters on site and we were to take them on, but since Lulu was still giving an appearance of being in charge they quite naturally thought they were working for her rather than us. I needed to see each one to learn their names and explain the situation before it became too confusing for everyone. Once the children had been fed and were watching television, I set about identifying who was there and what job they did. It was impressive to find that all of them spoke English. I had not learnt any Shona, which was the language of this region, as Ndebele had been the language spoken by most rural people further south. I was impatient to settle all the various household demands so that I could sit quietly reading letters from Muz and Ros and write back to them. There had been sudden startling news from each of them and with no other means of communication, letters were our only lifeline.

Chapter 3

While we were still on the farm at Hartley, back at Forest Lodge in England during 1971 two weddings were held that year. The first was Ros and Gary's wedding, which Fa did not attend, leaving Muz to preside with a reluctance and lack of enthusiasm that, Ros reported, had soured the whole proceedings. It was partly that Muz resented having to act as hostess without Fa to help and do his bit as father of the bride, but also because she strongly disapproved of a church wedding with Ros marrying in white after she and Gary had 'shamelessly' lived together for a number of years. 'You have to be a virgin to wear white,' she insisted. 'It isn't right to pretend.'

'I'm not pretending,' Ros told her. 'I can wear what I like. No one takes any notice of those silly ideas any more. Hardly anyone is a virgin when they get married these days.'

'Well, it's scandalous how morals are breaking down,' Muz said. 'Soon people won't bother to get married at all and will just go on living in sin.'

Due to such strained circumstances the wedding was necessarily a modest affair, but Muz had promised that she would arrange and pay for them to spend their wedding night in luxury at Gravetye Manor, as her wedding present to them. On the day itself, while going through the motions of a subdued ceremony and reception with just a few friends but none of the family except Muz (Elaine and Les were in Ethiopia), the highlight of the whole event for Ros and Gary was the prospect of Gravetye that night. It then came as a complete shock when Muz announced that she had changed her mind and no booking had been made. A wedding night at Gravetye was improper, she explained, since they had already been sharing the same bed for years, and moreover the wedding itself could not be a proper wedding in such circumstances. Her sense of satisfaction in having made this moral stand did nothing to ease the tension caused when there was no time to look for a suitable alternative hotel room. When Ros and Gary at last drove away from Forest Lodge that evening, they stopped at the first AA recommended roadside inn, glad to find somewhere half-decent for the night.

Muz's behaviour may have been provoked by misgivings within herself, I realised, as the second marriage that year, to everyone's consternation and possibly her own as well, was hers to Andy. He must have finally worn her down as there was no excitement or even pleasure in her letter telling me about the register office formality, followed by a honeymoon touring France. 'Andy is never happier than when he's behind a wheel, driving all day. He never stops to look at the view or learn the history of places where there are famous sights to see. He doesn't even feel the need to stop and eat somewhere until I insist,' she complained. 'Worst of all, he refuses to think about where we might stay the night, with the result that we arrive after dark in a strange town to find everywhere closed. We then have to hammer on the door of any place with a light showing, pleading with them to let us have a bed for the night.'

None of this was any surprise to me, but I was surprised when Muz said that Forest Lodge was to be sold and they were moving to Suffolk. Andy had spent his childhood there and had fond memories of life in a small village where nothing much had changed for centuries. 'He has always wanted to go back and recapture that idyll,' Muz said, 'and now we're married we can share his dream together.'

'What about Spindle?' was my first question when I replied to her letter telling me this news.

'He will be transferred to a hospital near enough for us to visit and have him home,' she wrote back. Muz had it all worked out. 'Ros and Gary can take the train from London to visit us, or they can drive up quite easily. The best thing of all will be the sense of liberation when Forest Lodge has been left behind with all its bitter memories. I can have a proper settled home at last and put down roots with Andy. It's still possible at our age to make a whole new life together.'

All Andy needs for putting down roots is a deep armchair, I thought. He'll be rooted to the spot for ever once they move, but if that makes Muz happy and, even more importantly, she takes her piano with her for comfort, it can be nothing but a relief all round.

My own situation was more pressing as attempts to prise Lulu out of our house continued without success, and what made it worse was that she and Adam seemed to have formed an attachment. Good grief, I thought, she's another one. It may be flattering to have a husband who is admired by other women, as long as it doesn't go beyond admiration, but to have one like this actually living with us, is really too much. Adam would often stay up late with her watching television on nights when she wasn't working, while I went to bed too tired to bother joining them. There was an occasion when, waking up at midnight and finding his side of the bed empty, I got up and went to investigate. 'Storming into the sitting room making a scene,' Adam complained, 'when all we were doing was watching the box together. I need to relax after a busy day driving round looking at bovines.'

'And what I need is a house all to ourselves with that woman gone. Do you really think sitting on the sofa at midnight with an off-duty stripper is the kind of relaxation you need before getting up early next morning for another busy day at work. She's got to go,' I demanded.

'Well, how do you propose achieving that?'

'I'll take the children to Fran's and stay at the farm with her until the coast is clear to come back. Fran says I can have her guest house for as long as I like. You will have to choose between Lulu and me.'

'Don't be ridiculous. Louise and Simon are due to start school in a week. You can't do that to them.'

'You can't go on inflicting Lulu on me.'

'I'll talk to her again. She knows she's got to go. She's waiting to hear about a flat she's been to see.'

'Why doesn't she get the housing officer to find somewhere else for her?'

'I think there was a problem with her tenancy here and she was given notice, so they are not keen to keep her as a tenant.'

'That isn't hard to believe. Why do you allow yourself to get taken in like this? She's just another scheming woman, using flattery to get the better of you.'

'She's had a lot of knocks in her life. She deserves a break.'

'Not at our expense. I'm serious about leaving and going to Fran's.'

'Please be a little more patient. She will be gone in days, I promise.'

Those few days went by and she was still there, drifting about in her pyjamas, giving orders to the staff and generally behaving as mistress of the house. So I took the children to Fran's and when term started we all did lessons together with Fran's children who were on an approved correspondence course. At first the children were excited to be back on a farm again, especially as Fran had horses and went riding every day, so we joined her, and mine were started on ponies. Of particular fascination was Fran's swimming pool (empty of water after a shortage) where she kept snakes as pets. All this was engaging for a while, but inevitably the children soon wanted to know when we were going home, and so did I. Adam's whole focus was on his new job, so that the situation with Lulu, coupled with my absence, seemed almost too much for him to think about. Each time I phoned to ask if Lulu had departed, he became more irritated with me, insisting that I was being unreasonable.

There had to be a solution to this impasse and Fran recommended a lawyer friend of hers for advice. I went to see him and he was able to assure me that I was not being unreasonable. He suggested starting with an informal approach. Fran would go to Salisbury and call at the house one evening when Adam was there, to have a friendly drink and introduce Mike the lawyer as a friend who had come with her, whom she would like Adam to meet. The conversation would gradually turn to Lulu, and if she was there Mike would be able to get a handle on the situation. All proceeded to plan, but it turned out to be one of Lulu's working nights and she wasn't there, so Fran and Mike took the opportunity to impress on Adam that the situation was untenable and he must force her to leave.

Fran reported all this to me on her return and was confident that Adam would be on the phone very soon to tell me that Lulu had gone and the house was ours. We waited a few days, and then a few more days, and when I phoned Adam for news it was as if no conversation between them had ever taken place. I asked him about this but he laughed it off as a social visit, saying how nice it had been to see Fran, and to meet Mike.

I went back to see Mike who was surprised at the lack of response and thought Adam was in a state of denial about the problem, because he didn't know how to deal with it at the same time as focusing all his energies on a new job. This sounded entirely plausible and it was very helpful to have a common sense opinion offered. 'In that case, what can we do about it?' I asked him.

'Since Adam and Lulu have been living in the same house, alone together for a significant length of time, whether or not there has been anything going on, you have grounds for divorce,' he said.

'I don't want a divorce. I just want the woman to go and leave us in peace in our own home.'

Mike continued, 'Although the threat of divorce sounds like an extreme measure, it is the only way to put pressure on Adam to get the woman out. As things stand, he is relying on you to relent and move back, accepting the status quo for the sake of the children.'

'I can't afford any legal costs.'

'You won't have any. I will ask Adam for a private meeting. A deadline will be set for the woman to leave with all her possessions and any hangers-on, never to return under any circumstances. I will explain to him that any failure to carry this out will result in instant divorce proceedings, indisputable grounds having been provided. If he feels unable to deliver an ultimatum to the woman, I can give him a letter to hand to her personally, to make sure she gets it. She will not argue. The last thing she needs in her line of business is anything to do with the courts.'

'Do you think Adam will agree?'

'Of course he will. I can guarantee it. He is in a hole, and I am offering him a way out, at no cost.'

'Why are you doing this for us?'

'Because you are a friend of Fran's, and I will always do what I can for any friend of hers.'

'Thank you,' I said, feeling close to tears. 'I don't know how we can ever repay you.'

'Go on being a friend to Fran,' he said.

Mike was as good as his word and Lulu left in a puff of dust the very next day after Mike had spoken to Adam, and, as it happened, to her as well. Adam was puzzled at the haste of her departure. 'She couldn't wait to leave,' he said on the phone to me, mystified. 'Mike really put the wind up her. I don't know what he said to her, but it was as if she'd got the law on her tail. All her things were flung into boxes and suitcases double time and she literally fled, bundling her poor blind brother into the car with her.'

'Maybe there was more going on in the house than we realised, with so many people coming and going, and you were a good cover, until she was found out.'

'We'll never know, darling, but thank God you're coming back. It's been a nightmare. You've no idea how chaotic it's been without you and the house being used as a drop-in centre. No one doing any proper cooking or organising any sort of routine. Just endless picnicking in the dining room and leaving a terrible mess for the servants to clear up. Do hurry back, darling.'

With Lulu and her tribe gone, it was bliss to return and settle back to the normal tumult of family life after such an unnerving experience. I was very relieved to find that the hiatus had not damaged us and I still had the same loving husband as before; his only fault that sometimes he was inclined to spread his loving nature too generously. Louise and Simon were excited to be joining Blakiston School just down the road, and best of all they had inherited second-hand bikes left behind by some of the younger members of Lulu's tribe. They could go off by themselves on these, riding along quiet streets in our suburb, avoiding a busy highway which connected this enclave to the city centre a couple of miles away. It was a very convenient place to live, with a short commute to the Bowmaker office for Adam, and close to Baines Avenue where several medical specialists had consulting rooms and a clinic. I promised myself a job at one of the surgeries as soon as the children were settled in school.

Peter was ready for nursery school, needing the company of other children his age, and a small nursery called Treetops was also conveniently close. He wanted to have a bike like the others but was still small for his age so he had to make do with a tricycle and, much to his frustration, he was not allowed out onto the road. Traffic laws were quite strict in Salisbury and children on bicycles had to pass a safety test before using public roads, while tricycles were restricted to gardens. This didn't prevent Peter trying to go out and making a dash for the gate whenever he saw a chance. Having hauled him back one day, I could hear the phone ringing in the house and went to answer it. It was Fran and we went on talking for some time until disturbed by the sound of a car arriving outside my house, loudly hooting its horn to indicate some kind of emergency.

The front door was open and a furious woman came running inside shouting at me, while dragging a reluctant Peter behind her. 'Is this your child?' she demanded. Not waiting for a reply, she went on, 'He was on a tricycle in the fast lane of the highway. In the fast lane – do you hear? Just pedalling along, oblivious to all the traffic swerving around him. A miracle he wasn't killed.' She paused to draw breath. 'It's a very fast road. Very dangerous. If I hadn't stopped to rescue him there would have been a terrible accident. No one else was stopping. I picked up the tricycle as well as him.' She stood there red in the face, trembling with anger and shock, her voice coming in gasps with the effort of telling me this. Peter had already run off.

I held out my hand to her in abject apology: 'I had no idea he'd gone out onto the big road. How could he have got there? I thought he was in the garden where he's supposed to be,' I added lamely.

'You were on the phone yakking to someone instead of keeping an eye on him,' the woman said accusingly.

'Yes, I know. But he also knows he's not supposed to go out of the garden on his own.'

'He's only a child. Children his age have to be supervised.'

'I know that, and I'm completely in the wrong, and mortified about what happened. Thank God you were there. How can I thank you enough? What can I do to make it up to you?'

'You can thank God, like you said. And keep your gate closed.'

With that parting advice she returned to her car, extricated the tricycle from the boot, set it down and drove off before I had a chance to ask her name or thank her again. I needed to find Peter and make sure he understood the enormity of his foolishness in going for a ride on the highway, but he was already entertaining the staff with a graphic description of his exploit, making them laugh and clap so much for its audacity that I didn't have the heart to be too cross. When he was told about it, Adam too was impressed, though not so much by my lapse in child care as Peter's daring escapade.

'He needs to go to nursery school instead of getting bored at home on his own,' Louise remarked after this incident, and I agreed. It was time, too, for me to get a job, and I was taken on as nurse/receptionist by a partnership of consultant paediatricians: Doctors Zilberg, Sanders and Pichanick, at their Baines Avenue rooms. Working for these three outstanding child specialists was a very happy and rewarding time for me because it was a great learning experience as well as a privilege to be part of their team. Each morning when I arrived at the surgery, phones would be ringing and this filled me with anticipation for the day ahead. GPs dealt with routine conditions and referred anything that was complicated or evading diagnosis, so the cases seen at Baines Avenue were interesting and unusual. Two other nurses were employed in addition to a book-keeper and secretary, and when patients started arriving each morning the surgery became a noisy hub of activity with children and toys spilling everywhere.

It was a time when Vietnamese orphans were being adopted by kind-hearted couples in different parts of the world, including Rhodesia. Some of these children had been through traumatic experiences resulting in disturbed behaviour which could be difficult to manage as problems became more evident. Other children brought for advice on disordered behaviour were often equally challenging, but the young patients whose conditions distressed us most were the child cancers. We became very involved with the parents and whole families in these situations for emotional as well as medical support, and when a child died it left all of us stricken. Bereaved parents often continued to come to the surgery for months or years afterwards, simply for the compassion and understanding of the doctors. Another group much in need of sympathetic care were refugees from Mozambique. They arrived destitute and speaking only Portuguese, as the battle for freedom in that country led to the disintegration of public services. The desperate plight of these people, who very often had sick children in need of urgent care, was met by Rhodesian relief agencies who made referrals to relevant professional specialities like ours.

Through all these varied demands the doctors dispensed kindness and expertise with a ready sense of humour, handed out with supplies of sweets from bowls in the waiting room and their consulting rooms. On Friday afternoons all three doctors left early, wearing prayer shawls, and the rooms went quiet, so the rest of us could clear up and put all the toys away that had been scattered around during the crowded week.

Unseen by most of us and for a time suppressed in national news outlets was that Rhodesia had its own liberation war, and this was gathering pace on northern and western borders. Young white men of military age were being called up to serve in the Rhodesian defence forces and when families began to lose sons killed in action, the truth of what was called the 'Bush War' began to be felt. Adam volunteered for the Police Anti-Terrorist Unit (PATU) which was a para-military force of civilian volunteers, requiring compulsory commitment to a set number of days on active service each year. It meant that he was often away, but all businesses and employers shouldered this burden willingly, in the cause of what they believed to be defence of the country against communist infiltration and takeover by a Marxist regime, as had happened in Mozambique. Prime Minister Ian Smith declared that Rhodesia stood as one of the last bastions against communism in Africa and this justification for the Bush War did not seem unreasonable at the time, since it was widely reported that insurgents were trained by North Korea and Russia. My own experience of the Mau Mau uprising which led to independence in Kenya, suggested to me that instead of war, a better strategy would be the inclusion of Africans in government, starting a process of integration. There were indications that Ian Smith may have considered similar options but his political party, the Rhodesian Front, was reported to be ideologically opposed to this.

During the early years of the seventies, the war still seemed far away and Salisbury was vibrant with social life. Adam soon became popular on the party circuit; his gift for mimicry and entertainment made him a favourite with hostesses so we were never without invitations and he was always ready for an evening out. It was a time of bottle parties when guests took a bottle and plate of finger food, providing a cheap way to get together at someone's house where the principle activity was dancing and circulating.

More elaborate parties were given by a friend whose family owned estates in both Rhodesia and England, and although she was titled she had no pretensions and was refreshingly scatty. An invitation arrived from her in the flamboyant handwriting style that went with her personality; this time for a fancy dress ball in one of the grand rooms of a mansion hired for the occasion. Fancy dress was one of my least favourite party themes, but Adam loved dressing up. We couldn't afford to hire costumes so it had to be something homemade or borrowed. Adam was already in a theatre group where they had been staging a production of South Pacific and had a selection of grass skirts, shell necklaces and gaudy flower garlands made of paper. Adam thought it would be fun to wear these and grass skirts could be twirled impressively during the dances.

When we arrived for the ball, our invitation was scrutinised and we were escorted by an attendant to meet the master of ceremonies who was announcing names of guests as they entered the ballroom. That is when we noticed that everyone else was wearing evening dress. Our hostess, who was greeting people, quickly took us aside. 'I'm so sorry,' she said, 'there's been a mix-up. At the last minute my dad arrived unexpectedly on a visit from London and brought with him a couple of cronies from the House of Lords. When he heard about the party, he insisted that some of the ministers in government who are friends of his, should be invited. Of course I couldn't refuse. But fancy dress had to go out of the window as soon as lords and ladies were to be present. I phoned in a mad panic all the people I could reach, but you must have got missed somehow.' She started giggling, and continued in a stage whisper, 'I love it though. You're not the only ones who didn't get the message. Come over here.' Huddled behind some potted palms we found others lingering in embarrassment, like ourselves dressed in ludicrous costumes. 'Don't worry,' she said, 'everyone will think you are the cabaret waiting in the wings. I'll make sure you have your own waiters looking after you with loads of drinks and food.' Adam, seizing on the idea of a cabaret with a chorus line already to hand, rehearsed us in an improvised comedy act hidden behind the palms while dancing was underway out in the grand room. After the inevitable speeches had been made and formality loosened with quantities of alcohol among the guests, we emerged from the palms with a piece of exotic folly that drew such gratifying applause, we found ourselves being congratulated instead of shunned as freaks.

To compensate the children missing out on parties when they either slept in the car or stayed at home with a babysitter, we took them to the drive-in cinema: a treat for all of us. It was an ideal family outing as we slumped in our seats with paper boxes of chicken and chips served from a café on site. The mess of greasy fingers and crumbs spilt everywhere was ignored as part of the evening's release from daytime cares, and if anyone fell asleep that was normal too. Our car had a bench seat in front so all of us could squash together, and in the interval the children ran around meeting friends from school. 'It's *lekker* having a drive-in,' they would say breathlessly, running back before the film started again. 'Not even England has one. I'm glad we're here.'

'They can't have them in England because of the rain,' Louise pointed out.

'Can I have a Lucky Packet?' Peter asked. His speech had improved noticeably since starting at Treetops where I could drop him off on my way to work each morning. Lucky Packets were another Rhodesian speciality much cherished by children. For fifty cents a small sealed packet could be bought and when opened there was a surprise object inside. This might be a miniature plastic animal or other cheap toy, or just a sweet, but it was the surprise element that appealed. As well as Lucky Packets there were Monster Packets of the same size and just as popular. Inside would be a small plastic monster of hideous deformity, thrilling the recipient, and many children had collections of these. Most shops sold the packets but I have never seen them anywhere else except in Rhodesia.

Adam's elevation to city slicker status (as he saw it) with a job in finance had not in reality enhanced our financial situation very much at all. We had a subsidised house and my own wage from the surgery, but we still struggled and there was nothing left for holidays or luxuries. Medical insurance was a big cost as there was no free health service, but it had been the same in Kenya. We had never needed any expensive treatment or thought about serious health problems until Louise unexpectedly became ill. For more than a year she'd had recurrent abdominal pain, but on numerous visits to our GP he said he could find nothing wrong and it was probably just a grumbling appendix.

As time went on, with more visits to the GP, I asked for a referral to the paediatric practice where I worked. I had already spoken to Dr Zilberg about Louise's problem and asked him, or one of the others, to see her, but these doctors had a strict ethic and would not see any child without a referral. In desperation, on a day when Louise was ill again, I took her to the surgery with me, and Dr Zilberg relented. After examining her, he admitted her to hospital straight from the surgery, and when tests were done these showed a serious kidney condition (hydronephrosis with bilateral reflux). Dr Zilberg explained this was due to congenital abnormalities which needed complex surgery. He recommended taking her to London for this to be done by an eminent surgeon, Sir David Innes Williams. 'The best in the world for this type of surgery,' he told us.

Instead of being alarmed by this news, Louise was excited to be going to England. 'We can see Gran, can't we? And go to stay at her new house, and Ros, where she lives in London. We can go to the fun fair and the zoo. The boys won't come with us. It will be just me and you, and then I can have the operation and get better.'

Ros and Gary had bought a flat in a terraced house in Battersea where houses still had pre-war features such as zinc tubs hanging on the back wall, and outside privies. By the time Louise and I arrived to stay, they had installed an indoor bathroom and modern kitchen/living room combined with two comfortable bedrooms; all very bijou and arty as would be expected. During this time traditional Battersea life continued as before with the rag and bone man calling 'Rag-Bones' as he drove his horse and cart along the street, to collect broken furniture, pots and scraps of anything that could be sold on. The paraffin man was another regular, filling cans from a tank on wheels to supply all household heating as well as some cooking stoves and even the occasional lamp. The fumes given off by burning paraffin permeated the interiors of these houses with an oily smell, always there, as familiar to household aromas as tobacco smoke.

One morning I noticed that all the windows in the street had their curtains drawn and Ros said there must have been a death, as, when this happened, curtains would stay closed all day as a mark of respect. We were still in the seventies and many of the old ways carried on, slowly.

Too slowly it seemed for Muz who, having moved into her dream cottage in Suffolk, found herself exasperated by its many age-related drawbacks after leaving behind the modern comforts of Forest Lodge. The cottage, in a small village, was several hundred years old, thatched and quaint to a degree that looked more suited to occupation by the Seven Dwarfs than real-life people. It had been built by Flemish weavers escaping persecution in their own country, and in honour of this connection Muz named the cottage 'Flemings'. Ros seized on this and insisted on calling it 'Phlegms', which she remarked was appropriate since Andy had become even more of a slob since marrying Muz, no longer needing to keep up appearances now that she was his.

'After they were married,' Ros reported, 'Muz discovered he hardly ever changes his underwear. He only has a bath when Muz insists, and due to a phobia about getting his head wet he can't bear to have his bald head washed, so it pongs.'

My own observations when Louise and I arrived at the cottage, were more concerned with its impracticalities as it had no modern heating and was very cramped inside. A staircase of steep twisting steps was poked into one corner of the sitting room with a ceiling so low that we were forced to ascend in a crouching position like hunchbacks. 'How did you ever get any furniture upstairs?' I asked Muz, and she explained that all the beds and cupboards had to be taken apart to enable this feat. 'After a great struggle dismantling them and getting them upstairs,' she said, 'nothing would stay in its place and kept sliding down the sloping floors. But Andy very cleverly solved this by suggesting bricks could be used as blocks, and it worked perfectly.'

'I bet he didn't carry the bricks up the stairs himself,' I ventured.

'Poor Andy. He developed a bad back just as we were due to move, and it's still troubling him. But he finds a good massage helps, so I do my best as a masseuse and he likes that.' I didn't want to think about Muz giving Andy massages, and turned my attention to other irksome features such as the damp chill which seeped through each room of the cottage, adding to its discomforts. 'I admit there are some problems,' Muz conceded after noticing how unimpressed I was. 'But we have got used to them, and Andy feels at home now he has his armchair and books to hand. We do a trip to the library in Sudbury once a week for him to change his books, while I do the shopping.'

'Does he help with the shopping?' I enquired, knowing what the answer would be. 'He seems to do nothing all day except read,' I pressed on, now we had got onto the subject of Andy's indolence.

'Yes, of course he's a great reader, very well informed on any topic. He was never one for taking exercise. He does rather take his ease and expect to be waited on, but I don't mind that because I like to be busy.'

Just as his sister Mary predicted, I thought, Muz has become his housekeeper and is blind to any deficiencies in him or the cottage. Except that she did allow herself a complaint when it related to her precious piano. She had to leave her beautiful Bechstein grand piano behind when they moved, but managed to fit an upright Bechstein into one end of the sitting room. Practising and playing the pieces that flowed from her fingers so readily was a joy but also an important therapy for her. Throughout the turbulent years of moving from country to country and place to place, wherever we went, a piano always came with us. After she and Fa were married and went to China as missionaries, all their wedding presents and other possessions followed, including her piano. When subsequently all was lost in a Japanese bombing raid and we later found refuge in India, Muz located another piano and this was carried by porters up the steep Himalayan mountainside to our house perched on a ledge, where earthquakes regularly rattled the ivory keys.

The piano installed at Flemings was, in this way, one in a long line, but no less treasured than all the others. Each day of her life Muz looked forward to a lull in household chores when she could sit down and play. Andy had not objected before they were married and was happy to sit with his book at Forest Lodge while Muz played, but now he said the music disturbed his reading. 'I can't concentrate with all that noise going on,' he grumbled.

'You can wear ear muffs,' I told him, 'and allow Muz the liberty of enjoying her one pleasure while you are indulging yours sitting in that chair all day.' He looked up from his book with a baleful glare. 'Don't be ridiculous,' he said.

The one big success of this visit was the pleasure that Louise and Muz had in being together again, with relief for all of us in the London surgeon's assurance that Louise's condition (which a few years before would have been fatal for most children) could be cured by a relatively new surgical procedure. He would not do this himself he told us, and explained: 'You have an outstanding surgeon, Mr Honey, right there in Salisbury where you live. I should know, I taught him myself. You can have complete confidence in Mr Honey. I will give you a letter for him, with my compliments.'

When Fa heard about our visit with its medical and surgical implications, he hurried down from Herefordshire where he and Babs now lived since returning to England to look after her elderly parents. A bed was found for him at Ros and Gary's tiny flat and we all squeezed in after leaving Muz and Andy to resume their mundane lives in the rickety cottage. 'Like two hamsters in a biscuit tin,' Ros remarked.

Chapter 4

Simon and Peter had gone to stay with Fran at the farm while I was in England with Louise and had a great many stories to tell about their adventures when we got back. Fran was inventive in finding ways to entertain and enthuse children: the farm offering many more imaginative outlets for energetic activity than city life could provide. Simon, always eager to share bursts of graphic description on any new discovery or experience, was impatient to tell us about these. 'It was *lekker*,' he said. 'We went out with horses every day, and we went to polo as well. We had *braais* and picnics and went fishing in a river on another farm. Fran didn't mind how wet or dirty we got, and we could take all our clothes off if we wanted to.'

'Did you do any lessons at all while you were there?' I asked.

'Only when there was time. But there wasn't much time because we went out all day.'

'What about Peter?'

'I went on the ponies all by myself,' Peter said. 'And I fell off too. Because we haven't got any ponies in Salisbury, I want to have a proper bike, and go out with the others.'

'You can have a bike when you start at Blakiston, so you can ride to school. That won't be long now.'

It was a relief to have the family back together and find Adam in good form still happy with his cattle finance job, but spending more time away on patrols with PATU and coming back exhausted, his camouflage uniform torn and streaked with dust or mud. Each unit consisted of five men, known as a 'stick' (the number that could fit into a helicopter), all civilian volunteers, each armed with an assault rifle and trained in bush warfare. They would be flown by helicopter to a location where gangs had been identified, and dropped to follow and engage them. These would now be called freedom fighters, but were then seen as terrorists, a term often shortened to 'terrs' in conversation.

A close camaraderie developed between members of a PATU stick, as in any combat situation their lives depended on each other, and this bond became so important for Adam that our house started to become a PATU hub. Simon and Peter were enthralled by the presence of all these uniformed tough guys coming in and out with their formidable weapons, demonstrating how to take them apart and re-assemble them, with all the gun talk and activity that boys love.

Louise was not so absorbed and was in a worsening state of health, not always well enough to go to school and often spending days in bed. A daily intake of antibiotics kept her alive while waiting for Mr Honey to arrange the surgery she needed. It was an intricate operation requiring grafts with a surgical team working together.

I had been surprised when I met Mr Honey as he was much older than I expected. When I remarked on this to Dr Zilberg, he said, 'Some surgeons go on working for as long as their eyesight and skills allow. Honey is over seventy, but he's still the best you can get. Age is no criterion of ability.'

In addition to our good fortune in having Mr Honey to do the operation, we also had a world-class hospital in Salisbury, so everything looked to be in our favour when Louise went into the children's ward the day before surgery. Mr Honey had discussed the risks with Adam and me and was optimistic that all would turn out well. 'The procedure itself should not present any problems,' he said. 'The nervous part is afterwards, waiting to see if the grafts have taken.'

Louise was more concerned about missing school than anything else and remained composed in the face of this ordeal. 'When I'm better I want to go to Mermaid Pools and have my own rubber tube, so I don't have to share with the others,' she said, lining up a treat to look forward to. The pools were some miles from the city in a wild area open to the public where an outcrop of smooth rock rose from the bushy plain. Water bubbled from the top and flowed down in a gradual slope, forming large pools at the bottom. This natural water slide became known as Mermaid Pools and was a popular attraction for families at weekends, taking picnics for a day out where children could spend hours on the slide and in the pools.

A date was set for Louise's operation but it coincided with another PATU call-up for Adam. 'You'll have to get out of it on compassionate grounds,' I told him. 'We can't go through this without you. It's more important than PATU.'

'If I drop out, the whole stick has to cancel,' he said. 'It's impossible to get a replacement at short notice. Everything will be fine. She doesn't need both of us.'

'You're special to her; she always turns to you if she needs comfort. I'm the one doing the practical things, and you're the one with the special touch when it's needed. Please don't go away just now when we need you most.'

'Darling love, it's only for a week or ten days. Nothing bad is going to happen. Mr Honey was confident on that score. You mustn't get skitzy or Louise will get skitzy too. You have to stay strong for her.'

This argument won, as he knew it would, and he went off to join his stick on the same day that Louise went into hospital.

The next day I took knitting with me for its calming effect while waiting for Louise to be wheeled off to the operating theatre. 'Don't worry, Mum,' she said. 'I'm not worried, so you don't need to be either.'

It was nine hours before she came back to the ward and I hardly recognised her when she returned. There were so many tubes attached to her body it was difficult to see how they could ever be untangled as she lay surrounded by them. She looked drained of colour, and almost drained of life, too weak to say anything or even open her eyes. I held her hand and she responded with a whisper that I couldn't hear. It was a relief when Mr Honey arrived and took me to a side room. Despite looking exhausted, he was smiling and said: 'All done. Grafts were tricky for the new valves, but we were ready for that. Everything went to plan and came together well. She just needs time to recover now.'

All I could do was shake his hand and thank him profoundly. It seemed an almost unimaginable piece of good fortune to have a surgeon with this particular expertise right here in the far reaches of Africa. When I went home later, Simon wanted me to describe all the tubes and pieces of equipment, and what they were for. 'Will Louise have a scar? Will it be a big one?' He was very interested in anything gruesome, and when asked what he would like for his birthday, he said he would like a book on forensic science.

Louise was making good progress in hospital and starting to look less frail, when she unexpectedly took a turn for the worse, with a fever and other signs that Mr Honey said were indications that the grafts might be failing. This was bad news, and when the nurses said I must send for her father because the outlook wasn't good, I felt very alone and fearful. It was impossible to reach Adam. He was out in the bush somewhere with only intermittent radio contact. I needed an adult with me, and Fran once again came to my rescue, sharing the bedside vigil. Those were long days and nights of anguish, but slowly the drugs being pumped into Louise began to take effect and she rallied. By the time Adam came home she was sitting up, asking for ice cream, but it was a whole month before she was well enough to leave hospital. She did have an impressive scar, much to Simon's satisfaction. This later required plastic surgery to reduce the keloid effect, but in all other respects she was restored to perfect health, thanks to Mr Honey.

Since Lulu and her tribe had been cleared out of our house and the debris from their occupation disposed of, we had been able to spread ourselves and enjoy the sensations of space and luxury which, after the bean house, was a remarkable step up for us. Even the dogs seemed liberated, and were excited by all the new smells as we took them for walks and they met other dogs to exchange sniffs with, or growl at. At home there was a particular activity enjoyed at weekends or in the evenings with drinks on the veranda, involving all members of the family including the dogs. The big avocado tree in the garden had fruit hanging from high branches, too high to pick, even with ladders. Children and dogs would stand underneath the tree while Adam and I, sitting comfortably on the veranda, took shots with air rifles at the stalks of high avocadoes. It required skill to hit a stalk so that the pear would fall. If a shot hit the pear itself, that was counted as a miss because the avocado stayed where it was. Every time a pear fell, a child or dog nearest to the spot would jump to catch it, keeping score of the number of catches. Labradors have soft mouths and ours had been trained to retrieve so they brought their avocadoes to place carefully into our outstretched hands, to be rewarded with an affectionate pat.

We feasted on all these ripe pears and gave them away to friends and our staff whose capable and willing service I very much appreciated, but there was a problem. Such a big house needed a lot of staff to keep it running smoothly, and the expense that we had accepted as part of the deal at first, began to be too much. When, in addition, the rent was increased after the first two years in line with other government rents, we realised we would have to look for something cheaper. This had to be near the school now that Peter had joined the others. He was still small and underweight so I took him to Dr Zilberg for advice. After carrying out percentile measurements, he was laconic: 'Just as age is no criterion of ability (he reminded me), size is similarly no handicap to achievement, in the absence of evidence suggesting otherwise.' So I was put in my place again.

The new and cheaper house we found was one of the older town houses, small and compact, on Montagu Avenue where jacaranda trees lined the street; their leafy branches and mauve flowers spreading cascades of colour. If there had been an institution for displaying blue plaques in the city this house would have had one. A famous ballerina, Merle Park, who was now a principal dancer with the Royal Ballet in London, had lived there and her parents still owned the house. It can be a feature of old houses that they preserve an ambience from previous occupants, and this one had a quality of composure and tranquillity that I found very soothing in the various ups and downs of family life where, for us, money was tight and Adam very often away.

When he was home he needed to unwind from the tensions of warfare and for him the best outlets were parties and dancing, the livelier the better. He had heard about swinger parties among Salisbury's smart set and was curious to see what went on and how to get an invitation. When he succeeded in inveigling himself into one of these, I was dubious, thinking it would be horribly embarrassing and shaming and no fun at all for a gauche person like myself. 'Come as an observer,' Adam suggested. 'You know how you love to sit in a corner incognito and watch how people behave, without getting involved.'

This appealed to me in a Desmond Morris kind of way, but not if I was going to have to watch my husband doing things I would prefer not to see.

'If you are there, it will put a brake on temptations for me,' Adam said. 'All I'm interested in really is the dancing. I gather they have professional dancers joining in – it's not just the usual smooching around. I need you to be there, so we don't get too sucked in.'

This convinced me but I was a reluctant party-goer when the evening arrived and we went to join a gathering of people we had never met before, and were included only as a favour at Adam's request. I felt awkward before we even entered the house when we found ourselves parking the car among Ferraris and Porches, but Adam was upbeat. 'These are the kind of people we need to meet. You never know when connections might come in useful and give us a leg-up.' An unfortunate choice of words, I thought, when associated with swingers.

I lost sight of Adam almost immediately as he went ahead as usual to make an entrance and disappeared into a room with lighting so subdued that his moment of drama, I thought, had little possibility of being noticed. Among those present, all focus was on a group of male dancers as they moved with hypnotic grace to the sound of soft music, exotic as birds of paradise. No one was being introduced to anyone else or new arrivals greeted by anyone as I sidled in, relieved to be anonymous and find cushions scattered around the sides of the room where I could sink onto one that was unoccupied. The mood in the room was not at all disagreeable and the dancers were mesmeric, but I soon felt the need for a drink, and a cloakroom.

Dim lighting in a strange house caused difficulties in finding my way around as I ventured into other rooms, and when a staircase appeared ahead I noticed a man sitting all by himself on a stair. He was wearing a blue boiler suit and looked distinctly out of place. 'You look as if you've come straight off a tractor,' I said, glad to find another misfit like myself.

'I have,' he replied gloomily.

'What are you doing here, then?'

'This is usually a perfectly normal house, with normal people in it, where I come to stay when I'm in Salisbury doing farm shopping.'

'Do you have a farm? Where is it?'

'Centenary. A bit far away. Would you like to join me on this stair and let me tell you my troubles?'

'I need a drink first. I was on my way to get one, while at the same time trying to find a cloakroom, and failing on both counts.'

'Tell me what you drink, and while I'm getting it, if you go to the top of the stairs there is a nice quiet bathroom on the left. I'm Richard Sims, by the way. I do have a wife, but she prefers to stay on the farm while I do the shopping.'

I introduced myself and when Richard came back with drinks for us both, we sat on the stairs talking, and shifting along when couples wanted to pass on their way upstairs.

Later when Adam came to look for me, he was surprised to find me settled on the stair with a partner, neither of us having any interest in activities elsewhere in the house. I introduced him to Richard and they chatted briefly, but Adam had not found the evening's exhilarations to his taste and was surprisingly ready to go home.

'You must come for a weekend at the farm,' Richard said. 'I would like you to meet Felicity, my wife, and she would be delighted to entertain your children as we have none of our own, so it's a treat for her when families come to stay.'

'Yes, we would like that, thank you,' I said, as we left him, still looking forlorn, sitting on the stairs.

'What did you think about the evening?' I asked Adam on the way home.

'A bit disappointing really,' he admitted. 'All those people are in a clique. I've never felt such an outsider before.'

'What did you expect? We're not into that scene. You knew that before wangling an invitation. We only went out of curiosity.'

'Yes, quite so, but I'd like to have another go since you have teamed up with Richard. He could show us the ropes.'

'He doesn't want any part of it, that's why he was sitting on the stairs still wearing his farm clothes. It's just a convenient place to stay when he's got shopping to do in Salisbury. His wife refuses to go with him. Probably terrified of getting trapped in a session with that lot.'

'I'd still like to go again.'

'This wife also refuses to go. One night in that house is enough.'

We were soon distracted by news from Adam's parents in Kenya telling us that the family farm, Glanjoro, had been sold to the country's president, Arap Moi, and renamed Technology Farm. His parents, Cen and Alison, had moved to another farm, this time at Gilgil, and were building a house where they could retire and live peacefully with no concerns about rainfall or other frets that farmers are daily obsessed with. The site chosen for the house was on a ridge with extensive views across dry grassland where herds of zebra and impala grazed on slopes above a tumbling river full of rainbow trout. This was the Malewa river which fly fishermen held to be one of Kenya's finest trout rivers. Adam was impatient to visit and since he'd had shares in Glanjoro Farms Ltd, now that it had been sold we were hoping to be able to afford fares when there was a distribution of proceeds.

Meanwhile, money remained short and there was little to spare for treats, let alone holidays, so I devised off-beat ways to entertain the children. A free ride could be had on lifts at the Monomatapa Hotel: a new and prestigious building in the centre of the city, it was a useful place to visit when shopping. The hotel rose to sixteen floors and lifts were a novelty for children who had not lived in a city before. We could enter at ground level and experience the thrill of elevation all the way to the top, where stairs led to the roof with a grand view and competition among the children to spot landmarks. We might descend afterwards to visit the hotel's swimming pool, and even have an ice cream by the pool if we were able to dodge questions about our eligibility as non-residents. Inevitably a time arrived when the hotel manager, noticing our family like vagrants entering the lifts laden with shopping bags yet again, politely suggested that we might agree to a moratorium on this activity for the sake of the hotel's reputation. I apologised to him and we shook hands on the agreement, my thoughts turning to other tall buildings in the city where we might look less conspicuous.

Normally children are bored by any kind of shopping trip, but the big stores in Salisbury with their glittering toy departments offered a whole world of exploration for mine after farm life. They knew that toys outside of birthdays or Christmas were off limits, but they could roam around looking at the toys, deciding which ones they would choose if they had the choice, making sure that I took note for future reference. Enticing displays of sweets were another magnet despite knowing they were not allowed any, to protect their teeth, but sometimes I would relent, or it might be Lucky Packets for a treat.

At supermarkets there were African packers who put all the check-out items into bags for customers and carried these out to their cars. It was a service I very much appreciated and regretted that we were not supposed to tip the packers since the service was offered free, so I would sometimes ask a packer to choose something out of my shopping bags for himself. The item most favoured, to my surprise, was toilet paper. 'My wife will be so happy to have this,' a packer would say, and the memory stays with me that such a small luxury could bring that amount of pleasure.

Shopping trips were always combined with a visit to the post office to collect our mail and this was a highlight when there was a letter from Muz, who wrote every week, or Fa or Ros, who wrote occasionally. Adam's mother Alison also wrote every week, always on blue aerogramme forms supplied and pre-stamped by the post office as more convenient and cheaper than using envelopes. Her style of writing was compact and direct, so she was able to convey a week's worth of news in the minimum amount of space. It was mainly about the dogs, and polo with scores noted, and how tiresome the chronic water shortage was, conjuring up an immediate sense of life in their new house with its daily dramas so that we could feel we were not so far away after all.

Letters from friends who had scattered to live in various countries around the world were just as important in helping me to feel less of an exile, and one day there was a fat letter from England with wavy handwriting that I recognised with a shock. I opened it in the car and sat reading, trying to pretend that my sudden agitation was due to the heat of the car park.

The letter was from Lanner, telling me that his father had died, and how this had affected him; continuing then at length with news and emotions long suppressed, as if his father's death had opened an outlet. I knew his parents and had grown close to them during the time of my nurse training in London, when they had been kind and hospitable to me. Replying to Lanner's letter would inevitably invite further contact but I could not ignore it. I was still owed an explanation for the heartbreak he caused me those many years ago in Tanganyika, when he had gone '*wasi wasi*', as that state of mind is described in Swahili. Refusing to communicate and shutting me out of his life had led to the wilderness years, and maybe now there might be some enlightenment. I replied to the letter with genuine sympathy, and wrote to his mother with the same feeling of loss for a good and courageous man.

He had fought in the First World War and talked to me about the terrors endured, as well as friendships and lighter times. They took it in turns, he said, when each day two of them would go back to base from their trench to collect rations and supplies. It was a dangerous sprint over rough ground, dodging German snipers. After one of these forays returning safely with the packs, when these were opened it was discovered that they had forgotten to bring the all-important cigarettes, so this was a major crisis. There was no option but to go back, and this time they found themselves under fire. They ran like hares to stay alive, getting lost at one point in the muddle and sweat of the dash. But the cigarettes were safe.

Nearly all letters were written by hand, even business letters, as few people had typewriters and there was pride in writing a good letter and having legible handwriting. The children enjoyed writing to their grandparents, often with candid observations which it might have been better to avoid, such as: 'Mum forgot where she parked the car today and we walked all round looking for it. Then we nearly got arrested because we thought we had found it and we all got in, but it was someone else's car and they called the police.'

After that incident I was careful to memorise parking places, but another occasion was reported in a letter that caused grandparents to reply in some alarm. The children were as usual sleeping on mattresses in the car one night at a hotel where Adam and I were guests at a party. Several other cars were occupied by sleeping children and all was proceeding normally until staff alerted us to a commotion in the car park. When we went to investigate we found our children and others running about outside in their pyjamas, all in a fever of excitement. When we had rounded them up and calmed them down, Louise told us what had happened, and now, these many years later, she relates from memory:

We were in our usual places in the car that night, supposed to be sleeping, but bored, unable to sleep. My place was on the front bench seat, Simon on the middle seat, and Pete was in the back. An African man came to the passenger window, knocked on it and asked me to wind it down. I obliged. He was quite polite and asked if he could look inside the car and in the glove pocket. In our childish innocence we said Yes because we didn't suspect anything nefarious and couldn't think why not. We thought he was just being curious and friendly. As he was leaning into the car a large white man came up and grabbed him from behind, started shouting at him, and threw him to the ground. This alerted the security guards and all hell broke loose. The thief was beaten up and restrained while they waited for a police van, which duly came and he was bundled into the back. We were pretty bemused by all the commotion, and I was distressed at what was happening to the window-peeping man since I thought he'd been quite nice. But it was fun to have the attention and have a break from the boredom of sleeping in the car. The great thing was that we never had to sleep in the car again after that incident!

There was no more partying that night as we questioned whether it was sensible to leave children in cars in a public place, and Louise had her own objections. 'It's too hot in the car so we often have to open the windows, and then anyone can get in. We could get kidnapped as well. Anyway I'm getting too big to be squashed up with the boys in the car now I'm nearly twelve.'

It seemed that a babysitter was a better idea and since we had moved to the Montagu Avenue house and taken on new staff, we had a very capable housemaid, Hilda, who was glad to earn extra money in the evenings. This avoided further such incidents reported with glee by Simon in letters to grandparents, aunts and great-aunts. But when he was involved in a seriously dangerous escapade which had been all his own idea, I noticed that no reports appeared in letters to relatives.

Adam had a Citroen company car but often walked to work to keep fit, so his car would be left in the drive next to our old Cortina Estate. One very hot afternoon during the school holidays when I had finished work and had shopping to do, I went to check on the children before going out. Louise was in her room but the boys were nowhere to be found. They knew they must not go off by themselves without telling me where they were going, and Hilda said she had seen them a short while before, playing in the garden. We both searched and called, but there was no sign. I decided they must have gone to a friend's house and forgotten to tell me, so I went to get in my car, uneasy about leaving without knowing where they were, but Hilda was there if they needed anything. Walking past Adam's car, I thought I heard a muffled noise but when I looked inside they were not there. I walked on and then heard the same noise again, faintly. It still seemed to come from the Citroen and going back to have another look, this time I opened the boot and there were the boys, jammed inside, their faces scarlet with heat and dripping with sweat, looking very shocked and shaken. 'Whatever are you doing in there?' I gasped, feeling shaken myself.

'We got in, just for fun,' Simon said, 'but we didn't expect the lid to shut completely and not open again. We tried to open it but there isn't any handle inside.'

It was the merest chance that I found them in time. Had I carried on to the shops thinking they were at a friend's house, by the time I got back they would have suffocated. When Adam heard about it, he was more angry than shocked. 'The boys know they are not supposed to play in the cars, especially my work car. Hopefully this will teach them a lesson. They're such idiots.'

'Don't be so sanctimonious. You're not above doing mad things yourself. All that running around in the bush doing PATU commando stuff.' Adam's constant absences were beginning to ruffle me.

'Don't knock it. You've no idea how serious the situation really is. What you call commando stuff, along with army and air force operations, is what's keeping us alive. Anyway, turning to a happier subject, what about our anniversary? Let's celebrate and do something special this time.'

'Such as?'

'It's a twelfth anniversary, so it has to be a slap-up dinner at the Twelve Thousand Horsemen.' This was a very expensive restaurant at the Monomatapa Hotel.

'We can't possibly afford it. Just one dinner could swallow a week's wages.'

'We have to afford it. Just this once. It's time we had a bit of romance in our lives to set us off again. Life has become too humdrum with all the endless family stuff. I'm going to book a table and take you out. No argument.'

It was enchanting to think this time I would be going up in the lift at the Monomatapa, wearing my best long skirt and top, without shopping bags and children trying to keep out of sight of the hotel manager. When the anniversary arrived it was like going out on a date again, just the two of us, keyed up. Adam was wearing a suit and looked as fine as any man at the age of thirty-eight in his prime. We were given a table by the window, looking out at the city sparkling with neon lights and a sense of prosperity and purpose as traffic hummed and people strolled in the avenues. When menus were brought Adam said, 'Don't look down the right-hand side first to see what's cheapest. Don't even look at the dollar signs. Choose whatever you want. Go for your favourites.' So we indulged ourselves and even had starters and a bottle of wine in an ice bucket.

At the end, when the bill was handed to Adam and he felt for his wallet, a familiar look came over his face and I wilted. Surely this could not be happening again, I thought. He was always losing his wallet or mislaying it, or the car keys, or important papers that somehow drifted away at vital moments. 'Please don't say you haven't brought any money,' I whispered so the waiter wouldn't hear.

'I know I had my wallet when we started out,' he said. 'I must have left it somewhere. Maybe in the car,' he suggested.

'I'll go and have a look, and if it isn't there I'll drive home and get my purse, then come back to pay. You'll have to wait here pretending that I've gone to the loo.'

I had not brought any money with me, as an act of faith that Adam would not lose his wallet this time and would be ready to pay the bill without any hiatus of the kind that often accompanied outings. This was especially embarrassing if we had guests but Adam was never embarrassed, assuming that the sudden unexplained absence of his wallet when the bill arrived would be accepted as momentary forgetfulness, covered by me paying, or the guests.

A quick search of the car revealed no wallet and it took only minutes to drive home and return with my purse containing money put aside for contingencies. I handed it over and Adam paid the bill with just enough left for a tip. We drove home in silence. 'Don't be like that,' Adam said, putting out a hand to take mine as I sat in glum silence. 'You have to admit the dinner was outstanding, great food in a fabulous setting. It was everything we could have wished for.'

'Except the bill at the end when you did your empty-pocket routine,' I said sourly.

'I'll refund you when I find my wallet.'

'And I'll look forward to hearing where it was, if you do find it.'

The next day when I asked if the wallet had been found, Adam said rather vaguely that, yes, it had turned up after all.

'Where?'

'Just lying around,' he replied.

'Remember, you owe me,' I reminded him.

Soon after this most memorable of anniversaries an invitation arrived from Richard and Felicity to spend a weekend at their farm, a long drive north to Centenary. The children were excited but there were always fights on extended drives when they complained of getting hot and bored. To avoid this we decided that their recently acquired pet rats could come along to provide distraction. There was a plan to teach the rats tricks, since one of the staff at our previous house had a clever rat who lived in his pocket, and emerged when called to show a variety of skills that were both entertaining and comic. The journey in the car turned out to be more entertaining for the rats than the rest of us when they dispersed to explore the many interesting nooks and crannies of the car's interior bodywork, while the children were kept occupied in efforts to extract them. We had not thought to ask the Sims if they minded rats coming to stay, having assumed that everyone was as charmed by rats as we were. It didn't occur to us that anyone, let alone a country farmer's wife like Felicity, could be phobic. So the pets were banished to their cage in the children's room, where they were fed and played with as regularly as at home, but not allowed out to scamper around the house.

Centenary was an important centre of tobacco farming and the fields of tobacco in those northern regions lay among landscapes of surpassing beauty. Great rocky hills of grey granite rose monumentally between the golden and russet colours of trees and bush under the bluest of skies. These were the colours of northern Rhodesia in its wild glory, where tobacco fields added ribbons of green. Tobacco was a principle export crop that contributed substantially to the prosperity of the country, where producers like Richard laboured in the many complex processes required to deliver high-quality bales. During the curing season when harvested tobacco leaves were hung on racks in tall barns to dry out, farmers and their assistants checked the temperature of the drying process at intervals throughout the night, with very little sleep to be had for several weeks.

I enjoyed being back on a farm again with Richard showing us around, absorbing the familiar sensations of farm life, but not those of recent developments in the Bush War which was spreading now with attacks on farm houses and worker compounds. The Sims had built a fortified bunker inside the house where we retreated each evening before sunset, dinner being served early to accommodate this routine. The danger time for coming under attack we were told was usually between 5.30 and 8.30 in the evening, and SMGs (sub-machine guns) were carried by both Richard and Felicity from tea time onwards. We did not sleep in the bunker, but it was an uneasy feeling all the same as we lay in our beds later on, listening for any unusual night sounds. All the windows in the house were covered with sandbags piled up outside to repel grenades, but these were no defence against the bush fighters' RPGs (rocket-propelled grenades) which could penetrate buildings.

Richard told us the story of a local family who had come under attack. They were alerted one evening by their dogs barking outside, and when shots were fired the wife ran to let the dogs into the house so they wouldn't get shot. Before she managed to open the door it was blown off its hinges by an RPG, but instead of flattening her as it crashed inwards, she fell onto it and was propelled by the blast like a missile along the hall corridor. Her only thought during those moments was a determination to hang onto her gun, still on its strap across her chest. Simultaneously another grenade collapsed the end wall of the corridor and she hurtled through the gap, landing in a flower bed outside. Stunned but unhurt and seized with adrenaline, she steadied her gun and let off a burst at members of the gang she could see silhouetted against flames rising from the house that was now burning. Surprised to be caught in a volley of shots, the gang dropped their heavy RPG launcher and fled.

Her children and husband who had been taking cover during the barrage, now emerged, and finding all of them alive, including the dogs, they drove to a neighbour. Refusing to be daunted and with no fuss, the house was rebuilt, this time with a grenade-proof bunker.

It was the first time we had experienced the reality of a war that seemed previously far away. Richard was a member of PATU as were all farmers, who were also on a radio network known as Agri-Alert for communication if they were attacked. The PATU connection provided Richard and Adam with hours of absorbed conversation while the boys sat listening with rapt expressions, hoping to be allowed to help with the loading and unloading of gun magazines. These held thirty rounds of 9mm ammunition and it was a tremendous thrill for Simon and Peter to handle the pouches of shiny bullets and count them as they were clicked into their metal slots.

National news broadcasts were sparing in the way incidents were reported, to avoid alarm, but I suspected there was an element of propaganda so that supporters of the regime (which included most non-Africans) went on believing that they were engaged in a just war against the forces of communism. The belief system held a notion that the world didn't understand this and that we had few friends outside the country, so a sense of isolation took hold. As nervousness about the future increased, professional people began to leave, with some of Salisbury's most distinguished doctors joining the exodus. When Dr Pichanick, a partner in the practice I worked for, left to go and work in America, I became anxious myself. I asked Dr Zilberg about this: 'When Jews start leaving a country, does it mean the writing is on the wall?'

'Put it another way,' he said. 'When Jews start moving to a new country, it could be seen as a good sign for that country.' Within two years he had moved to Texas, and Dr Sanders left for Cape Town in South Africa. But before this happened it was still 1975 and we had Christmas to think of.

The big department stores each had a Santa in residence in a glittering grotto complete with elf helping to give out presents to children. Louise declared herself too old for such events but the boys loved to visit Santa each year when he arrived from Lapland. The post office ingeniously ran a service at these times that intercepted letters addressed to him, posted by children, and these were passed to a team employed to send replies. It was advertised in advance that children should include an address with their letters, the advertisement coming from Santa himself of course. Simon always wrote and always received a reply. Peter was still learning to write and was shy about writing, so Simon wrote for him. Replies from Santa were typed instead of handwritten and this raised questions. 'Santa is old, and old people don't do typing. They do writing instead,' Simon remarked. 'So do you think the letters really do come from him?'

'His elves probably do the typing for him,' I suggested.

'When are we going to Greatermans (a large department store) to see him?'

'As soon as we hear that he has arrived.'

When the day came for our visit to Santa, the city was full of Christmas shoppers all trying to find parking spaces in crowded streets, stifling in December heat. I was flustered and hurried the children along, not wanting to spend longer than necessary on this expedition. Clutching Peter's hand I steered him past a bunch of people who were surging into a shop and was pulling him on, when a shout came from Simon. 'Mum, you've walked straight past Greatermans.' In my haste I hadn't noticed where we were.

'It's all right,' I said. 'There's another Santa at OK Bazaar a bit further on. We can go there instead.'

'Don't be silly, Mum. Santa can't be in two places at once.'

You can't fool children, I thought, as I turned to join the throng in Greatermans.

The biggest surprise that Christmas was Adam's announcement that we were moving again. Eric Hornby had not found a suitable replacement for him at Rogate Farm and was offering enhanced terms to entice him back. 'We're barely making ends meet here,' he said. 'It's been a struggle ever since we arrived, even with you working. Eric has made me the kind of offer it would be foolish to pass up. And I know you miss the farm,' he added.

'I'm not living in the bean house again,' I told him. 'I like our house here in Montagu Avenue. It's convenient for everything, especially the school. We can't move the children back to Hartley School after Blakiston, that would be a backward step for them. And what about all their friends? And ours?'

'We can invite them to come and stay. They'll jump at the chance for weekends on a farm. Eric is moving to Salisbury. This has been his plan for a long time, to concentrate more on his various directorships. We can move into his nice big house, you'll love that, especially the garden, and the swimming pool. The children will think having a pool makes up for any drawbacks like changing school. The clincher is the salary, a lot more than we've ever had before. Eric has gone over to zero-grazing and has increased his herd substantially with all the cows kept indoors now in big new sheds. This has almost doubled production but led to management problems which need sorting out. Hence the big salary. It's flattering that he's asked me to take it on. What do you think?'

'Have you already accepted?

'Provisionally, yes, but I need you to agree before it can become official.'

'I thought you had got disillusioned with dairy farming and wanted a nice clean city job, which you found with Bowmaker. And what about PATU? It's such a big part of your life now.'

'I'll transfer to the Hartley Police section. That won't be any problem.'

'When are you supposed to be starting?'

'When I've worked out my notice with Bowmaker, so it will be about a month from now. I feel ready for a new challenge and the Rogate herd fits the bill, since reportedly things have got a bit out of hand trying to integrate the new system. Eric is aiming to have the biggest dairy herd in the country, and this shed-based system is essential for supporting maximum numbers where there is insufficient natural grazing.'

'Do you feel up to coping with such a big intensive scheme?'

'It's a challenge, as I said, and if Eric thinks I'm the one who can get to grips with it, then we should both have faith in his judgement.'

'If it's really what you want, I'll go and bang my head against the wall a few times to feel better about yet another upheaval, and go along with it, I suppose.'

'I knew you would come round. Come and have a kiss, darling.'

'No thanks. I'm not in the mood just now.'

The boys, of course, took it as another family adventure and were easily persuaded, as long as they could take their bikes and ride them on farm roads, which was agreed. But Louise was desolate at the thought of leaving Blakiston School where she had a large group of friends who were all due to move to senior school together the next year. 'I will have to go to boarding school from Hartley and that will be horrible,' she protested. Peter tried to cheer her up: 'Roger and Ruin will like being farm dogs again, and we can have more cats this time. The farm will be fun for our friends to come and stay, yours too.' So it was that after four years in Salisbury we were heading back down the road to Hartley, with the same furniture van and Cortina filled with boxes and suitcases as before.

Rogate farmhouse stood serenely in a spacious garden with wide lawns and mature trees. The swimming pool I was glad to see did not dominate, and was screened by shrubs and flower beds laid in pleasing curves instead of straight lines. Water sprinklers kept the lawns green and flowers bright with colour. There was even a vegetable and fruit section with mango and avocado trees and, best of all, two gardeners on the farm payroll in charge of it all.

The dairy buildings were fifty yards away which was convenient for Adam and I didn't mind the usual farm noises of machinery and general activity, while the warm smell of animals and silage at close range was, for me, comforting. The dogs were ecstatic the moment their noses encountered these scents and they could go off investigating cowpats and the rich variety of detritus that is always to be found in farmyards. The boys too were jubilant with the freedoms they could explore on their bikes, homing in on the workers' compound to find new friends as soon as they had tired of jumping in and out of the pool. This was a magnet for the dogs as well as children wanting to cool off in the long hot months of summer. Even the arduous milking times seemed more tolerable in the context of such an enhanced lifestyle, and Adam said he had found his slot at last. Not only did he have a superior office attached to the dairy from which to oversee operations, he had two excellent African assistant managers, Francis and Morgan.

All I needed now was a visit from Muz or Ros to show them all this. Muz said she could not afford the fare, and Ros said she and Gary could not visit a country in the grip of a rebel regime that denied its indigenous people their rights. I told Muz that I would save up the fare for her to come, and started putting aside money from my housekeeping allowance each month. Meanwhile we continued with our letters, writing each week as we had done regularly whenever we were apart. Muz, indomitably, had found a niche for herself in village life, joining the church and playing the organ which she particularly enjoyed at weddings and festivals when she could 'let rip', as she put it, with stirring music pulling out all the stops. Happiness had returned for her since she had an instrument to play once more.

As soon as word got round that I was back in Hartley the hat ladies welcomed me with one of their gargantuan tea parties, delighted that I was now living in the Hornby house with plenty of space to invite them back. We had new friends at the police station due to Adam's PATU connection, where parties were given of a completely different sort, with prodigious amounts of alcohol instead of tea. Tessa who was married to a police officer, gave epic parties. 'The best shindig ever,' Adam raved after one of these when he had recovered enough to comment after stumbling back from early morning milking. 'Tess really knows how to lay it on, and Phil is a cracking host. We're on the way up with this move. There are some first-rate people at the police camp where I'm joining one of their sticks, and you'll have the other wives to commiserate with.'

I thought the children would be excited to be seeing their Hartley friends at school, but they were scared of the headmaster, a tyrant who had children lined up outside his office each day waiting to be beaten for minor errors. Corporal punishment had been abolished in most schools by now but the regime at Hartley remained stern, while the teaching itself was of a very high order. I advised the boys to lie low and keep out of trouble.

Girls did not get beaten and, in any case, Louise would be leaving soon. Hartley girls went to Roosevelt School in Salisbury as boarders which was a dreaded prospect for her, and for all of us, but she was philosophical. 'Don't worry, Mum,' she said, 'Other girls from Hartley will be going, so we'll be together. We can share lifts with them.'

When the farm workers and their families heard that I was a nurse they started coming to the house for medicines and treatment, but I soon noticed that many of the children were malnourished and was surprised that this could be happening on a dairy farm. At Glanjoro, our farm in Kenya, milk was supplied with workers' rations but there was no milk ration here, or provision for people to buy it on site. I discussed various options with Adam to help the most needy children, but as soon as word got round, the idea was scotched by neighbouring farmers who warned of the dangers of going soft on labourers. Another idea presented itself when I noticed quantities of skim milk left over from the cream-separation process. There was no market for skim milk and it went to feed pigs, so I thought no objection could be raised if I asked for enough of this to give each underweight child a daily pint. This was agreed on the basis that children receiving the milk were nominated by me to avoid any unregulated distribution, while in view of skim milk being a waste product, it had no value anyway. In fact it retains valuable protein, vitamins and minerals, and most of the malnourished children responded remarkably quickly, so I began to hope that all the farm children could benefit in time if I introduced this ration by slow stages.

It was not just the general health of children on the farm that became a preoccupation, but their mothers as well. Large families, welcomed by men as proof of fertility, could soon turn into a burden as more children came along and mothers were worn out looking after families in addition to working as cotton pickers and weeding crops. In their culture a man's status was measured in the number of children he fathered, regardless of the effect on his wife, wives, girlfriends, or ability to support them. The women were forthcoming in their views as they brought new babies to my back-door clinic. Conversation would turn to protest: 'Men are like cockerels making a lot of noise and jumping on us all the time to make more of these to feed and look after.'

'You can get pills or an injection from the mobile clinic,' I told them. Mobile family planning clinics provided by the government came round every three months and were a very well-resourced service, but not very well attended, which surprised me.

'The pills are no good, we forget to take them, or our husbands find them and throw them away.'

'What about the injection?' This was safe and easy.

'We're afraid of the injection. The grandmothers say it is bad medicine.'

'Next time the clinic comes, I will have the injection myself so you will see nothing bad happens to me.'

The injection, Depo-Provera, was a new form of birth control that I wanted to try, so the mobile clinic offered an ideal opportunity. When it arrived at the farm I joined the queue of African mothers, and as soon as they saw me having the injection they wanted it too. 'What about your husbands objecting?' I asked.

'They won't know,' the women laughed. 'Inside the clinic van they will think we are just being given a check-up.'

Pleased with the outcome of the clinic visit I was unprepared for any reaction from other farms. When it was reported that I had been seen entering the van with African women, there was disapproval from neighbouring farm wives. 'Adam's wife is making a spectacle of herself and setting a bad example. Lining up with all those nannies, getting so familiar.' The term 'nannies' was often used in the form of a collective noun for African women. 'And do you know,' the gossip continued, 'Wendy was seen outside the post office the other day in full view, shaking hands with a black as if they were the best of friends, and then having a long conversation with him. She is completely shameless. Adam won't last long in his job if he lets her carry on like this.'

'Oh yes, we have heard there are problems, and Adam doesn't do anything about it,' the hat ladies reported back to me. 'Even worse,' it was confided, 'you were seen at the dip helping to put *mombies* (cows) through when Adam was away, and you were laughing and telling jokes with the blacks. It's very unwise. We are just warning you.'

'Take no notice of them,' Adam said when I asked if it was true that this could affect his job. 'They're the most terrible bigots. It's a small-minded thing. Combined with a Rhodesian version of apartheid. We'll have to get used to it, darling, and we'll have to win this Bush War, that's the focus, not petty gossip.'

Chapter 5

I had promised the boys that we would get a tent when we moved back to the farm so they could fulfil a long held wish to camp out in the garden. In the absence of family holidays or safaris, a tent in the garden was the best alternative during school holidays outside of the rainy season. Sleeping bags that had come with us from Kenya were unrolled and put into a small tent we bought from friends, so all was ready at bedtime for the camping experience. Louise teased the boys with stories of hyenas that gnawed their way into tents at night and dragged people out with jaws clamped around their heads, or snakes wriggling in, but nothing put them off. All was quiet as darkness settled on the garden that night and the boys crawled into the tent and zipped it up.

Hours passed peacefully without interruption and the rest of us were asleep when sometime after midnight we were woken by screams and sounds of commotion outside. This was accompanied by the deep-throated bellowing of large animals, followed by two frightened boys hammering on our window. 'The bulls have escaped and they're charging all over the garden, and one has fallen into the swimming pool,' Simon shouted. 'It can't get out and the tent has been squashed by the others.' When we looked out in the moonlight we could see and hear mighty splashes in the swimming pool, while dark shapes galloped among the flower beds. 'Hurry up and open the door so we can get in,' the boys urged, panicked by the stampede.

'We'll have to rope the beast in the pool to get it out,' Adam said glumly, pulling his clothes on as he went to get help. 'Keep the children out of the way. And the dogs.'

When he got back with ropes and several assistants roused from their beds as it was too early for milking, he called me. 'None of us can swim, so it will have to be you going in to fix the ropes,' he said. I reminded him that he was supposed to be able to swim after so many years of strenuous efforts by me to teach him, and that he was considerably more experienced in handling hysterical farm animals than I was.'

'I'm needed on the pulling team,' he replied. 'We haven't got time to argue about it.'

I could handle bulls in a calm controlled situation but this one was highly stressed, plunging about in the dark water, with a fierce pair of horns, while the other bulls had stormed off into the night.

'Good practice for you for when I'm away in PATU,' Adam volunteered, getting ropes ready, aided by light directed from a vehicle parked so that its headlights lit the scene.

'Why can't you just lasso it?' I suggested.

'Don't be daft. A loop has to go around its body, and another one around the base of its horns.'

Oh, that's all right then, prepare to die, I thought, as I lowered myself fully clothed into the water which was now like sewage from the bull's panic-induced defecations. With its neck stretched above water and legs pumping to keep afloat (the pool had no shallow end), I hoped the bull was too distracted to aim a kick at me as I wrestled with the ropes. These had to be secured around those portions of its body that Adam indicated as it thrashed about, and the wet slippery ropes pulled tight before I heaved myself out of the pool in my water-logged clothes. It was a tug of war from that point, with pulling power available from a vehicle standing by if required, but the bull was able to help by scrambling out once its front legs found a purchase on the side of the pool.

'Don't frigging let go of the ropes,' Adam yelled to the team as the bull roared off – the pulling team holding on frantically while trying to control the wildly bucking animal in its attempts to break free and run off to join the others.

The boys' tent had been pulverised by so many pounding hooves, and disappointment was intense. 'We didn't get even one night of camping,' they wailed. 'And now our tent is smashed up as well.'

'To make up for it you can go on one of the school camping trips. I'll find out about the next one and put your names down for it,' I offered. This produced instant perking up.

'That's *lekker*, Mum. We can tell our friends to put their names down too.'

When the next school holidays started, the boys went off with their small suitcases packed, joining friends on the camping trip, all boys, eager and impatient to be off, leaving parents behind. A week later they returned, barely recognisable, brown all over from sun and dirt, their hair sticking out like fur, stiff with dust. They looked like ragamuffins but they were smiling the widest of smiles. When I opened the suitcases to unpack them, nothing had been touched, nothing had been used. Toothbrushes and flannels were still dry, pyjamas and changes of clothes remained neatly folded. The boys had worn the same shirt and shorts (no underpants) for the whole week, and evidently slept in them too. 'Did you wash at all?' I asked Simon.

'No one told us to wash, so we didn't. No one minded about those sorts of things. That's the whole point of camping,' he said in a condescending way as if that needed to be explained to me.

I noticed children at a certain age adopt an assumption that their mothers are not very bright and need to be enlightened. Mums like me, distracted by multiple chores, may begin to seem dim-witted due to being in a perpetually preoccupied state. Seeing me like this, Simon was inclined to use a superior tone when announcing some new idea or piece of news. When schoolboy jokes were brought home and giggled at by him and Peter, if I asked what the joke was, Simon would say, 'It's no good telling you, Mum, you wouldn't understand.'

Peter was growing at last and speaking fluently enough to express a passion for horses and wanting to be a jockey when he grew up. Riding lessons seemed a sensible first step and when these were suggested Simon didn't want to be left out, so both boys were enrolled in a riding school at Gatooma, a small town about twenty miles south on the main road to

Bulawayo. A routine of long hot Saturday mornings developed as they joined others on a line of ponies trotting around a dusty sun-baked ring, while mums sat on a bench at the side, bored beyond endurance in the heat and tedium of such a droopy display. At Fran's farm the children had gone for canters across open country, but that was not part of the curriculum here and Peter soon decided he didn't want to be a jockey after all.

Growing up was what the children were doing faster than I was prepared for, with none of them shy about expressing strong opinions that often clashed with mine and those of each other. Louise's resentment of Simon frequently erupted from a state of armed truce into open warfare as he, soon to be a teenager, became an even more overt presence than usual. Peter's role, whether he was aware of it or not, was that of buffer zone and this was being challenged, particularly on car journeys if all three were sharing the back seat. Louise could not sit next to Simon due to a morbid fear of being touched by him which, if it happened, made her feel contaminated, so Peter was expected to oblige by sitting in the middle between them. He in turn resented never getting a window seat and this led to fights when the noise and scuffling became insufferable for me in the front trying to drive. I would take one hand off the wheel and lash about blindly behind, attempting to slap as many heads as possible regardless of whose they were. It usually produced a temporary ceasefire, but on one occasion driving back from school when the fighting became too much, my patience exhausted, I stopped the car on the grass verge and made all the children get out. I had threatened to do this on several previous occasions of violent disorder, and now the time had come. They did not believe that I could drive off and leave them there, but every parent who has been driven to fury by children fighting in the car, knows that sense of near madness induced in the person trapped behind a steering wheel.

I left the trio standing on the grass verge looking surprised as I drove away, and carried on until they were well out of sight before stopping to decide how to play the next step. They needed to be taught a lesson but not put in danger. It was a busy main road with fast traffic and the farm was only two or three miles away, so they would start walking home, obviously, I assumed. But then it might be better, possibly, on second thoughts, to turn round and meet them, to be sure.

When I got back to where I had left them, they had disappeared. There was no sign of them in either direction. Surely they could not have simply vanished? They could have got a lift, but I would have seen them on my way back. They may be taking a short cut across the fields, I decided, and went to have a look. They can't have got very far. Miles of fencing lined the sides of the road and I climbed through a fence, expecting to see the children making their way across fields in the distance. The land was flat so figures on foot would be easy to pick out, but the fields were empty. On the other side of the road there was a railway line and I crossed to have a look, walking through long grass between the road and the line. When I got there, far away I could see a small straggly group of children walking slowly down the line. They must have decided this was the quickest way to get home, while watching out for trains. Once I had collected the car and caught up with them they were very relieved to see me arrive and climb back in, so they were spared the remainder of a long hot walk. The experience did lead to a short lull before car warfare resumed, but the threat of ejection now carried more weight.

The proximity of a railway line with passenger as well as freight services reminded me that the children had never experienced the marvel of rail travel, and here was an ideal opportunity with Hartley station virtually on our doorstep. I booked return tickets to Salisbury where we could spend the night with friends and then come back the next day. No refreshments were supplied on trains so we took our own food, and settled into an empty compartment where we could watch an ever-changing view of scenery seldom seen from a car window. I was enthralled by this, but the children to my surprise and disappointment showed no interest in joining me at the window. Louise preferred to read her book, while the boys spent their time visiting lavatories to gaze down the hole at railway sleepers flashing past underneath, mesmerised by the sight. Far from becoming bored with such a mindless occupation they seemed captivated by it. 'We never knew the train had holes like that to pee through,' Simon declared with the kind of wonder only schoolboys would understand. 'We wanted to see what it was like peeing down the holes with the train rocking to and fro and going so fast.'

We hardly saw Adam during this time as he was either away on operations with PATU, or when he was home, the demands of his job took over completely. It was like being married to a zombie but a happy one, as these preoccupations brought the kind of satisfaction he said he had always wanted, and I reasoned my job was to fit in and provide domestic support. My normal household and farm activities now had extra duties added and these included calf-rearing. Since the size of the milking herd was steadily increasing in line with Eric Hornby's desire to be the biggest milk producer in Rhodesia, this meant more calves were being born. Dairy calves need close attention after being removed from their mothers soon after birth, when they are taught to drink milk from a bucket or other system such as a 'calfeteria' with rubber teats and tubes. I enjoyed doing this just as I had done at Glanjoro, while training dairy workers to care for these infant animals with kindness and expertise so they could thrive and later join the herd.

The difference at Rogate was that this was a pedigree herd and bull calves kept for breeding needed to be raised on a specialised regime. They were milk-fed from a bucket until they were six months old and then released into a paddock where they grazed together in a bull-calf herd, receiving extra care and nutrition. They grew fast and became very friendly so I had to be wary on entering their paddock when they ran to greet me with head-butts. This was their way of saying Hello but such a boisterous welcome could easily knock me over. Later, they would have a ring put through their noses and a tug on this was enough warning to be more gentle.

We had several bulls ready for sale one year when Adam was away and I was left to prepare them and take them to auction. Agricultural shows had been the highlight of our farming year in Kenya, and grooming cattle to peak condition for the ring was something I knew how to do and enjoyed. The Rogate bulls really did look splendid when each one was led into the sale ring that year, but I hadn't bargained for a slump in sales due to political instability, and only one bull sold which was a big disappointment. No one was buying bulls that year when they could use commercial semen for artificial insemination. It was unthinkable for me to return with the unsold bulls and only one cheque, so I ran around the cattlemen at the auction and bargained prices with them, having seen how far they were prepared to go when the animals were in the ring. I know that I did a lot of smiling and wheedling of the sort that would annoy feminists, but I didn't care about anything except selling those bulls, and by the time a few drinks had been swallowed in the bar, all were sold.

Managers' wives had to step up to these challenges on farms where husbands were increasingly subject to call-up. Most managers were white and the white population of the country was small in comparison with indigenous Africans who were not subject to conscription, although many joined the Rhodesian forces voluntarily. Many Africans as well as non-Africans were fearful about the future now that the Bush War was taking hold, and the Marxist ideology of the leaders held more threat than comfort for people who only wanted peace and security.

Morale generally needed a boost and here on the farm, I decided, we could do that with support for the farm football team so I asked the players for ideas. 'Boots and strips,' they said without hesitation. Adam agreed to allow a small budget for these under the heading of 'welfare' in farm accounts, and matches were booked against other teams to show off the new kit when it arrived. The farm lorry provided transport and there was cheering when the Rogate team left for their first away match, which they won, and when they returned I could hear loud singing from the open back of the lorry as it turned into the farm road. The team were singing a triumphant song in the spontaneous harmony that comes to African people who have in their souls this sublime natural ability. When I ran to them with congratulations I noticed that the players were wearing their boots, unworn, hung around their necks like trophies. It turned out that they chose to play barefoot as they had always done, the boots displayed as proud emblems of their status now that they had entered the inter-farms football league. They were wearing their strips, in the colours they had chosen, and these would be washed by their wives or mothers and hung up to dry like flags around the compound, relieving its usual bleak appearance.

Those times when I went to visit sick people in their huts, or collect my children when they were so busy playing with friends that they had forgotten to come home, the workers' compound depressed me with its long lines of identical houses looking drab and comfortless. There was no cheer or colour adding brightness to the scene, so a visual up-lift could further boost morale, I thought. If each family was given a tree or shrub to plant outside their door, it could provide shade and interest, with a sense of ownership. We had a very good local plant nursery with far-sighted owners who supported my idea enthusiastically and kindly donated plants and tree seedlings. There were enough of these for every household to have one each and when the plants arrived, families chose the one they wanted and carried it off to a ready-prepared hole. Dairy farms are never short of manure and plenty of well-rotted stuff went into the holes along with a gallon of water for each plant or tree and, just as importantly, beer for the hut occupants. This often included a grandmother or sometimes both grandparents.

It was these elderly people who I might be called to visit if they were ill and could no longer get around. Also, occasionally, disabled children in the same predicament. One grandmother, whom I had been to see several times, was not ill but simply incapacitated due to age and frailty. Unable to help anymore with child care or cooking, I could see the difficulty her helplessness posed for a busy family where both parents worked. On most farms in our district men were employed as labourers while women weeded crops or picked cotton in season. I felt concerned for the grandmother in her feeble state and visited as often as I could. One morning when I called to see her, a young girl came to the door and said she wasn't there. The child giggled in an embarrassed way behind her hands and muttered that the grandmother had died in the night, which did not surprise me, but the girl's response was unexpected as she stifled more giggles before running away. I had an impression that the death might not have been entirely natural, but that it may have been merciful for the family.

I wanted to ask one of the African farm assistants, Morgan, what he thought about this, and waited for a suitable time. We often worked together when Adam was away, and during a break at the cattle dip one day I turned to him with my question. Morgan was a young, capable, articulate and well-qualified assistant who, together with Francis, helped run the farm during Adam's absences. All cattle on the farm were driven through a chemical spray race once a week to kill ticks. These were potential carriers of deadly diseases so this regular spraying was essential, with supervision to make sure it was done properly and no animals were missed. Counting them as they went through was my job as I stood with Morgan at the rails, glad to have breaks in between different herds arriving when we could discuss issues of the day. I wanted to understand more about the grandmother's death in the wider context of tribal customs and culture, existing as they did in Rhodesia alongside western norms. Morgan rather dismissed the notion of deaths among older people as being anything other than entirely normal in these circumstances. 'Old people die,' he said. 'Old age is something to be respected, but there is no point in being old without purpose,' he added, as if that concluded the matter. The conversation then wandered around contrasting attitudes between different societies and progressed to the vexed question of colonial occupation, when I was glad to be able to talk to him about this in the most informal of situations when neither of us felt the need to stand on ceremony.

Living as a colonial in Kenya and now in Rhodesia, held conflicting emotions for me and exercised my thoughts a great deal as I acted out my own part in this mix, with accompanying qualms. I asked Morgan if he felt that we (Europeans) had imposed foreign concepts which may have destroyed in this process the integrity and innocence of their lives while bringing doubtful benefits in return. Would it be better for them to have been left in their original tribal societies, undisturbed physically and spiritually by external influences? His reply was expressed in a way it seemed to me at the time (July 1977) important to write down and keep:

'There was no such thing as peace before the colonialists came to Africa,' he said. 'The tribes traditionally preyed upon each other, and my tribe, the Mashona, was being wiped out by the Matabele when Rhodes arrived and stopped the war. I am extremely glad to have had an education and to be a farm assistant earning a good salary with good prospects, instead of an illiterate person herding goats on my father's land. No one wants to go back in time, and even if there are bad things about modern life, there are plenty of good things. I am happy in my position, only worried about the wrong African nationalists taking over the country. If it's Bishop Muzorewa it will be all right, but if it's one of the others we will all be ruled like slaves.'

It was being noticed that I was indulging in 'over-familiar' talk with Africans, whether these were employees or businessmen who came to buy or sell products, and Adam was warned that he could face dismissal if he allowed me to continue with what was seen as trouble-making behaviour. He laughed at this and the notion that I could be controlled like a subservient wife, but it was intimidating to live in a community where such views persisted and made me aware that I was very much in a minority here in Hartley.

The warning to Adam had further emphasis due to my support of cotton pickers the previous year, when farmers had set the hourly rate for pickers at such a low level that they refused to work until a fair rate was agreed. There was a stand-off and the women were told that their husbands would be sacked if they did not go back to work. I was furious with what I saw as shocking exploitation and put pressure on Adam to pay a fair rate on Rogate, but this would have broken the cartel and the attempt rebounded on Adam who was threatened with losing his job if he caused trouble. He reasoned with me that getting the sack would not help the pickers, so please would I desist on this occasion and he would do his best to negotiate better terms next year, if the price for raw cotton held up.

As so often in farming, fate intervened. October turned out to be a blistering month: the hottest month of the year in that part of Africa. The air hummed with heat, tarmac melted, cattle stood listless in fields and cracks appeared in the baked earth where grass had withered. Through all this our cotton survived in Rogate's black soil with its moisture-preserving density. Everyone waited breathless for the November rains when thunder clouds came rumbling and growling around the sky for several days before at last bursting in torrents. That November when the rains broke with streaked lightning and claps of thunder sharp as rifle shots, I ran outside with the children and dogs, jumping like dervishes on the wet grass in a mad frenzy of relief and joy. We put our tongues out to catch the cool water which fell in heavy drops, and were soon soaked, our clothes sticking to us as we danced. I knew it was dangerous to be out in the open, careless of lightning strikes, but the ferocity and splendour of the storm was too exhilarating to hide from.

The rain continued steadily all that day and night, and the next day and night, until the elation of dancing among rain drops on the lawn stopped because the lawn was ankle-deep in water and it was no fun anymore. The extravagant flower beds I had planted and tended diligently all year were flooded, and even some of the trees which gave merciful shade to the garden during long hot months, now started to die.

'The garden is the least of our worries,' Adam said. 'If this rain carries on, we're going to lose the cotton.'

The rain didn't stop, and the river between us and Thornby Farm overflowed, forming water meadows where fish released from the river swam freely. Soon there was the weird sight of fish swimming in the cotton fields among bushes which had drowned. There was misery in the workers' compound as flood-water swept through their huts destroying meagre possessions and causing an outbreak of the type of sicknesses associated with such conditions. Adding to the calamity, every single one of the treasured shrubs and trees planted beside each hut, drooped and died. The people were stoical and fatalistic, appearing to accept happiness and disaster as interchangeable on the whim of an unseen power; though for some the fury of the season was interpreted as an omen.

Usually the rainy season, for me, was more comfortable than winter because rain was warm and the temperature stayed constant, but this time the air was filled with so much moisture that it turned cold. My church friend, Anne, the one whose curtains were chosen by God, felt so chilled one night that she got out of bed and put on a fur coat which normally she kept for visits to England. Back in bed she reached over to give John, her sleeping husband, a hug. He woke up thinking he was being attacked by a large furry animal and sprang terrified from the bed to run in panic from the room. 'It's only me,' Anne shouted, but he was so unnerved he didn't hear her and returned with a bucket of water to throw over the dark shape in the bed. This roused Anne who leapt from the bed with furious shrieks, lunging at John in retaliation and the two of them ended up on the floor yelling at each other like maniacs. Pausing for breath they started laughing, and laughed so much they had to revive themselves with brandy before going back to bed, the fur coat having been peeled off.

The exceptional rains brought an unexpected discovery to neighbours across the road when a large hole opened in their garden exposing a lump of something solid and glittering which the gardener brought to their back door. It was a piece of rock containing specks of gold and in no time they had a mine with a stamp mill pounding excavated rock loudly and monotonously all day and night, too close to us to be ignored. This may have been music to miners' ears but to ours it was an unwelcome industrial noise and we suspected that it disturbed the farm animals too. Milk production had fallen, but this may have been due to persisting damp conditions.

The weather made no difference to security operations and Adam was away when the milk lorry skidded into a ditch one morning on one of the muddy farm roads with hundreds of gallons of milk on board. The milk was in churns that were tilting ominously as a crowd of workers arrived, but did nothing except stagger about doubled up with laughter, thinking the sight hilarious and likely to provide entertainment when the churns toppled over. It took a lot of shouting from me and the farm assistants to get the churns unloaded and the lorry manhandled back onto the road, so the whole operation of delivering the milk to the creamery could get underway again.

Hardly had this potential disaster been averted than another skidding incident caused alarm, this time on the main road outside the farm entrance. Loud knocking on my back door revealed an agitated group saying there had been an accident and I must come quickly. An army vehicle had gone off the road into a ditch where it had sunk in a morass of what appeared to be sewage filling the ditch. Army officers travelling in the vehicle had been pulled out and were now sitting dazed by the side of the road, covered in slimy filth. Main road ditches, maintained by the public works department, were intentionally wide and deep enough to provide capacity for flood water run-off. The ditch outside our gate also, coincidentally, provided a run-off for slurry from the cow sheds, and now with all the recent rain had become a roadside river of sludge. This was camouflaged by long grass growing along the verge so the festering contents of the ditch remained undetected, except to anyone passing by on foot with a sensitive nose, or anyone falling in. It was easy to blame excess rain for the effluent problem when the officers, gloomily wiping muck from their faces, recovered enough to splutter expletives on the very un-military experience of nearly drowning in sewage. Offering them hot baths and whiskies while they waited for a rescue party to be despatched from Salisbury, helped to defuse the situation.

All these sorts of incidents seemed to wait until Adam was away; his absences becoming more frequent as the war grew more savage and widespread. Since Africans were exempt from compulsory call-up I was seldom without Francis or Morgan and relied on them totally. Sometimes they were called to help on other farms under company management and these were the times I dreaded most, when I was left in charge and assumed to possess a capability I neither felt nor had acquired.

Most dreaded of all were power failures when the milking machines cut out and long lines of cows stood with bulging udders, looking peeved. If electricity reconnection was delayed they would start bellowing in pain as their udders swelled, and the noise from hundreds of stricken animals increased the level of tension and stress. It was obvious that we needed a back-up power source to meet this kind of crisis which was costly in several different ways. Since it was expected that I would step in when Adam was away, I started lobbying for a range of improvements. Farmers' wives all over the country were having to deputise for their husbands and attend to demands outside their normal range of expertise.

Harvest times were always strenuous, especially for me with almost zero mechanical skill. Farms like Rogate with large dairy herds relied on growing and harvesting vast quantities of maize to make silage which was an essential feed for cows, while silage-making was an art form in itself. When peak time for cutting the maize arrived, the crop was brought in by three giant forage harvesters working continuously, and this of course would coincide with PATU call-up for Adam. Rogate had several expert African mechanics but they were often over-stretched at these times, so the company directors decided that we needed a white engineer to help out, due to Adam being away so much.

The engineer appointed was elderly, too old for call-up, and may once have been a competent operator but now had memory problems, particularly when it came to remembering anything to do with machines. 'I'll have a look,' he would say helpfully, setting out to examine a stranded tractor or harvester in a field, but very little remedial action followed, and I would be sent for. The enormous machines were terrifying in their size and the noise they made, but most of all (to me) was the danger they presented in the deadly clanking and clashing of their moving parts, seeming ready to dismember or crush any unwary investigator. Somehow solutions were always found, but not always in the best agricultural traditions.

Repairing machines became routine, but injuries and illnesses among animals were more of a worry because there were so many of them and, unlike machines, they were live sentient beings that needed careful and competent handling. Almost every day there were cows calving and this was not always an uncomplicated process. During one of Adam's absences there was a query in the farm accounts about the number of times the vet had been called out, so I decided to phone him each time for free advice over the phone, avoiding a visit and rolling up my sleeves to do whatever he suggested. The vet soon rumbled this ploy. 'Farm wives like you need to get more professional. I'm going to run a wives' course and I want you to be on it,' he said firmly.

The course took place on a farm near his surgery and I was relieved to find some of my friends there, all of them as nervous as I was, not knowing what to expect. The vet was a no-nonsense young man with unlimited kindness and patience where animals were concerned, but a low level of tolerance for inept handlers. 'You will all wear suitable clothing,' he told us in advance, 'and bring your own rubber arm-gloves.'

'Now ladies,' he began at the start of the first lesson, 'by the end of this course, all of you will be able to judge what is likely to be wrong with a sick animal simply by looking at it from ten paces, observing its stance. Only then will you obtain a temperature reading and other useful indications to confirm what you already suspect. In addition,' he said, 'you will be proficient in the techniques of artificial insemination, confirmation of pregnancy by internal examination, correct diagnosis and treatment of diseases, the handling of all types of livestock and, most importantly, you will have become competent bovine midwives.'

Despite these assurances I never did succeed in establishing any bovine pregnancies regardless of the time spent with my arm in a rubber sleeve ferreting about in the deep recesses of a cow's rear end. The vet was not impressed with my progress. 'Your problem is you're not getting properly stuck in. You're frightened of hurting the cow so you're nibbling at the job. You're not cut out for bovines because you've been trained on humans,' he told me. 'Some of the others have caught on, but here I am, stuck with all of you women now your husbands have gone.' Farms are lucky to have us at all I reminded him, and women still have houses to run and children to look after.

When they were not at school, mine went off every day immediately after breakfast and often didn't come home before evening. The boys joined their friends from the compound for a day spent roaming the wilder parts of the farm, or fishing for cat fish at the dam. 'Be sure to come back before dark,' I called after them as they ran off, barefoot, carrying nothing but their fishing rods and penknives. They would drink at cattle troughs and eat scraps of cold boiled mealie meal brought by their friends. Often they would be given food at mealtimes back at the compound with workers' families, eating *sadza* (mealie porridge) which they scorned at home but happily ate with families living on borderline wages, who were unfailingly hospitable despite having so little to share. It posed a dilemma for me, as, had we reciprocated in the same way, we would have had fifty or more children crowding into the house for whatever was offered, and I would not have been able to cope with such numbers. Louise had friends next door at Thornby where the farm store was a hub of activity with shoppers and cheap clothes on sale, setting her off on a lifelong passion for jumble sales or anything on special offer.

During the rainy season, flying insects invaded the house in swarms after dark, attracted by the lights, battering themselves against these and dropping stunned onto beds, chairs, carpets and food on our plates while we were eating. Most annoying of all were hordes at bath-time when they fell into the water and formed a twitching layer before the taps were even turned off. The children refused to get in until every sodden corpse had been removed and disposed of. Kneeling on the bath mat, I dripped with sweat while scooping insects with flannels until the last drowned creature had been extracted and Louise climbed in. She always had her bath before the boys, to avoid any possibility of pollution from 'their water' when accumulated dust and dirt floated off in a murky layer.

Simon's birthday had been in October before the rains started and what he wanted more than anything was a new bike after crashing the old one so many times that the frame had buckled. He would be eleven this birthday and we thought this was an age when he might be expected to become more sensible. 'You've got to promise to be more careful in future if you get a new bike for your birthday,' I told him.

'A new one will have better brakes and won't be wobbly like the old one,' he said, failing to see that it was his recklessness rather than any defects of the bike that caused the problems.

'The only reason it's wobbly is due to so many accidents,' I told him.

'It will be different this time,' he said confidently. He was always confident. Nothing was ever a problem for him. Optimism triumphed whatever the circumstances.

The birthday arrived and so did the bike (not new, of course, but good second hand), early enough for him to ride around before leaving for school. Friends came for a birthday tea and party later and when all were assembled, eager to show them new skills with the bike he set off at speed down the drive. Reaching the gate at the end he executed a turn with such flourish that control was lost and he bounced into a barbed-wire fence. Nonchalant as ever, he extricated himself from the wire and walked back up the drive to the house with blood dripping from his head, his friends lending handkerchiefs. I was so used to Simon's mishaps, this didn't seem any worse than others, but the jagged cut needed stitching so we spent the rest of his birthday at Gatooma Hospital. 'Will I have a zigzag scar?' he asked the doctor. 'I'd like one to show Granfa when he comes to see us. My Granfa is a doctor and I am going to be one too,' he informed the medical officer at Gatooma.

'You'll have a scar all right, but it's nothing to be proud of. You could have lost an eye on that barbed wire, it's lethal. My advice to you if you want to live long enough to be a doctor is to leave off doing any more stunts.'

My disappointment at Muz's continued reluctance to visit had been eased by Fa's enthusiasm to come and see us, expressed in his tiny precise writing on a blue airmail form, saying he would visit at the end of his next voyage. His latest adventures had become global, touring the world as a ship's doctor with Babs as his nurse. A life continually on the move exploring new places was ideally suited to his restless nature and passion for discovery. Letters posted along the way described in lively prose the peculiar diversity of life on board as they sailed between ports vibrant with activity.

Of all the countries visited, China excited him the most because he was seeing it again after an absence of nearly forty years when war interrupted the missionary career he had been enjoying there. He looked forward now to speaking the Mandarin learnt at Peking University and still remembered, so that he astonished the guides by greeting them in their own language when the ship made its first stop at a Chinese port. They were official guides appointed by the Chinese government with instructions on what they were allowed to say to visitors, but with no language barrier and curious to hear Fa's stories of China before the war, they relaxed and told him about their own lives. These were entirely beholden to government control as they were posted to regions far from their families, whom they seldom saw. It disturbed Fa to hear stories of enforced separation with its effects on these good people, while other aspects of this highly organised society impressed him. The extreme poverty which had been widespread when he was living in China, with the common sight of people dying in the streets from destitution, and summary executions in public, no longer happened he was glad to see. He contrasted his current impressions of China with a visit to Russia the previous year which he had found depressing, describing scenes and sensations everywhere as unfriendly and grim.

While Fa and Babs were cruising around the world, Muz was playing the organ at Long Melford church and immersing herself in village life. She liked to be busy and useful, as in a lifetime of perpetually moving from place to place she always found new people to help and work to do. Her weekly letters became more upbeat as these interests provided distraction from the gloomy presence of Andy, who remained slumped in his chair all day with a book, only rising when she called him to meals.

'I do worry about Andy's lethargy,' she wrote in a letter. 'Burglars could raid the house when I'm out and he wouldn't even notice the place being stripped around him.' As long as they didn't disturb his reading, I thought. The letter continued:

'There is something else, more worrying still, that Mary his sister told me about. I knew that his first wife, Olive, died of a stroke, but had never heard any details. Mary tells me that Andy woke up one morning to find Olive unconscious in bed beside him. He phoned the doctor, who said there was no point in coming round as she needed to go to hospital so he would call an ambulance. Andy went downstairs to make himself a cup of tea while waiting for the ambulance and when it hadn't arrived after an hour, he had breakfast, then settled himself to read while he went on waiting. Time passed and no one came, but he never thought to try and find out what had happened to the ambulance, or go upstairs to check on Olive. Eventually, when he started getting hungry and realised it was lunchtime, he phoned the doctor again. The doctor was very put out that no ambulance had arrived and sent one round within minutes. The ambulancemen went running upstairs with their equipment but it was too late, and Olive was dead, so it makes me nervous that the same thing could happen to me,' Muz wrote. 'It occurred to me that his lack of energy and interest could be due to thyroid deficiency, so I took him to the doctor for a blood test. This was reassuring in a way because the result showed normal thyroid function. But in that case, surely he should be full of energy doing things, instead of shuffling around in slippers all day because he is too tired to put shoes on with the bother of tying laces. The doctor thinks his lethargy may be due to depression, but when I talked to Mary about this, she said if it's depression then he was born depressed, because he has never been any different for the whole of his life. Anyway I was annoyed with the doctor for suggesting he could be depressed, when he couldn't wait to marry me and he's got what he wanted, so he should be happy. And do you know,' she continued, now she was roused on a theme of indignation: 'Babs has changed your father's name to Guy. She thinks it suits him better. He's gone along with it, of course. She's taken him over completely.'

I wrote back saying that Fa was much more a Guy than an Alfred, so I approved of the change, risking the displeasure this response would cause. There were times when I rebelled against agreeing with her even if it brought on spasms of distress. 'You're taking Babs' side,' she would say accusingly. 'I'll have no one left soon. Elaine refuses to discuss anything to do with Babs or Fa. She won't even allow Babs' name to be mentioned.' The subject was taboo as far as Elaine was concerned. Ros and I both thought that was very wise of her, but if we all took the same view, Muz would feel forsaken.

She was particularly affected at this time by a tragedy that had struck the Craddock family. Her divorce from Fa had not changed her affection for his brothers and her favourite was Frank, the eldest, who had married one of Muz's nursing friends. They had two sons and the youngest, Colin, was a first officer in the Merchant Navy. His ship was carrying a cargo of frozen meat from Argentina to Britain when it collided with a Chinese tanker that crossed its bows during early morning fog in the River Plate. There was an explosion and Colin's ship, the *Royston Grange*, was engulfed in fire so intense that fire tugs despatched from the shore could not get anywhere near it. All they could do was watch the ship burn, with the loss of everyone on board, including the captain. Colin had married three months before and his new wife was with him as part of a honeymoon trip, but no one could be saved, and no bodies were ever found. By chance, Frank and his wife had been visiting Muz when this happened and were watching BBC News on television with her and Andy, when terrifying pictures of the burning ship came up on the screen, with a breaking-news report. The impact on them, stricken with despair as they watched helplessly, was so devastating that Muz remained haunted by the horror of it, which only added to the recurring lows of anguish she poured out in letters.

If only I could persuade her to come to us for a holiday it would provide distraction, I thought, but she said Rhodesia was now too dangerous for her to contemplate visiting, especially since the Foreign Office had advised against travel to the 'rebel country'.

CHAPTER 6

The physical exertions required on combat operations with PATU were beginning to affect Adam's usually robust health and he was having trouble with one of his knees caused by the strain. On the latest PATU patrol he had needed a 'casi-vac' (the term used for casualty evacuation by helicopter) due to problems with this knee. He was seen by a military doctor and given blood tests which showed antibodies for rheumatoid arthritis, but no active disease. The doctor said that Adam was at risk of the disease becoming active if he didn't adapt his life to reduce physical activity, and offered to give him a letter exempting him from further active service. Adam refused the offer, saying (to me) that operations with PATU were more important to him than almost anything else, even his job. This explained his increasing absences, exceeding the number of days required to be spent on call-up. I had been puzzled by this because other men his age seemed to be less often away, and less eager than he was to fulfil these obligations. Each time he was away I worried about his safety as casualty rates began to rise. Young conscripted sons and husbands were the ones most at risk, and every night on the radio and television news the names of those killed were read out, so that we began to dread hearing the name of someone we knew. Those of us living in Hartley district consoled ourselves that the war was still far away in the north and east of the country, but this was a false impression as we were soon to find out.

When Adam had been flown out of the war zone and seen by the army doctor, he was told that he must give up smoking as his cigarette consumption had gone up to sixty a day at this point. The doctor recommended hypnosis and gave him the address of a therapist in Salisbury. We were sceptical about this solution but made an appointment and I went with him as moral support. In the waiting room he, like a condemned prisoner, had his last cigarette and gave me the remains of the packet to throw away.

'I'll keep it just in case,' I said. 'I don't want you going cold turkey on the way home if this doesn't work.'

He was inside the hypnotist's room for an hour and when he came out he was smiling, and so was the hypnotist. 'You won't need to come back,' the man said cheerfully as he shook Adam's hand and opened the door for us to leave. When we were outside I asked what had happened during the session. 'Did he put you into a trance?'

'No. I was fully awake the whole time, just answering questions and listening to what he was saying.'

'What did he say?'

'A lot of stuff about not needing to smoke; that I would find the taste of tobacco so unpleasant from now on that I would never want to smoke again, either cigarettes or a pipe.'

'Not ever?'

'Not ever.'

'Would you like a cup of tea instead?'

'Good idea. Let's go and find somewhere to have one and celebrate.' Much to my surprise from that day Adam never did smoke again, and said he was not even tempted to pick up a cigarette, or the pipe that previously accompanied him everywhere with its tin of Sweet Nut tobacco. But PATU was something he couldn't give up, and if anything he felt more energised for the conflict, confident in being extra-fit since he no longer smoked.

Just as in Nakuru, Kenya, before we left there had been concern about the situation of elderly widows among expatriate communities needing support, the same demographic feature was becoming apparent among the European community in Hartley. One of these widows was Esther Brightman who had lived in Burma, so it was thought a good idea for me to visit and see if she needed any help, since I too had a connection with Burma. Esther, like many of her compatriots who had been the wives of senior British Army officers, was feisty and forthright. She was also small and stout like Queen Victoria. Dressed in black with a beady expression, she remained sitting in her chair when I was shown into her presence by a servant. 'Sit down,' she said, 'and I will tell you about myself.' After a short preamble during which I sat patiently wondering what possible help I could become to such an assured person, she made a startling statement. 'I am eighty-two years old and was married to my husband Chummy for forty years before he died, and I am still a virgin. What do you think about that?' Her tone was so defiant it made me laugh and I was relieved when she laughed too. 'That is some achievement,' I said. 'Chummy must have been very tolerant, or simply very shy.' Ignoring this remark, she went on: 'After we were married I made sure that I had my own room at the hotel where we went for our honeymoon, and he had his, each of us with our personal attendants. From then on, wherever we lived, these refinements continued. Chummy understood completely and was a perfect gentleman. He never made any demands.' She was silent for a few moments. 'Of course it meant that we had no offspring.'

'Didn't either of you mind about that?' I asked.

'We never spoke about it. Chummy gave no indication whether he minded or not.' She looked up, ready to change the subject. 'Now you may tell me about yourself and what you were doing in Burma.'

I liked Esther and visited often on shopping trips to the town, calling in to take a list for her or stopping for tea and entertaining her with stories of the latest mishaps on the farm. One day she was unusually agitated and said some kind of interfering government official had been to see her about security arrangements, due to nosy neighbours worried that valuable items of hers lying around the house might attract thieves. She drew my attention to a pair of paintings on the wall. 'Those are my Burma pictures,' she said. 'They are my most treasured possessions.' This surprised me since they were unremarkable small amateur watercolours in matching frames, each showing a scene of houses beside a lake. 'I know what you're thinking,' Esther said, 'that no thief would be interested in those. But Chummy painted them for my birthday one year in Burma and I have kept them safe ever since. There is more to them than meets the eye. Go and have a look,' she said.

I went to gaze at them obligingly and could see nothing on which to exclaim appreciatively for Esther's benefit, but I did feel a tug of reminiscence in the hazy colour tones and gentle landscapes. Though faded, they brought back a sense of the diffused air of the Burmese highlands. I was still looking at the pictures when Esther startled me, saying she would like me to have them. 'You are the only person I have met since coming to Rhodesia who has any connection with Burma. I'm getting old and the doctor says I could go at any time. There is no one for me to pass my things onto.' She waited for a response and when I didn't say anything, she asked directly: 'Would you like to have them?'

'Well,' I said, pausing to think what to say. 'It would be an honour, and of course I would treasure them and their story, but I'm not sure that you should part with them just yet.'

'Go on, get them down off the wall and take them with you,' she said. 'Then I can demonstrate to my bossy neighbours that I'm getting rid of things.'

The pictures were dusty and wedged on their hooks, and when the first one came loose I nearly dropped it, surprised by its weight for such a small object. Esther laughed. 'Chummy had solid backs put onto the frames. He was very particular about that.'

The framing had been done quite crudely and I knew Adam wouldn't like the pictures. The second one refused to be prised off its hook and I put the first one back so the pair would not be split up, feeling relieved that I didn't have to take the pictures away immediately; feeling uneasy about them.

'I'll get someone to see to the one that's stuck,' Esther said, 'then you can take them another time.' Somehow events moved on rather swiftly after that and I forgot about the pictures. Esther didn't mention them again and I was glad to see them still safely attached to her wall when I visited. Sometime later, when the war had scattered many of us to other places, a letter arrived from a friend in Hartley saying that Esther had died. But had I heard about the Burma pictures? These had caused a stir when they were rescued by a charity along with other overlooked effects, and it was discovered that the wooden backs of the frames were hollow on the inside, holding small sachets of precious gems. Clever old Chummy, I thought, remembering how Esther had said there was more to the pictures than met the eye, and careless of me to have shrugged off what that could mean.

Meanwhile, back on the farm in Hartley, letters arrived from friends dispersed around the world, including Mary Rooken Smith who I missed very much since she and Don had gone to live in Brazil. Their new home was on a cattle ranch with horses and cowboys in a remote region of the country, hundreds of miles from any larger centre where they might find other people who spoke English. Mary found this very isolating while she struggled to learn Portuguese and help their four daughters to settle at a local school for farm labourers' children. It was the only school nearby, otherwise they would have to be sent away. 'And that would break my heart,' Mary wrote in a letter. 'Everything here is totally foreign, except for the men all day on horses rounding up cattle: for them it's their ideal life. But a funny thing happened the other day – it will make you laugh. We do have some nice neighbours who are Swiss and they invited us for dinner with people from other estates. None of them speaks English. The Swiss speak French and Portuguese, but as neither Don nor I speak French, we had to rely on our very basic Portuguese for conversation around the table. Everyone got very animated all of a sudden when talk centred on a baby being born to the household, and Don, summoning his best Portuguese, turned to the host and congratulated him. All conversation stopped in mid-sentence as guests gasped and put their hands to their mouths in alarm. It was explained then, to Don, that it was the maid who had had the baby, and no one knew who the father was. Can you imagine the embarrassment. I don't think we will be invited again.'

Frequent letters came from David, full of endearing optimism for meeting up again when the opportunity arose. 'We could each fly to a half-way place, such as Athens for instance, from our current positions. That would be the easiest. Or Cairo. I have an assignment coming up in Blantyre, Malawi. What about meeting there?'

Lanner wrote infrequently but the letters were long, written on thin blue paper over several days with sometimes as many as forty pages folded into an airmail envelope barely able to contain such a fat letter inside. The sentiments expressed were often touched with nostalgia, but buoyant about his life in Kenya on a career ladder where he was now perched on the top rung, gratified with the view of his achievements from that elevated position.

Another letter brought news from Fa that he was free at last to come and see us in between voyages while Babs was busy helping her parents. He was planning an itinerary with trips to Victoria Falls and Kariba and wanted all of us to join him. We had not seen either of these marvels and excitement for such a treat was mounting, when suddenly with no warning a new and chilling situation engulfed our rural community and we had to advise Fa to postpone. The new year of 1978 had arrived with no hint of danger when, feeling a sense of relief that the rain had ended and dry weather returned, unknown to us this signalled clear nights for the Bush War to erupt in our own district of Hartley with savage brutality. We should not have been so surprised by this or felt so unprepared for the first attack, since for several weeks the police had been arming civilians and putting in place a regime of defensive measures.

I had been going obediently to compulsory firearms practice at the local police training centre, where farm wives like me and others who lived out of town were taught how to use a sub-machine gun. Anything lighter such as a pistol or shotgun would not be any use against the bush fighters' automatic weapons. Each of us had been issued with a gun similar to an Uzi, which had to be carried with us day and night. When I went to the supermarket in town, I kept the gun in the top basket of my trolley, close to hand, where it looked incongruous among the groceries. At night it rested against my side of the bed where I had only to stretch out my hand to reach it, and Adam had his own gun similarly beside him. I had been taught how to dismantle the gun for cleaning, and how to load and unload the magazine and re-supply it from a box of 9mm ammunition. The boys loved to help: inserting the bullets one by one into a magazine. It's all part of a varied education for children in Rhodesia now, I told myself, remembering how Muz used to tell us during my own childhood that we were acquiring 'a rich tapestry of knowledge,' whenever something outlandish had to be taken on board.

One of the wives on the training course with me was Camilla Breckenridge who had a son in Simon's class at school and they were friends, sharing an interest in falcons and falconry. Camilla and I both hated the guns and were nervous of them. Heavy and cumbersome, they were difficult to hold steady while firing, when a volley of shots made the gun jump and the noise made us deaf. 'Don't jerk the trigger,' the instructor shouted. 'Just squeeze it gently. You don't want to empty the whole frigging magazine in one go.'

'God, I hope we never have to use these things,' Camilla said. 'It's bad enough having them hanging round our necks the whole time.'

'Like albatrosses,' I said, and we laughed. But it was not a good simile. Hers was the first family to be attacked and the news hit us like an earthquake. It had become routine for families living out of town to send staff home and lock all doors well before dark, so Camilla and her family thought they were safe sitting around the table for supper that evening. One of their sons had a friend staying, and Camilla's mother was there too but, feeling unwell, she had gone to bed. Without any warning the gang broke in through the back door and into the dining room, spraying bullets around the table, killing Camilla's husband and one of the sons, as well as his friend, before going to the bedroom and shooting the old mother in her bed. None of the bullets touched Camilla who had frozen onto the gun in her hands, unable to move. The gang didn't wait to finish off any more victims and escaped into the night, so that Camilla was able to access the alarm system which all farms had installed by then, connecting them to the police station.

I was unnerved by this event, losing friends in such a savage way, and wondered if I, like Camilla, would freeze on the trigger if the same thing happened to us. I hoped that seized with fury I'd blast the devils with a full magazine, if I was still standing. Meanwhile, we were told that when husbands were away, wives and families on farms must now move into 'safe houses' in town. These were flats, rented for the purpose, very basic, but that was not a problem. The problem for me when it came to decamping to one of these flats the next time Adam was away, was that I found it impossible to desert the farm workers and leave them to fend for themselves. I was the only person on the farm with a gun if Adam wasn't there, and the workers with their families were just as vulnerable as the rest of us. Everyone was terrified of the gangs. No mercy was shown to either black or white if there was an attack. The tactics were aimed at pure terror, randomly applied, with the object of demoralising a whole population, and this was succeeding. Whole swathes of the country had now been infiltrated and Hartley was just the latest. I told Francis and Morgan that I would be staying on the farm whenever Adam was away, but I needed the compound to be my eyes and ears, to warn me of any suspicious activity or approach. The gangs had many different methods of attack. Sometimes, instead of breaking into a house, they would go with one of the workers after dark with a gun at his back to lure the farmer out on a pretext. 'We will have a code,' Francis said. 'If one of us comes to your window in the dark when all the doors are locked, we will knock on it and say, loud, so you can hear: "The cows are calving". That will be a sign because you will know, if it is plural, then it is wrong and you can use the alarm.'

One night, in the house on my own with the children, one of the workers came to call me, saying that someone at the compound was very sick. I suspected a trap but couldn't be sure. 'Why hasn't Francis or Morgan come to tell me?'

'I couldn't find them,' he replied. That sounded even more suspicious as one of them had to be on duty all the time when Adam wasn't there. The man persisted: 'This person is nearly dying. You must come quickly.' It sounded genuine, but I couldn't leave the children on their own in the house. Should I wake them and tell them it was an emergency so they must get under their beds and stay hidden until I got back? This was standard security drill. No, I thought, it would scare them, but leaving them asleep and unguarded while I went to the compound was a big risk, and a foolish one. On the other hand it was impossible to ignore a sick person. I would have to go.

Fumbling as I tried to hold my gun steady while unlocking the back door, fearing an ambush, I was determined not to blink or freeze if there was a burst of fire when I stepped outside. It took a huge effort of will to go out, leaving the children behind, but I was met by only the feel and sounds of the dark night outside when I locked the door behind me, until the click of a torch released a shaft of light and an urgent voice said, 'Come, hurry.'

Running with the gun strap tight against my neck and chest I was soon out of breath, the gun and a bag of medical kit heavy as I ran. What the hell am I doing running into a trap, I thought, as sounds of shouting increased the closer I came to the compound. The cause of this was soon obvious when several brawling figures staggered out of a crowd that had gathered to watch a drunken fight, where everyone was so inebriated they would barely have noticed a gang arriving. Ignoring the mob, I was ushered into a hut where a man lay bleeding profusely from a stab wound to his chest. 'This is going to need stitching,' I said impatiently, feeling not sympathy but anger at the sight. 'First the bleeding has to be stopped.' Others stood around impassively, increasing my sense of frustration that no one ever seemed to think of taking the most basic actions to save a life. 'You should have told me about the fighting and stabbing,' I said.

'We thought you might not come,' was the innocent reply. My own thoughts were turning to what an idiot I was to have got myself into this crazy situation, when a group of spectators arrived panting at the door of the hut to announce that there was another stab victim, who was lying on the ground outside.

'Go and get one of the drivers,' I told them. 'These people have to go to hospital. Someone must go with them to press on the wounds all the time. With a folded cloth. A clean one,' I shouted, exasperated, and panicky about the children at home on their own. What if they woke up and went looking for me? It's completely irresponsible to be messing about up here I thought as fear and shame made me dash back, my legs like lead as I reached the kitchen door and home. The dogs were standing guard and wagged their tails when they saw me. What could I be thinking of to have gone off like that? I was furious with myself and shaking as I went to the children's rooms in a sweat. Then tears of relief to find them asleep in their beds. The dogs had gone back to their baskets and all was quiet. I poured myself a shot of whisky and took a couple of gulps before sinking into an armchair and removing the gun strap from around my neck. The gun could lie across my lap ready to be snatched up for any other alarms, or I could prop it against the side of the chair close to hand. Later it would come to bed with me and I would sleep intermittently, reaching to touch the alien metal from time to time, to reassure myself that the gun was still there, never allowing myself to lie down completely and go into a deep sleep. Instead, as always, I half-sat in bed with pillows piled up, listening for sounds outside: footsteps, dogs barking, or the sudden blast of a grenade.

Some farmhouses had sandbags walled across their windows as defence against grenades, but we had grenade screens which were effective against hand grenades but probably useless against anything fired by a rocket. The screens were made of reinforced metal mesh to allow light into the house. 'No bloody terrorist is going to make us live like troglodytes,' Adam said bitterly when it was suggested that we might be safer with sandbags.

However well prepared we were, it was impossible to spend every hour on alert, watching and waiting for something to happen, not knowing what to expect or where it might come from. I had been in a state of dread for such a long time, even before the war reached Hartley, going each week to firearm practice at the police station, and rehearsing security drill at home. The drill followed a set pattern and was impressed on the children with military precision so that they would do what was required, automatically, at any sign of attack. Some farmhouses had concrete fireproof bunkers, but in houses like ours with no bunker, children must take cover under their beds while adults stood ready with their guns.

One evening, when the children were in bed and the dogs not yet put out for the night but sitting at our feet as Adam and I watched television in the sitting room, there was the sound of heavy boots outside the window. These could not be from innocent intruders stumbling about in the dark, we thought, as there was a strict curfew in place. Adam raised a finger to the dogs to be quiet, and a quick glance at me to make sure that I had picked up my gun and torch before he switched off the lights and TV. It was standard drill for all internal lights to be switched off and external security lights switched on, if anything suspicious happened. I went straight to the children's rooms to get them under their beds, which was part of the drill. The children, sleepy and alarmed, whispered urgently, 'Don't leave us in the dark, Mum. Give us your torch.'

'You can't show any light and give away where you are hiding,' I told them before going back to the sitting room where I could make out the shapes of Adam and the dogs, motionless, listening and waiting. A loud thud followed by a shout outside the window was too much for the dogs who broke from Adam's restraining touch and ran around in a frenzy. I was trying to steady my gun and keep my balance in the commotion when one of the dogs, excited and confused, knocked into me and the gun went clattering to the floor. The noise brought the children running, too scared to be left on their own. If a gang had burst in at that point with all of us falling over each other in the dark, we would have stood no chance. Adam, who was the only one remaining calm, took command as he hissed: 'Get down and shut up, you bloody idiots.' At the sound of his voice the dogs went to him and lay at his feet. The rest of us huddled on the floor, listening for more sounds from outside. Everything had gone very quiet and this felt ominous as the strain of waiting for something to happen began to wear us down. Adam indicated that he was going on a recce and was leaving me on guard. The dogs wanted to go with him but he made them understand they must stay obediently with the rest of us.

The silence stretched out as we remained crouched on the floor and the children were fidgety with whispered questions: 'Where is Dad now? What is he doing? When is he coming back?'

I explained, softly, that gangs sometimes pretend to have gone away, and then wait in ambush for anyone who goes outside to have a look.

'Will Dad get ambushed?'

'No. With his PATU training he knows exactly what to do. Our security lights cover all sight angles from the house. He will soon know if there is anyone outside.'

'I'm glad Dad's here,' Simon said. Yes, I thought, just as well it isn't me on my own this time.

'I'm thirsty,' Louise murmured. 'Dust from the floor is getting in my throat.'

'We'll get a drink when this is over,' I told her.

'You can make spit in your mouth and swallow it,' Peter suggested. 'I do that sometimes.' Louise gave a big sigh.

We didn't hear Adam slip back into the room, but we heard the catch on his gun slide back into place which made us all look up expectantly. 'Not so much as a frigging mouse fart out there,' he said. 'If it was anyone, they've buggered off. Probably drunks staggering about in the dark, hopelessly lost. The coast is clear. We can all go back to bed, thank Christ.'

Going back to bed did not bring much rest that night, or any other night. Needing to be on constant alert coupled with genuine fear for our lives was causing nervous strain and exhaustion, which I felt could not go on being ignored. Since the Breckenridge attack I questioned whether it was irresponsible to expose our children to these dangers. Another worrying element entered the war situation when we heard that our section of the country was under the command of a particularly aggressive battle group known as ZIPRA (Zimbabwe People's Revolutionary Army) whose fighters were trained by the Russians. Many of these were Ndebele speakers of the Matabele tribe with origins among legendary Zulu warriors from the south, traditionally much feared for their superior fighting skills and stamina. The ZIPRA gangs were well armed and we were given instructions now to move the children's beds into a central corridor safely away from windows, and reinforce all our defences, such as they were. Going out at night to have dinner with friends was now a distant memory, and the closure of Gatooma's much-loved Bio-scope (drive-in cinema) was another casualty of war.

Families with sons of military age were losing too many of their young men: would this be the future for ours? *The Rhodesia Herald* of Wednesday, 4 January 1978, carried the photo of a teenage soldier leaning to kiss his mother goodbye from a train window, with the caption:

TEARS FLOW AS 500 LEAVE FOR ARMY LIFE
They were the Salisbury contingent of Intake 160, one of the largest ever, which left last night on a 'special' train bound for Bulawayo's Llewellin Barracks and 18 months of military training. In an emotion-charged farewell, mothers and girlfriends wept, while most of the men looked as if they were willing to go, if not actually happy about it. Five army officers mingled with the crowds of about 2000 relatives and friends, answering parents' questions and allaying their fears as to whether or not their sons would be given breakfast this morning.

Our neighbours next door at Thornby Farm had already lost a son, killed in action. They had another son in the army and the youngest would be called up as soon as he left school. How would I be able to bear losing sons in this way, I kept thinking, looking at Hazel who, always strong and capable as she went about a multiplicity of tasks, seemed diminished now with grief and anxiety.

An invitation from Richard and Felicity Sims for a weekend at their farm offered a break and Adam jumped at it. 'It will be fascinating to see how they're coping with the war up there, and what sort of crop they're having this year,' he remarked with enthusiasm. I had no enthusiasm for observing life in a different war zone as if this offered a refreshing change from our own, but any change of scene suggested temporary relief from the restrictions which now dominated our lives. The invitation was tempting, except that Centenary was a long day's drive from Hartley, and we would have to negotiate a dangerous piece of road known as 'ambush alley' on the way there. This was a narrow section running through a gully where gangs could position themselves above for an ambush, as had been demonstrated several times already. I reminded Adam about this and suggested that our drive to the Sims' farm must aim to pass through the gully during mid-afternoon, which was a time less favoured by the gangs. Their preferred times were around twilight when they could shoot up vehicles and melt away unseen.

'I can't leave until after the milking on a Friday morning if we're going away for the whole weekend,' Adam said.

'That's all right, as long as we leave immediately milking finishes and then drive straight through with only a short stop for lunch, so we're well past the alley by tea time,' I told him. When all had been organised for the weekend, on that Friday morning I had the children and bags packed into the car waiting outside the dairy at the precise time that milking was due to finish. All Adam had to do was climb into his seat and we could be off. After a few minutes when he hadn't appeared I looked at my watch. We could not afford to lose too much time, so I left the children in the car and went to look for him. He was in the dairy office sticking pins into a map on the wall. The map showed all the fields and paddocks on the farm and each pin corresponded to the ear-tag number of an animal, indicating its location. The pin-map was updated with cattle movements each day and Adam was meticulous about it. 'I've got to finish doing this before we can go,' he said.

'Let someone else do it,' I said impatiently. But I knew he liked doing it. 'Please don't make us late for the sake of getting the map done,' I tried to reason. 'The children are sitting in the car waiting. We're all waiting. We're ready to go. You absolutely promised to leave on time, otherwise I wouldn't have agreed to go.'

'Stop nagging, I'll only be a few minutes. Let the children out of the car so they can run around.'

'Don't be mad. They'll run up to the compound and we'll have a devil of a job getting them back. I'm giving you five minutes.'

After five minutes there was still no sign of him appearing, so I leaned on the car horn and kept it blaring, which brought everyone running. All except Adam. 'Baas Adam, he is busy in the office,' the dairy workers told me as if that was something to be treated reverentially. 'He don't like to be disturbed by anyone.'

Well, that doesn't include me, I muttered, and went to disturb him so violently this time that he would be forced to give up what he was doing and submit to being dragged out. When I arrived in a rage at the office I found it locked. Going round to the window to shout and bang on it, mysteriously he had disappeared from his desk and the office was empty. 'Where now is Baas Adam,' I enquired of the dairy workers as politely as I could through clenched teeth.

'He has gone somewhere,' was the vague reply. 'He did not say where he is going.'

He may have gone back to the house to get something, I thought, as I went to the car to check on the children. They were hot and restless and ready to jump out. 'Why are we stuck here like this, not even starting to go?' they demanded.

'We're still waiting for Dad, as usual,' I said crossly. 'I'm going to see if he's at the house collecting something he's forgotten. Don't get out whatever you do. We're running out of time. Soon it will be too late.'

'What do you mean, "too late"? Why will it be too late?' I preferred not to have to explain about that particularly uncomfortable issue, and was spared any hasty prevarication as there was no time to reply, making sure the car doors were firmly closed before running to the house. Adam was there, packing spare magazines for his gun. 'For God's sake, hurry up,' I spluttered at him, breathless from running. 'We've already gone past the deadline for leaving.'

'I know, I know, you don't have to tell me. But there will be a different sort of dead situation for us if we don't have enough ammo loaded up.' I knew it was no good chivvying him. He would take his time since procrastination I had come to realise was in his DNA, and regarded by him as a virtue which he liked to demonstrate at the most inopportune moments, such as now, when staying alive might be seen as a priority.

A whole hour had been lost before we eventually set off and then more time wasted when we had a puncture and found that the spare was flat, but luckily we had a foot pump. We were going to reach the gully just when passing through was most dangerous, but Adam was unconcerned. I almost felt that he relished the chance of what he called a punch-up. 'Stop fussing,' he kept saying as I became increasingly jittery. 'We've each got a gun and plenty of ammo. The children can get down on the floor when we go in. I'll put my foot down and we'll shoot through. It'll be a breeze. You'll see.'

When we reached the notorious alley, Adam drove through so fast I closed my eyes in fright, thinking that if we escaped being ambushed then the car would go out of control and we'd crash instead. But we shot out the other side into open country like a cork from a bottle, and kept going flat out until well clear. When we arrived at the Sims they told us we were lucky because a car had been shot-up there the previous evening, but not to worry, as, on the way back, they would get the latest *sitrep* (situation report) before we left.

Happy as we were to see them again and enjoy an exchange of news and opinion, it was not a relaxing stay while the crackle of their Agri-Alert radio provided a constant reminder that no time of day was safe. Each evening towards sundown we retreated to the bunker where everyone now slept on bunks, so there was no privacy. Even the children found the novelty of eating and sleeping squashed together in a reinforced concrete cell soon wore off when no night-time alarms broke the monotony. We passed the evenings playing cards, notably a game called Oh Hell, which can include any number of players or abilities, with children having just as good a chance of winning as adults, so this was a successful distraction.

'We are allowed to say "Oh Hell" as much as we like in this game,' Simon remarked, 'but not allowed to say it any other time because Mum says it's swearing. Why is it only all right in a game? And anyway Dad swears all the time.' Avoiding the subject Adam commented, *apropos* of nothing in particular, 'Wendy is getting very skitzy these days.'

'She's not the only one,' Felicity told him. 'My nerves are in shreds, and the worst thing is not being able to plan for the future, or even for the next planting season while everything is in limbo. No one knows what's going to happen next and whether we are going to lose our land, or even our lives.'

'It's not as bad as that,' Richard was more optimistic. 'We just need to hang on and remember that tobacco, not religion, is the opium of the people. We grow the best Burley and whatever happens here, millions all over the world are going to keep buying it, and millions more are being born every day, so it's never going to end. What needs to come to an end is this bloody war so we can get on with our lives without having to dodge bullets all the time.' He was solicitous about our return journey, knowing how nervous I was about another dash through the alley. 'I'll come in convoy with you this time, and we might get some others to join us' he said. 'It's safer to go in convoy now things are becoming more hairy. I've got farm stuff to pick up in Salisbury so I might as well make a trip of it and go with you as far as the city.'

'Oh, Richard, thanks,' I said, almost in tears with relief.

We had shopping of our own to do on our way through and, starting very early, just managed to arrive home before dark when it wasn't safe to be on the road. We were surprised when the usual ecstatic welcome by two excited dogs running out to the car didn't happen this time. No dogs appeared and we felt instant alarm. Amos, the cook, who was waiting for us, came out and said both dogs were sick and had been taken to the vet who was keeping them at the surgery. 'What kind of sickness?' we asked, worried at having left them, especially Ruin who was old and coming to the end of her life, but Roger was still strong and healthy.

'It is a sickness of the stomach, the vet said maybe from eating something bad,' Amos told us. Labradors are notorious for eating filth wherever they can find it and farms provide rich pickings. Crusty cowpats can be irresistible along with any putrid maggot-infested morsel dropped in a field where cows have given birth. A dead rat or other decomposing scrap lying around brings tail-wagging delight, and the generous nature of Labradors inclines them to want to share these finds, so that something grisly was often picked up to be offered to us as a gift. Our lack of enthusiasm for receiving such treasures was a puzzle to the canine mind. Like all retrievers, Labradors love to demonstrate their skill in fetching objects: best of all when retrieving birds during shoots, while in between times any unresisting substitute will do. Small kittens were favourite objects in our household. These were gently removed one by one from their baskets if the mother cat was not present, to be carried around until someone noticed a bedraggled kitten lying helplessly in the drooling mouth of one of the dogs. It would come obediently when called and drop the wet kitten into an outstretched hand as another charming gift for us. The trusting guilelessness of dogs can be endearing, but now they had got themselves into trouble by picking up something repulsive and our usual rapturous homecoming was empty without their welcome. 'We better phone the vet straight away and find out what happened,' I said, thinking it must be serious if the dogs had been kept at the surgery overnight.

'They're in safe hands. We can phone in the morning.' Adam was tired after the long drive. We comforted ourselves with the cats who strolled out when they heard us arrive and curled themselves around our legs. Each child had been promised a cat of their own when we moved back to the farm and Louise had a black and white tom called Prince Socks. Simon's was a ginger tom named Brian, but Peter's was the star: a luxuriant fluffy grey female he called Puffer. We failed to realise that toms are fiercely territorial and mark out personal patches as theirs wherever these might be. They lost no time in dividing up the territory of our house, spraying scent onto curtains, table legs and strategic pieces of furniture; considering it an additional right to pounce on poor Puffer so that a state of almost perpetual motherhood was imposed on her. This was the starting point of a cat population that multiplied until underneath every bed there were baskets and cardboard boxes containing litters of kittens. The scuffling and mewing mesmerised the dogs while infuriating Adam who eventually insisted that all the toms were unmanned by the vet.

In the absence of dogs this time when we arrived home, the cats took over and made a big show of welcoming us, but it wasn't the same. 'I can't go to sleep not knowing about the dogs,' I said to Adam as we lay in bed that night, stupefied with fatigue after the long drive.

'Just close your eyes and stop flapping,' he muttered, turning over to put an end to discussion of the subject as he reached down to check his gun before sliding into that easy sleep which seems to come naturally to husbands, while so often eluding wives when the niggle of an anxiety keeps batting away at the edges of consciousness.

Long before the first chirp of a bird at daybreak, Adam had slipped out of bed and gone to the dairy. There were no dogs waiting to be let into the house as he opened the back door, and no dogs padding into our room to flop down and doze with the cats before getting-up time. Phoning the vet out of hours was restricted to emergencies so we had to wait for the surgery to open. The children were as anxious as I was about the dogs and as soon as they were awake that morning had been full of questions: 'Are Roger and Ruin all right?' 'How soon can we go and get them?' 'What do you think was wrong with them?' 'Who will be looking after them at the vet's?' 'Will someone be there all night with them?'

A veterinary assistant was employed to look after any sick animals that were kept at the surgery overnight, I told them. 'Anyway we'll know soon,' I said, and almost as I said it, there was Adam arriving back, though it was still early for breakfast. He was looking shaken. 'It's bad news, I'm afraid. The vet phoned which was good of him.' I was holding my breath. 'It was some kind of poisoning, maybe from licking something at the dip. They never recovered. They died in the night. Both of them, last night. There was nothing anyone could have done. Andy [the vet] did everything possible. They were on drips and antidotes. It's a massive blow for all of us, happening so suddenly.' The children looked at him in disbelief. I had to sit down, faint with shock before breaking down in tears, so that when he brought me a cup of tea I was too distraught to be able to drink it. 'Ruin was on her last legs anyway,' he said gently. 'She could hardly drag herself around at times. I'd been thinking we should get Andy to put her down. You saw how she was. She couldn't go on much longer; in dog years she was into extreme old age.'

'Yes, but Roger was still bouncing around. He wasn't that old. He was the best companion, coming with me every day on my rounds checking animals and water troughs. It will be too lonely without him. He made me happy and I felt safe with him. He always watched for snakes when I was gardening, and barked to warn me if there were any in beds where I was weeding. Dogs have distinct personalities, more than humans sometimes, don't you think?'

'You're as bad as Mum with her Pointers. Remember, this is a farm; we can't afford to be soppy about animals,' he said, trying to sound reasonable, but in reality he was just as upset as the rest of us.

'They're not just animals, they're part of our family,' Simon sobbed, in such distress it set me off again and we clung to each other, while Louise and Peter kept calm and asked sensible questions about what had happened, and whether we could get puppies so they could have one each like the cats. I can't bear to have another dog, I thought: I can never go through this heartbreak again. Then an even worse thought occurred – if I'm like this with a dog, what if it was a child?

The hiatus caused by a long weekend away and the sudden loss of the dogs distracted me from normal routines such as collecting the post while shopping. When I remembered to call at the post office there was a letter from America among the envelopes in our pile of mail. Several Rhodesian farmers had emigrated to America in a group with their families the previous year and the letter was from one of them, Jim, who was a good friend. The group had found opportunities in agriculture where experienced managers were needed by wealthy Americans who bought farms and plantations as tax havens. Jim thought we might be interested in joining him if we felt up to making another move. He had established a company offering agricultural services and there was a place for Adam if he wanted to go and have a look at what was on offer.

'This could be a big break for us.' Adam seized on the prospect enthusiastically. 'What do you think, darling? There's no future for us here the way things are going. We can do a quick recce using the holiday time we had put aside for your father's visit.'

My response needed no more than a moment's thought because America held a deep attraction for me. I owed my life to American Air Force pilots who rescued Muz, Elaine and me from Burma where we had been trapped during the war. Risking their own lives they flew under the noses of Japanese fighter planes to scoop us up with other refugees from a remote jungle landing strip, saving our lives, and these memories stayed with me. Further memories of American big-heartedness came from my first school which was wonderful Woodstock, high in the Himalayan mountains at Landour in India. An American school for the children of missionaries and others, it was the happiest and most friendly school anyone could imagine. This encounter with American culture made an indelible impression such that I had always wanted to go to America and feel again the energy and dynamism of people who had been born and raised there. These qualities seemed to me excitingly different from English reserve and inhibition. I liked the way that Americans treated failure as no more than a useful stepping stone on the way to future success with no sense of shame about it. My admiration for this attitude had been a tug pulling at my subconscious for years, and now there was an opportunity to connect with that fondly remembered American ebullience again.

'How soon can we go?' I said, the urgency in my voice reinforced by the weight of my gun as it hung like a shackle from my shoulder, combined with the gloom of grenade screens at the windows and a foreboding that had come over me since losing the dogs.

Chapter 7

In my excitement at the prospect of seeing America I completely forgot what it might cost to move. 'How can we afford it?' I asked Adam, remembering the usual state of our finances.

'I got a good pay-out from my shares in Glanjoro when it was sold. The money is in Switzerland where it's safe and I haven't wanted to touch any of it except for emergencies. You could say that this is an emergency, or at least a contingency, due to our lives here being in danger. We can afford the move if we decide it's the best thing to do. If I can get a decent job in America.'

Adam had not mentioned that he had money in Switzerland, or details of any distribution from the sale of Glanjoro. This was surprising since he was highly critical of families who never discussed money, especially if it was his own family, and he frequently complained about Granny Hill's refusal to let Cen help with her investments, or even see her Will. When she died it was found that many shares she owned had become worthless, and bequests which may have seemed generous many years before, looked meagre later on in modern money. She left five pounds to each of her grandchildren, including Adam, which barely paid for a round of drinks by the time this amount had passed through the hands of executors and solicitors.

'I'll write to Jim and ask for more details,' Adam said, 'and ask if he can put us up at his place in Boston while we look around. We'll need to get the children planted somewhere: the boys can become temporary boarders and it won't make any difference to Louise who will be at Roosevelt if we're only away for a couple of weeks.'

'We'll have to get visas. I'll see about that,' I offered confidently, but the visa process was complex. Certified copies of personal documents had to accompany detailed forms and other documents verified by a government official. Hartley had its own local government office serving a wide area and provided a notary service. While I was there one morning, two African chiefs arrived from a tribal homeland where they still held traditional roles and powers. I had never seen chiefs like these before. They wore impressive metal breast plates like silver quarter moons across their chests, but their clothes, which were government-issue uniforms, were well-worn and shabby in contrast to these regal symbols of status. They went to speak to the white female clerk at the reception desk while I sat at a table filling in forms, and began with the customary courteous exchange of greetings, but the clerk was in no mood for pleasantries. 'What do you want?' she asked irritably.

'We would like, please, to request new uniforms. These are no longer respectable for our work.' The clerk looked at them and laughed. 'Do you think the government has money to spend on clothes for *muntus* like you,' she said rudely. I stood up, scraping my chair back loudly in a show of annoyance at the woman's disrespect. The word *muntu* translated from Shona means 'man', but in this context was being used in a deliberately derogatory sense.

'Last time we came, it was allowed,' one of the chiefs said reasonably, taking no offence.

'Haven't you noticed what's going on?' the clerk responded. 'There's enough problems coming into this office without you bothering us as well.'

I wanted to object to the clerk's attitude, but soon realised it would be futile, just as any attempt to get her to re-consider the chiefs' request would fail to register with someone as prejudiced as she was. The chiefs had already turned away, and left the office with their backs straight, walking tall and looking dignified even in defeat.

This is why I can't stay in Rhodesia, I thought. It isn't the war, or fear of the future, it's the alienating culture.

People who left were despised for giving up instead of staying and fighting, but we couldn't fight for something we didn't believe in any more. When we told the children our plans, the excitement of a new adventure was overshadowed for the boys by the imminent prospect of boarding at Hartley School. 'We'll get beaten every day,' they protested, terrified. 'Boarders get beaten more because their parents aren't there to save them.'

'You'll have to be very good and stay out of trouble,' Adam advised.

'You don't even need to do anything wrong, you just get beaten for the heck of it.'

'Better that than getting shot on a farm somewhere off in the bush if you go to stay with any of your friends. Anyway it's only for a very short time and then you'll be leaving Hartley School for ever if we find a nice place to live in America,' Adam told them.

'Will we have Kentucky Fried Chicken?' Peter asked. He had seen this on television.

'As much as you like. With a bucket of fries and big bottle of coke. That's a promise.'

Jim was very prompt in replying to our many questions and helping with arrangements for our trip. He organised an itinerary which took us on a series of plane hops to different states and places where he had identified prospects and opportunities, suggesting that we should see as much as possible of the country and what it offered while we were there. With our visas and documents finally collected together, we booked tickets and arrived for our flight at Salisbury airport on a glowing morning that shone with the glorious umber colours of Rhodesia, making me feel a pang to be looking for somewhere else to live. When the plane took off, instead of climbing at the usual angle it went off like a rocket, straight up. The force of the ascent pushed me into my seat so that I was almost lying on my back, panic-stricken that something had gone wrong. 'It's OK,' Adam said. 'The plane has to get out of range of SAMs (surface to air missiles) pretty damn quick before they lock on. It's standard practice since the bastards found out how to bring down passenger jets.' These new atrocities marked a recent escalation in tactics with further outrage when survivors from a crash had been shot. An echo for me of Japanese savagery in Burma, and now, here I was, trying to escape yet another conflict.

Boston, when we arrived, was like stepping onto a film set. The contrast after living in a small rural town in Africa was startling as we emerged into a world which felt very established, leafy and privileged, with deep coffers. Jim took charge and whisked us round on a tour of prosperous suburbs with clubs where we were introduced to people Jim thought might be useful contacts. It was all very different from anything I had seen before. The cars were big and shiny and the men wore expensive-looking suits. When they shook my hand they gripped only the ends of my fingers instead of a proper handshake, and when I remarked on this, I was told it was the polite way to shake hands with a woman so that her fingers would not be crushed by her diamond rings. I noticed the rings, and the stylish clothes, but particularly the hair. Everyone seemed to have thick glossy hair, and dazzling teeth. They radiated health and good cheer and astonished me with their candour, freely talking of personal finance and relationships which I found refreshing after a lifetime of English modesty. One very convivial Italian businessman told me he had started a bank with $10,000, borrowed from a friend. 'It is very useful to own a bank, especially a successful one,' he said, laughing, and looking at him I didn't doubt it.

Jim outlined our itinerary: 'You don't need the frenzy of New York so I haven't included a visit, but Washington is a feast for the eye and soul. You can't miss that on your way south.'

We had friends, Jyll and Mike, who lived in Washington where Mike now worked for the World Bank after their family farm in Kenya had been sold. Meeting members of the white Kenyan diaspora who had successfully transplanted themselves was reassuring, so we looked forward to this after spending our first day in Washington visiting monuments and museums. It needed no more than one day to convince me that Washington with its sublime symmetry and spaciousness was the most beautiful city I had ever seen, and when we walked into the Air and Space Museum my sense of wonder was complete. There, suspended on wires in a great hall, was the actual *Spirit of St Louis* aeroplane which Charles Lindbergh had flown across the Atlantic, while in another hall the Apollo space craft that had landed on the moon was displayed beside a small moon rock. The rock was mounted on a plinth where it could be touched and felt, like a pebble on the beach.

Intending to be abstemious, we had booked ourselves into a budget hotel and this, when we found it, was in downtown Washington where we were the only white guests. Being part of a tiny minority was normal for us after Africa where we were always vastly outnumbered, and the other guests were charming, but surprised to hear that we lived in Africa. 'How come you living in those parts with lions and tigers?' they asked, seeming to have a limited concept of Africa as a continent of great splendour and variety, but no tigers.

The only problem with the budget hotel was the breakfast menu where we had difficulty translating items such as 'grits', but then found this was simply mealie porridge which we were used to at home. Jyll laughed when she came to collect us after breakfast. 'You'll wise up in a blink when you come to live here,' she said. 'You have to. America isn't the Pilgrim Fathers bringing Englishness from across the sea. It's a foreign country. Being smart for instance has nothing to do with clothes, it's a state of mind. Life is a bandwagon. You'll see.' We were walking out to her car parked on the kerb. 'You can't even start without the right sort of car,' she said as she opened the door of a flashy beast and then drove like a bat through the traffic to Georgetown, where we were to meet Mike. The plan was to stroll around, absorbing the very different and more intimate sensations of that district in contrast to the powerfully expansive character of Washington city, and then have lunch at their favourite restaurant. There would be no grits, Jyll teased, but we could try something else traditional which was special to that region and shouldn't be missed. These were cherrystone clams, so princely and rich I was almost defeated by my portion, but Adam wolfed his and the expression on his face told me that he was already won to the American dream – good food being high on his list of desirable objectives.

Filled with the particular satisfaction of a good lunch we went outside to Jyll's car and found it hemmed in bumper to bumper with other cars, making it impossible to move. Adam and Mike surveyed the problem from various angles and were discussing options, when a bunch of men in loud shirts who happened to be passing on the sidewalk, stopped to offer assistance. Mike took charge, distributing members of this improvised workforce around Jyll's car, so that each one stood ready when Mike shouted, 'LIFT', and the car was shifted bodily not just a few inches but right out into the road. We piled in for a quick getaway, yelling thanks to the helpers, but someone had already called the police who stopped the traffic and tried to arrest us for public disorder. 'You can't arrest us, we're English,' Adam attempted to charm them. 'We didn't know we were committing any offence.'

The officer ignored him and asked gruffly, 'Who is the driver of this car?' Jyll declared herself, putting a hand out to shake his, which surprised him and he responded gingerly, 'Are you English too?'

'Yes,' she said. 'We would like to apologise for our ignorance, causing you this trouble.'

'What about the other guys?' the officer looked around for the lifting crew, but they had disappeared. He sighed and looked at Jyll, who gave him a dazzling smile. She was the kind of girl who had what was called back then 'winning ways'.

'Try not to cause any more trouble,' he said graciously, 'and have a nice day.' We shot away after that, hoping not to add a speeding ticket to our crimes.

Jim was not impressed when we told him what had happened. 'Getting arrested isn't going to help you get a green card, and you can't mess with the Police here. But I would have liked to see you bumping that car out into the traffic,' he laughed. He was taking us to the airport for the next leg of our lightning tour, which was to Arkansas.

When the plane left Washington and turned to fly over western Virginia and then northern Tennessee, I watched, gripped by the view from my window as we passed over hundreds of miles of seemingly uninhabited country. Range after range of green forested mountains passed below with only an occasional road to be seen cutting through the dense tree cover. I strained to see patches of cleared land or houses in the immensity of that environment. So much land, so much rich land. The diversity of this giant country was phenomenal, and I was only just beginning to see it as we continued to fly south. By the time we arrived at Little Rock it was dark and we were tired, grateful to be met by a car taking us to the Rockefeller Center at Petit Jean Mountain, arranged by Jim. The Center is a campus founded by Governor Winthrop Rockefeller at his 188-acre home and cattle farm on the mountain, providing a place of learning and inspiration for people to meet and exchange ideas.

The campus included a training facility for agricultural students from all over the world and this was where Adam came in. Some of the East African students were homesick and finding it difficult to adjust, so the Center wanted to employ a lecturer who spoke Swahili and understood their culture. As soon as Adam was introduced to these students and started speaking like one of them, they were overjoyed. Other students at the faculty were mainly from South America and appeared more sophisticated than the East Africans, so it was easier for them to fit in. We felt instantly bonded to 'ours' and wanted to spend longer chatting, but our hosts wanted to see how we might fit into the academic and social life of that specialised community. I was taken to meet the wives of lecturers and administrators who had gathered in one of the staff houses and served me something I had never encountered before. This was iced tea poured from pitchers filled with ice cubes, which was appealing in the muggy air of that region, but I was disappointed to find the tea surprisingly flavourless. A more insipid and utterly limp infusion would be hard to devise, I thought, and it wasn't even refreshing. I could imagine Adam's father, Cen, bellowing (as he used to) if weak tea crept into his cup: "This is gnat's pee, revolting, not fit for humans!"

That evening when I felt a strong urge for something more reviving after the day's exertions, and enquired about a gin and tonic, I was told that Arkansas has strict laws on alcohol and this was a dry county. 'That's it then,' I told Adam. 'I'm not coming here if I can't get a drink. Those poor Africans will have to be left to their fate.'

Before we left Arkansas Jim wanted us to visit a dairy where they were milking sixteen hundred cows on a production line. He seemed to have contacts everywhere and people to collect and drive us wherever we needed to go. On the way to the dairy we passed an enormous sign at the side of the road saying: 'CAT FARM'. 'Oh that's horrible, farming cats, and what for?' I asked our driver.

'It's not those sort of cats,' he said, amused at my ignorance. 'It's cat fish. It's a big market. When you see them on the menu you should order some.'

Further down the road another big sign declared: 'MUMS' for sale. 'I expect you have a perfectly reasonable explanation for selling mums as well,' I teased the driver.

'Chrysanthemums,' he said. 'You should see those farms. Spread out like rainbows.'

But the mums were not displayed close enough to the road for us to see, and we went on driving for miles through a landscape which was flat in every direction to the horizon: fenced, cultivated or grassed, and seeming limitless.

The mega cow unit, when we arrived, was similarly a marvel to eyes like ours which were used to less opulent endeavours, but I was beginning to look more critically at these countrywide 'Biggest is Best' systems of production, and wanted to see if the cows looked happy. They were healthy and looked content, strolling from machine bays to stalls where they could lie, munching and resting their distended udders. 'They are just as happy as any factory workers anywhere in the world, and probably a lot better looked after than most who spend their lives on a production line,' Adam remarked. 'Remember, they're bovines, with a bovine temperament. They're not looking for a hammock and good book for contentment.'

'No, but they're not so daft they wouldn't prefer green grass and the open sky.'

'What you've never had, you don't miss,' Adam said, and moved on to talk about yields and lactations and all the issues that are of such absorbing interest to dairy farmers, rather than what cows are thinking about.

Back in Little Rock we were dropped off at the Greyhound bus station to start the next and very long leg of Jim's itinerary, taking us down to the middle part of Florida where he had a major project underway. It was not his recommendation to ride the Greyhounds but we wanted to see the southern states at ground level instead of flying overhead, and thought some of the stops might be interesting. They were, but not in the way we expected. Interstate highways are not built to be scenic and the 'stops' at bus stations were often in seedy downtown areas frequented by junkies, which was not a feature of American life that I had prepared myself for. The states I so much wanted to see, associated in my mind with vibrant robust characters from *Show Boat* and those firebrands of the Civil Rights movement, passed in a blur from the windows of our bus. But our route couldn't miss the mighty Mississippi river flowing as majestically as ever it did in my imagination, busy with the traffic of a great waterway. I saw, too, Birmingham Alabama in a hazy dawn when my biggest surprise was the density of rush hour traffic with everyone going to work at 6 o'clock in the morning.

We were impatient by now to reach Florida and when the Gulf of Mexico came shimmering up in front with palm trees, white sand and the salty breath of a gentle breeze, we knew this was where we wanted to be. After the panhandle there was Ocala, its avenues of oaks draped in silvery Spanish moss, like a town dressed for Halloween. Further on, as we emerged into open countryside, there were horses grazing in paddocks as green and smooth as any English meadow, with stables and barns like palaces. This ribbon of plenty merged further south into flat pine-studded forests of featureless palmetto scrub which ran into the distance seemingly without end. Palmetto is a tough saw-leafed plant with a spread that covers most of inland Florida, where the highway runs straight and fast through these backwoods and along the gulf coast. Jim had flown down to meet us at Fort Myers and take us to see his new project.

This was a ranch, or potentially a ranch, on fifty thousand acres of virgin land, dense with palmetto and swamps where it was easy to get lost on rough tracks weaving through the wilderness. As we drove around in a truck with four-wheel drive, Jim identified occasional small islands of elevated ground with a cover of holm oaks where we could stop to take a view. These islands were called, 'hammocks', which may have been simply a different way of pronouncing 'hummocks' because this is what they were, mercifully offering shade under the oaks. The islands offered places to rest as the trees invitingly spread their branches above carpets of fallen leaves for weary wanderers, and animals too. We sometimes disturbed shy deer sheltering from the intense heat of the flatlands, and there might also be wild turkeys among the trees Jim told us. These were fair game for the syndicate of investors who had bought the ranch and looked forward to hosting hunting parties as soon as the main business of the ranch was up and running. This is where Adam might see an opportunity, Jim suggested, if he was attracted to a pioneering job in helping to plan, develop and run the cattle side of the ranch. It was a huge job and a daunting one, but Jim himself would be in charge as general manager with several others attending to different parts of the project. Adam's section would be entirely centred on beef cattle, starting with the basics: putting in fences and handling yards; feed-lots; building up herds and breeding stock; all the things he was familiar with and good at. But while he was enthused, I was more cautious.

I wondered where we would live. There had been no visible buildings of any kind during our tour and everywhere looked barren and baked. Some evidence of previous attempts to develop this vast tract of land was evident where canals had been dug to drain the swamps, and along the canals I noticed there were alligators sunning themselves on the banks. Some of the alligators were big enough to be a menace, I thought, and remarked on this to Jim. He laughed, 'Oh, they can grow to enormous sizes, but they are protected by law and we're not allowed to shoot them.'

'Do they ever attack people?'

'Usually only dogs or small animals if any come within reach. But out here in the boonies, it's snakes you have to watch for, and it's OK to shoot them. You'll meet plenty of nasty ones,' he said, as if I might find this piece of information encouraging. Adam, of course, was very engaged by this. 'What kind?' he asked, eager as ever when snakes were mentioned.

'The worst ones are rattlers, copperheads and cottonmouth moccasins. Rattlers are aggressive, so you move quick not to step on one when you hear rattling in the grass.'

I didn't want to hear too much about snakes, and asked about schools instead.

'The nearest ones with a bus service are about thirty miles distant at Punta Gorda, but you can run your children by car and there's a fast road once you get off the ranch.'

'Is there a shop nearer than Punta Gorda?' was my next question.

'Yes, but it's the other direction. Arcadia is about twenty miles and it has a Winn-Dixie (supermarket) which is quite handy.' I thought about that for a moment and hoped the ranch might support a couple of cows to avoid running out of milk if we were going to plunge for a life among the swamps and hammocks.

'Where would we live?' I asked Jim.

'It would have to be a trailer at the start until more people come and we can put houses along the river. I haven't shown you the river yet. It's pretty, and not too far from the road. We've already surveyed the site for building.'

I looked at Adam whose interest was further sparked by the mention of a river, with the prospect of fishing. There was also the Gulf, famed for its deep-sea fishing and long white beaches as fine as any we had known along Indian Ocean shores. 'I'll take you on a drive to Boca Grande Island for lunch tomorrow to show you how unspoilt this coast still is,' Jim said. 'One thing about the ranch is having all the islands and beaches so close. Great for families. And fishing,' he added as a nod to Adam.

We might almost have been back at the Kenya coast the next day, walking on sand like icing sugar, beside water the colour of jade. Each tide brought a fringe of tiny shells strung along the shore. 'See if you can find a sand dollar,' Jim said, 'for luck.'

Within days we were on our way home, leaving Fort Myers on a tiny American Eagle plane for the short hop skimming above the Florida Everglades to Miami, and then a rather larger plane for the Atlantic leg. We were impatient to get back and rescue the boys who we knew would be frantic to escape the ferocious grip of Hartley School's headmaster. As expected they were tearful with relief to be collected and taken back to the farm then, as soon as we arrived, more concerned to be reunited with their cats than to hear about our adventures. There were letters from Louise, anxious to come home, reminding us about her next exeat from Roosevelt. Other letters were official ones about petrol-rationing, added security arrangements and those from PATU for Adam, with dates for call-up. We were dismally back in a world of guns, sandbags, curfew lock-down and war fatigue, but however unappealing this was in contrast to the many attractions of America, I was on familiar territory here while many aspects of that country had felt distinctly foreign.

'How do you feel about going to work for Jim?' I asked Adam after each of us had recovered enough to collect our thoughts.

'It's a dream job, there's no mistake. And the pay's good. Much better than we would get anywhere else. Best of all, ranching is a picnic after dairy farming. I'd never have to look at a frigging milking machine ever again.'

'You said that before, when you couldn't face another day stuck at the back end of a cow, and we went to live in Salisbury.'

'That was different. I ended up in an office handing out loans for other people to go off enjoying themselves as ranchers. This time I'll be handed the money to do it myself, plus spending all day with horses out on the range.'

'Apart from work, what about the lifestyle there?'

'What do you mean – lifestyle?'

'Friends. Social events; not just for ourselves, for the children as well.'

'Jim is moving to the area with his family so we will have them, and he's recruiting other Rhodesians.'

'Why doesn't he recruit Americans? It would be a lot less trouble and expense, and avoid all the green card complications.'

'Americans don't want to live out in the sticks. Farming and ranching are low status occupations there. They prefer to live in cities where they can work in air-conditioned offices, leaving a head honcho in charge of anything agricultural. Jim sees big potential in supplying expert on-site management for properties with absent owners where there is a growing demand for this kind of service. Not just farms and ranches; orange groves too, up and down the state. We would be in on the ground floor of this new enterprise. It's a great opportunity, especially as there is nothing to keep us here any longer now that Rhodesia is going the same way as everywhere else in Africa.'

He stopped, waiting for me to say something, and when I didn't reply immediately he looked surprised. 'Don't you see?' he asked.

'I was hugely impressed with America. It didn't disappoint, in fact it massively exceeded expectations. The energy, enthusiasm and vibrance of the country is extraordinary. When you arrive you automatically get plugged in, it's truly dynamic so you can't help feeling you want to be part of all that. But now I've had time to think about it, there is a part of me with big reservations niggling away in the back of my mind. '

'What do you mean?'

'All the time we were over there, I was registering impressions on a conscious level, while at the same time my subconscious was absorbing and brooding like some kind of internal fat frog sitting there pulsing with its own interpretations.'

'What the hell are you on about?' Adam interrupted irritably.

'Just that now I've had time to process it, America, despite all its attractions, feels foreign. I'm basically too English, or too African, to adapt easily to that culture and way of life.'

Adam greeted this little speech with silence before composing himself to reply, and when he did so, it could not have been more unexpected or startling. 'I didn't tell you about it straight away, darling, because I didn't want to spoil our first day back, but when I arrived at the office there was a letter waiting on the desk for me. It was from Eric, terminating my employment, with three months' notice. Due to restructuring the company, he says. Which is a polite way of saying they don't want my services anymore. So you see, darling, Jim's offer is a godsend. It couldn't be better timed. We have to go willy-nilly. You can see that now, can't you?'

My initial reaction was disbelief. How could Adam be dismissed just like that with no discussion or warning; it didn't make sense. But it was some consolation that the decision had been made for us, and we had somewhere to go, even if it wasn't by choice. 'It's just as well we've got the Florida option, then,' I said, feeling resigned whatever my reservations. 'You'll have to contact Jim without delay and get the offer in writing.'

'I knew you'd see it like that, dearest. The whole thing is providential.'

'You know we're going to be called traitors, leaving the country like rats.'

'Better to be live rats than dead ones.'

Events moved swiftly after that as Adam's new job was confirmed and we faced the dismay and sometimes hostility of friends who felt we were abandoning them. The next time I saw Andy the vet I asked him if he knew what had led to Adam losing his job. Andy said that it had been of concern to Eric and the other directors that Adam was away so much with PATU, as this was affecting the farm's performance. It could not function properly without a fully committed manager and no one could understand why he was volunteering for so many missions. Andy was well aware this was a cause of concern for me too, left with a gun to help defend and run the farm as best I could during his absences.

With new prospects underway and only three months left on the farm, there can be no more excursions with PATU, I thought, and instead Adam will be able to help me pack up. Our boxes would be setting out on a long haul after going overland first to the port of Beira in Mozambique, then by ship sailing around the Cape of Good Hope before crossing the Atlantic to Miami. The next stage would be overland again – this time to the ranch if all went to plan. I had started sorting what needed to go, when Adam revealed that he had volunteered for one last PATU mission. This left me feeling completely exasperated, thinking that he didn't need to give himself any more chances to get killed at this point. I had a bad feeling about it. He was tempting fate, apart from which there was a lot to do and organise at home, and on the farm too, so that it was left in good order for someone else to take over.

'Please don't go,' I implored him. 'It's madness. You don't need to. You know you're pushing your luck this time.'

'You don't understand. It's something I have to do – going out with my stick one last time, backing them up.'

'What will they do without you when you've gone, then? They will find a replacement, you know that. You're not indispensable to them, but you're indispensable to us, your family.'

'Stop bitching. I'm doing what I have to do, and you can do what you have to do.'

We had delayed telling the children the news about moving until Louise came home for a weekend so we could tell all of them together. It was a big announcement, received with delight. Louise was pleased because it meant she would not be boarding anymore, and the boys saw prospects ahead of horses and cowboys and fishing. They had heard of Disneyworld and the theme parks of Orlando, and when we said these were within easy reach of the ranch, excitement was intense. But when we told them the cats couldn't come with us in the same way that the dogs had accompanied us to Rhodesia, faces fell. 'I can't go without Brian,' Simon protested. 'And I can't go without Puffer,' Peter added.

'You'll have to stay behind with them in that case,' I told them, and Louise commented, 'Cats hate moving, it really upsets them. We can find nice homes for them.' That seemed to settle the matter, leaving the boys looking glum, but they cheered up when it was suggested that we could get new pets in America. 'Can we have horses too?'

'I don't see why not,' I told them. 'With so few roads on the ranch we'll probably need horses to get around.' The boys were elated by this news, conjuring up images of wild-west galloping about. 'Will we have guns as well?'

'I hope we're leaving guns behind. The whole point of moving is to live in a place where we don't have to carry guns all the time.'

'We'll be able to have airguns, won't we?'

'I'm going to need one myself. For snakes,' I told them, which drew immediate attention.

'Are there lots of snakes?' The boys were agog.

'Millions,' I said, deliberately exaggerating. 'Some very poisonous ones, so we'll have to watch out.'

'Dad will love having lots of snakes around.'

'Dad will be too busy to bother much about snakes. It's going to be a huge job for him, the biggest job he's ever had. We'll all have to be extra helpful and make sure he doesn't get too tired.'

'Dad's always tired.'

'That's dairy work, milking three times a day. It's a killing regime for both man and beast. We're escaping all that to a completely different life which is going to be incredibly exciting and full of new experiences.'

'When do we actually go?'

'As soon as the tax department has worked out how much we owe them and it has been paid, then we're allowed to leave.'

A complex obstacle course of regulatory hurdles had to be cleared before anyone could leave the country. It was made as difficult as possible, with procedures deliberately protracted to discourage leavers, it seemed.

During our last weeks at Rogate, Adam went on his final PATU assignment. The boys were eager to help as usual in assembling his equipment that included what were called 'rat-packs'. These were packs of food supplied as tinned or dry rations, much coveted by the boys who were allowed to keep any leftover packs for themselves. When all was ready, Adam in camouflage uniform and everything loaded into the car, the boys piled in and we drove to the police station rendezvous point.

The boys didn't want to miss a moment of the thrill as other members of Adam's PATU stick arrived, similarly kitted out, ready to drive to Salisbury and be flown from there by helicopter to a battle zone.

I looked forward to meeting other wives who were dropping off their husbands and felt a bond with them as we all shared the same apprehension and fear for their safety. This time I felt embarrassed because we were leaving. I knew the others must feel we were deserting them, even if they were too polite to show it. One of the wives, Audrey, was a close friend and gave me a hug as the men went off. 'Don't feel bad, hey, you're doing the right thing. Anyone who gives you the finger, they're just jealous.'

'Thanks Audrey, we'll keep in touch, I'll miss you.'

The boys were subdued on the drive back to the farm now there was no more excitement to occupy them, except taking it in turns to hold my gun while I was driving. I hoped there would be no alarms back at home to deal with during this last stint on my own. There had been no sign of a replacement for Adam, and Francis was in charge, very competently, so that I wondered if he might be promoted to Adam's job, and hoped that he would.

The next few days passed without incident as I set out on my usual long walks around the herds each morning, checking animals and water troughs, but the pleasure had gone out of these walks without Roger beside me. I missed him every day, and surprised myself by feeling such grief that tears still came whenever I thought of him. I could never have imagined loving a dog so much. I will get over it as time goes on, I told myself, but I will never be able to replace him.

These thoughts and the sadness of my walks were interrupted one afternoon by a message from the police station telling me to go there immediately. I knew this meant something must have happened to Adam, and drove the five miles to Hartley with dread for what this could be, and what it might mean for our plans. At the station an officer told me that Adam's stick had been involved in a contact. A 'contact' was the term used for engagement with one or more heavily armed gangs. During this contact it appeared that Adam's stick had been outnumbered and had taken cover among the rocks of a small *kopje* (hill) from which they fought fiercely and there had been quite a battle. Unfortunately the sustained action was too much for Adam's unreliable knee, which gave out and he went down. The stick leader called on the radio for a helicopter evacuation, and when the helicopter was heard overhead it spooked the bush fighters who retreated temporarily, but returned later and the stick came under heavy fire again. No further *sitrep* had been received from them since this point, the officer reported, but reinforcements had been sent in. Meanwhile, Adam had been flown to hospital in Salisbury and was receiving treatment for his knee.

Audrey told me later that with one man short, the others thought they were goners and fought for their lives with ammunition running low, but they were saved by another stick arriving. 'Adam mustn't do any more patrols,' Audrey said. 'It's too risky.'

'Don't worry, that's absolutely the last time,' I assured her. 'I didn't want him to go, but he's obsessed with PATU and feels he is letting the others down if he doesn't go.'

'It's worse if he leaves them short during a contact.'

'You don't need to tell me. I'm sure he feels terrible about it, and extremely fed up to miss the rest of the action. It's almost an addiction, craving a good fight, and it's not healthy. No one should be addicted to danger.'

'I don't think the others see it that way. They like being together out in the bush, sleeping rough, being invisible, surviving. It's a bond between them. But the fighting is a job. No one wants to be killed. Adam doesn't want to get zapped any more than the others.'

I do wonder sometimes, I thought to myself, but why? It doesn't make sense. I was still going through this in my mind when I went to collect him from the police station on his return. I didn't know what state his knee would be in, or his mood after this latest setback, so I was glad to find him buoyant though seething with frustration. His knee was puffy and painful and he was limping. 'What did the doctor say this time?' I asked.

'Not much. He told me to avoid any strain on the knee and rest it as much as possible, not to walk around too much. Just the usual guff, nothing special. It's simply a blip, nothing to worry about. I'll soon be running around again, you'll see.'

I was so relieved to have him home that all other thoughts went out of my mind except those involved in getting ready to leave Rogate, disposing of furniture and trying to limit the number of packing boxes to keep shipping costs down. Books were bulky and heavy and took up a lot of space but my books were like friends that I could not bear to part with, and both Louise and Simon felt the same about their books. They were compulsive readers and had many favourite books which could not be left behind.

Simon had surprised us by winning the Children's Library Prize one year when we lived in Salisbury. The city library awarded this prize in a competition for children who were invited to write about the library book they had most enjoyed that year, and why. Simon chose one of the Doctor Doolittle books and his prize was a set of the books, so they were among those impossible to leave behind. Peter had been slow in learning to read because Simon read to him from an early age, so he saw no advantage in doing it for himself and had no interest in owning books. His main concern was for the cats and finding homes for them where they would be properly loved and appreciated; also our hens who lived outside the back door and were cherished by Peter who carried them around, one under each arm, talking to them. It was the hardest thing to leave the animals, and had Roger and Ruin still been alive, we probably would not have been able to go at all.

Once all the boxes had gone, we had just our suitcases and the car, but still no tax clearance allowing us to leave the country. We needed somewhere temporary to stay and Adam suggested renting accommodation at the police camp in Salisbury while he was still officially a member of PATU. I was surprised that he had not resigned after the last crisis with his knee, and was even more surprised when he said he had applied to join a Salisbury stick so that he could do more call-ups while waiting for clearance to leave. 'What about your knee?' I protested.

'It's almost better. I can't sit around idly doing nothing, just waiting for the bloody government to hand over a ruddy piece of paper.'

'You won't be sitting idly. Remember Jim sent a stack of books about cattle raising in Florida. I've kept them handy, so the moment we've got somewhere to stay you can sit down with the books and read all about it.'

'I don't need books to tell me about bovines. Florida is tropical like Africa. The breeds and breeding programmes are roughly the same. The whole process is similar. They all eat bloody grass.'

'The types of grasses there are different – we saw that. You'll be running feed-lots as well and you haven't done that before. One of the books is all about feed-lots. You can't just dismiss the chance to brush up on all this. You need to be fully ready by the time we get there.'

'Stop fussing. You never stop nagging and getting on my tits.'

'Darling, this is serious. It's nothing to do with fussing or nagging. We need to be sure of success in this job, for you and for all of us. Are you totally sure about it? Can you handle it if you don't even look at the books beforehand? I can only give a hundred per cent to this move if you are a hundred per cent for it yourself.'

'I'll give it a go – does that satisfy you?'

We were committed to our plan and there was no other way to go. I would have to make it work and there were the children's expectations to live up to as well. They had been taken out of school when we moved to the Salisbury police camp and needed to be occupied. I suggested that while we were waiting, instead of languishing at the camp we should go and see famous sights like Victoria Falls and Great Zimbabwe which had not been included in any family excursions before. 'While the children are missing school this would be educational for them, and we all need a break,' I told Adam.

'I can't go away. I need to be on hand for PATU, in case anything comes up.'

'Just forget about PATU. We've got to look ahead now, and you need to be careful with your knee so that you're fully fit when we arrive in Florida. Please, darling, be sensible.'

Part of keeping fit for PATU involved daily runs which had been routine for Adam on the farm where he was running on dirt paths, but city paths where he was going for runs now, were tarmac, and the effect of these hard surfaces caused his ankles to swell up. I was worried that the constant pounding might trigger full blown rheumatoid arthritis as the doctor had warned. Adam dismissed this as medical scare-mongering and continued to run several miles a day along city pavements until both his knees and ankles became so painful that he was forced to stop. At this point he finally handed in his PATU uniform, and agreed to join family visits to the Falls and Great Zimbabwe ruins.

We were very cramped in the utilitarian police bungalow, living out of suitcases, so it was a relief to escape, having booked a package holiday to Victoria Falls with flights there and back on a cheap deal due to a shortage of visitors. People were wary of flying after the earlier airline atrocities, while security at the Falls had deteriorated to the point that visitors were now accompanied at all times by armed guards. We knew we were taking a risk, but as Fa used to say: 'Taking a risk is all right as long as it is a calculated risk,' and I calculated that the benefits of the trip outweighed the risks.

The children of course were ecstatic with excitement as family holidays were a rare event, and Adam's disappointment at being denied further PATU excursions was mitigated by the prospect of action at a different kind of hotspot. Adding to the excitement, a letter arrived from his parents inviting us to visit them in Kenya before we left Africa for good, and then, hearing about this and not to be outdone, the aunts said that a visit to them at Howleigh must be fitted in too. If we were stopping off in England, there was my own family to see, and all these extra diversions fed into an idea that had already been growing in my mind.

Leaving Africa behind was one thing, but leaving my European identity behind as well had made me feel uncomfortable from the start, and apprehensive about moving to America. Despite my admiration for that great country as a nation of boundless opportunity, purpose, endeavour and achievement, there were some less appealing aspects to do with culture that I found unsettling. I would adjust to this and the children would become Americans, but I didn't want them to grow up knowing nothing of their European heritage. For me, the capital of Europe was Paris, and if we were having a stop-over in England then I would take the children to see Paris first, knowing that Adam would be glad to stay longer with his parents while we did this, even if he disapproved. As soon as I mentioned it to him he reacted as expected. 'What the devil is the point of taking the children to France? Costing money and wasting time. It's just one of your daft notions and nothing but an indulgence.'

'We're going to America because we've run out of options here. It wasn't my choice, but I'm backing you because it's what you want, and this very small detour is part of the bargain.'

'It's the first time you've uttered a word about any bargain. But I'm not going to argue the toss if it gives me an extra week at Naitolia.'

Naitolia was the farm where Cen and Alison now lived in retirement on the hills above Gilgil in Kenya. Their new home occupied a great sweep of land with very little farming activity taking place, so wildlife had moved in, protected by Cen. In a few years this became a safe refuge for all kinds of animals and subsequently the area was bought by Kigio Wildlife Conservancy to run as a low-key tourist attraction. A lodge with individual thatched rooms for visitors was built on the banks of the Malewa river, creating a happy outcome for Cen's nurturing vision during the last years of his life.

There were few other passengers on the plane to Victoria Falls and when we arrived at the airport we were taken to the hotel in a small convoy of vehicles with mounted machine guns. Armed guards patrolled the hotel perimeter emphasising that we were in a war zone after leaving the comparative safety of Salisbury. This of course energised the boys and Adam while Louise and I resigned ourselves to a holiday dominated by that kind of buzz, but nothing was going to spoil the magical experience of seeing the Falls. As we flew in, we had a dramatic view of the cataract with its towering mists of spray above the Zambesi's mighty plunging waters, and when we reached the hotel we could hear the river roaring as it hurtled into the gorge. We would not be walking to any viewpoints until the next day, and meanwhile there was the rare luxury of staying in a hotel with hotel food and comfort and, best of all, Adam with us.

Later as we sank gratefully into soft beds, all was quiet outside with only the distant muffled thunder of the Falls and sleep was instant, so it was entirely unexpected when we were woken around midnight by the clatter of a helicopter overhead. 'I know precisely what that is,' Adam muttered, instantly alert. 'There's a punch-up going on.'

'Well, I'm glad you're not involved this time,' I said, and went to see if the children were awake or alarmed. They were at the window listening and watching the flashing lights of the helicopter as it hovered overhead. It was a novel experience to see and hear one so close. 'What is it doing?' the boys asked eagerly. 'Can we go outside and see?'

'No, you can't. It probably means there's a fight happening somewhere. We'll find out in the morning. Back to bed now and back to sleep.' Louise, who was in the same room and had not got out of bed, remarked irritably: 'We're supposed to be having a holiday away from all this.'

Next morning when we asked what had happened, we were told there had been suspicious activity during the night and a helicopter patrol had come in to back up forces searching the area. 'There's nothing to worry about,' staff at the desk said. 'You will be escorted to the viewpoints and there are safe places for taking photos.' It was a short walk to these narrow clearings with a lot of scrambling up and down wet paths before we reached the safe points. We had been given waterproof capes but still got drenched with spray and felt like tiny stick figures against the enormity of the great tumbling water. All sensations were extreme in the sheer scale of such power so that it felt other-worldly, and more was to come that evening when we went on a sundown cruise along the Zambesi river. There were guards on board the boat manning machine guns on a raised platform while we sipped Pimms on deck, and watched animals coming to drink at the river, unperturbed. I thought if we were attacked and the boat disabled, we would be carried on the current downriver and tipped over the Falls, but our escorts assured us this could not happen. There are safeguards in place they told us, but when I asked what these were, they just smiled and topped up our glasses with more Pimms.

The next day Adam was twitchy, complaining that he had seized up through lack of exercise and what we all needed was a good walk. 'Elephant Hills (hotel) is only a couple of miles away and it will do us good to walk over there and have a look around,' he said.

'No one is allowed outside the hotel grounds without an armed escort, you know that,' I reminded him, 'and if we ask for one, they will insist on driving us over.'

'If we go in the middle of the day when it's too hot for most people to go outside, no one will see us and the gangs don't operate at that time. It's usually the evenings when they come out.'

'I don't think we're going to be popular bumbling about like idiots on a stroll out in the open during the worst heat of the day.'

'We'll take water bottles, and you can let the children wear hats if you think that makes any difference.'

None of us normally wore hats. In Adam's case because they fell off or got caught on thorn bushes so they were just a nuisance. In my case because Fa maintained that wearing hats in a tropical climate caused over-heating of the brain and thinning of the hair, so it meant that no hats were allowed during my childhood. Since I seemed to have developed no ill effects from going bare-headed all my life, I saw no reason to make my own children wear hats despite the fad among everyone else. Hats were not an issue of any consequence in these particular circumstances anyway, and Adam was being frivolous to make it seem that my objection to the walk on security grounds was silly.

I didn't want to go on the walk. I thought we would be arrested. Or shot. It was completely irresponsible to put the children into this kind of danger, I wanted to protest, but they were already running out of the door with their water bottles, eager as spaniels let out for a run. Adam had promised them ice creams at Elephant Hills and there would be no holding back now.

'We'll have to sneak out,' Adam said, ' so we give the hotel *askaris* (guards) the slip.' This was not difficult as no one expected hotel guests to be setting out on a scorching plain just before lunchtime. The view in front of us was flat for a mile or two, dotted with dry-leaved mopani trees offering no more than scant shade between our hotel and Elephant Hills. 'Don't walk in a bunch,' Adam instructed. 'It will present too much of a target if there are any *terrs* prowling about. Spread out. And don't walk in a straight line. If you want to stop for a drink, do it under a tree.'

I watched the children scatter playfully ahead, dodging between the trees while I followed on, eyes narrowed against the glare of the sun, looking out for any distant movement which might not be friendly. The heat was intense. It seemed to rise from the baked earth under my sandals while at the same time beating down from a sky which was not blue but drained of colour in the furnace blast. I'm never going to make it, I thought, trailing behind the others as they went ahead. No longer skipping from tree to tree but steadily pressing on, after a while the children fell silent while Adam went striding purposefully in front. At last after several stops for water, the high fortress-like walls of the hotel appeared distantly through trees and the relief I felt was overwhelming.

As we got closer we could see armed guards high on the roof looking at us through binoculars, and then there was the sound of a vehicle approaching, winding its way through the trees, having been sent out to 'rescue' us. We were greeted by anxious hotel staff thinking we must have got lost when their guards spied us from the roof, alarmed to see a tourist family wandering in the mopani bush with no security. Adam laughed it off, but they clearly thought we were mad and not the kind of guests they normally welcomed to their prestigious hotel, insisting that an armed vehicle escort was provided for the return journey.

The children had been standing by patiently all this time. 'Can we have our ice creams now?' they asked at last, impatient to get down to essentials.

Chapter 8

Without further incident at Victoria Falls we had just enough time to wash our clothes and open our post back at the police compound before the next trip, which was to Great Zimbabwe. This ancient stone-built city had been deserted by its inhabitants and fell into ruin at some point after the Middle Ages without leaving any record of it origins or history. There are no burial remains and only one inscription which, mysteriously, is in an obscure language. Other sources suggest the city was extremely prosperous and an important centre for mining and trading gold throughout Africa in mediaeval times. Legends connect King Solomon and the Queen of Sheba with Great Zimbabwe through stories of its renowned wealth.

The ruins stand monumental in their isolation, rising from a dry plain in a sparsely populated part of the country which was not at that time thought to be a danger area, so this was a relief. Adam was content to go along with a low-key excursion since his knees and ankles had become painful again and he was willing to accept gentle walking around the old city.

When we arrived there were few other visitors and no guides so we could wander by ourselves, absorbing the sensations of this enigmatic place. The remarkable design and construction of the citadel stood stark against a barren landscape. High stone walls built with extreme precision and no mortar surrounded what was left of the old city that had been ruthlessly plundered down the years by fortune hunters. Narrow passages led the way between parallel outer walls and there were sections where these had collapsed into piles of stone, while other structures remained intact. Among them a perfectly preserved and inscrutable high conical tower dominated. The boys ran ahead exploring by themselves and when we caught up with them at the ruined royal palace, they were eager to show us a discovery. This was a midden outside what may once have been the palace kitchens where they were busy scavenging for 'treasures'. Any kind of rubbishy detritus left in a heap was inevitably a magnet for them and I went to remind them that this was a historical site and nothing must be disturbed. They had already collected a small hoard of broken pottery and coloured ceramic beads, and were curious to know more about these. 'We'll have to take them to the museum,' I said, having noticed a small building announcing itself as a museum beside the ticket office at the entrance.

The museum attendant was unimpressed when the boys handed over their find. 'We already have plenty of those,' he said dismissively, and was reluctant to pursue the subject when we asked about the beads. They were unusual in shape and colour; clearly not of African origin. 'They could be from Persia,' the attendant suggested. 'Yes, they're probably Persian.'

'What will you do with them?' Simon asked, hoping that he might be allowed to keep some.

'We will put them with the other pieces,' the man said indifferently as if the subject was of little interest. This was disappointing as we thought identification of the beads could connect the finds with a definite period in history and would make the whole experience of our visit more relevant, instead of leaving us with a sense of frustration at such apathy towards the history of Great Zimbabwe.

The name itself however, and what it stood for, was seen as highly significant by those who were fighting for independence. When this was achieved, the image of an eagle found among the ruins was adopted as Zimbabwe's national symbol.

Despite protestations that nothing was the matter, Adam was limping badly by the time we returned to Salisbury and I went with him for further advice from the police doctor. He recommended seeing a rheumatologist and gave Adam a letter of referral to a consultant in Cambridge who could see him while we were in England on our way to America. The main worry, now, was whether Adam was going to be well enough for a job that demanded a high level of physical fitness, but he was optimistic. 'We can't abandon our plans so late in the day so we'll have to go buggering on, and at least get out of this bloody country, then see what the Cambridge quack says. By then I'll probably be doing five-mile runs if this present idleness is a cure,' he said blithely. 'You always worry too much and that never solves anything.'

I was glad to see him rested and confident while contentedly passing the time on jaunts with the boys to places of interest like firing ranges, in between visits to PATU members who were still actively engaged in bush operations. The children were happy to be back with their Salisbury friends, leaving me free to look for cheap flights to Paris. A French airline, UTA (Union de Transports Aeriens), operated a service for people living in French-speaking African countries and there were regular flights from the Comoros Islands to Kigali in Rwanda, before going on to Paris. It would be a short hop from Nairobi (where we would be at that stage) to join the plane at Kigali and proceed to Paris. All we needed now was tax clearance so I could book tickets and we could be off.

Restrictions had been placed on cash leaving the country with a limit of $500 (Rhodesian dollars) per person going out. Any balance that remained in our bank account after we left would have to stay there or be given away. We expected this could amount to a few hundred dollars and I wanted to give the money to our neighbours at Thornby Farm, who were not well off, in return for their unfailing kindness to us during our time at Rogate. Adam said this would embarrass them so it would be better to give the money to one of the national charities. Others leaving the country were faced with the same dilemma and all kinds of ingenious solutions to get around the restriction were devised. Some people bought valuable stamps which were easy to take with them and sell in another country, while others bought gemstones. For those with large sums of money there was said to be a route through an underworld contact who could transfer funds to a bank anywhere in the world, for a fee of thirty percent of the money transferred. No one using this method had ever been cheated, we were told, but it was only for those with substantial means, and that definitely excluded us.

The children were becoming bored and impatient with the prolonged delay and it was frustrating for all of us, living in suspense, when abruptly we were handed our tax bill and told to leave immediately. We needed no urging and were on a plane to Johannesburg and then Nairobi as fast as we could get tickets.

Arriving back in Kenya after long years away was like coming home, with a welcome at Naitolia so touchingly warm and emotional it made me feel that I was accepted at last. Alison was visibly overcome with pleasure and amazement at the sight of her three grandchildren now grown almost beyond recognition and, as she remarked within minutes because such things mattered to her, 'Such beautiful manners too.' Her delight in the children made me wonder how she could have let them go ten years before when we might have stayed if she and Cen had agreed to let the farm help with school fees. It was a trifling sum for a wealthy farm, but they feared it could set a precedent when other grandchildren came along in the future. Now, looking at the house they had built for themselves on Naitolia, the same penny-pinching was evident in its utilitarian design with no relieving features. Plain as a shoe-box on the outside, the rooms inside were arranged in a cluster of similar boxes spared of any imaginative detail, with only one bathroom however many people were staying. From an ecological point of view, the austerity had purpose, allowing the house to blend seamlessly into a landscape where herds of zebra grazed and at times wandered into Alison's garden, where they had to be chased off her few struggling plants.

Cen had his polo ponies, now retired, in stables nearby and a syce brought them each morning for Adam and the children to ride. They would go off in a string with Adam leading while I stayed to assist Esau the cook in producing some kind of lunch from Alison's kitchen. This was daunting in a kitchen so primitive it defied even the most basic hygiene standards, while offering almost zero culinary aids. Alison explained this by saying that she hated cooking and never went into the kitchen, so she left it to the servants. 'I am like Queen Victoria, I do not cook,' she would announce loftily when catering arrangements fell short.

Her hapless kitchen staff might have overcome the deficiency of their working conditions with additions such as a gas cooker, but Alison would not hear of it. 'We've always had a wood stove. It's what they understand. Gas is much too dangerous. And expensive.' A cast-iron *kuni* (wood) stove had been hauled in to belch black smoke and fumes into the suffocating room, so that in no time the walls were caked with soot and every surface similarly encrusted. This provided perfect camouflage for swarms of flies which rested undisturbed on the walls until stirred by the flick of a dishcloth. I inspected Alison's dishcloths for colonies of bacteria ready to infect my family with gastroenteritis. Fingertip examination of these slimy rags at arm's length identified them as strips torn from discarded shirts and underclothes. Even underpants I noticed were still doing service in a different kind of unspeakable role as I recognised half a Y-front among the breakfast dishes. There was no detergent or soap, but plenty of Vim (a scouring powder) and hot water from a boiler which huffed outside the window blowing off steam like a Stephenson engine. In the absence of mains electricity these wood-fired boilers were ubiquitous in Africa, burning merrily all day with very little attention apart from regular feeding with firewood: a task usually assigned to the gardener. A paraffin fridge rusting away in a corner of the kitchen added its vapour to the mix of odours in Alison's kitchen as I looked around to see what might be achieved among the smuts in this black hole. Esau and the 'kitchen toto', who was sous chef at the age of ten, observed me expectantly as I opened the fridge door to see if anything useful might be lurking inside. Deferring to Esau at this point for advice on the menu would seem diplomatic and from there we worked amicably together, with the toto scurrying at Esau's command to fetch and carry.

Cen expected lunch to be served promptly at one o'clock and dinner on the stroke of eight, with fresh meat or fish for the main course. Any male guest who happened to be staying was sent out with a rifle to shoot something edible, or directed to the river with a rod to catch a few trout. Both these activities were routine for Adam who now had the added pleasure of teaching the boys how to hunt and fish. I enjoyed trout fishing as much as any of them, and the Malewa river which flowed through the farm, was familiar territory for me from the many weekends spent with Fa casting a fly over its rills and pools during my childhood growing up in that part of Kenya.

In the soft light of evenings at Naitolia, Adam and I, leaving the children to walk dogs with Alison, took rods and went down to the river while trout were rising, knowing that supper that night would be in the bag. The quiet of those companionable hours renewed the sense of contentment we found in being together when alone without distraction, doing the things we both enjoyed. While walking along the river bank on one of the golden evenings, there was a sudden explosion from thick bush ahead as several buffalo crashed out in alarm when they caught wind of our approach. They looked as surprised to find us on their patch as we were to see them on what we thought was ours. Buffalo are completely unpredictable and it was a tense moment as the group paused, snorting and lumbering, while we stood there, quietly motionless. With some tossing of heads and a few more derisive snorts they turned and galloped up the slope away from the river, so we could breathe easily again and walk on to a spot we called the beach. This was in a bend of the river with a wide pool and a sandy shore on one side. It was a good swimming place but the water was always icy cold in its tumbling run from the high Aberdare mountains.

In the evenings, if we were not fishing, there were safer walks to be had along the ridge where Cen and Alison's house stood in an open landscape of dry bush and scrubby trees. The buffalo preferred to stay lower down in a riverine environment where they could lie up in the heat of the day shaded by thick cover, coming out later to graze where the grass was green, close to water. High on the ridge as we walked in the thin air of altitude, there would be warthogs trotting across the path in front, while shy dik-dik and sometimes a mongoose or genet cat emerged from bushes at the side. Most special of all were the wild dogs (also called painted dogs) in a pack that had its territory less than a mile from the house and always appeared when we were walking. They would bound along the path in front and then stop to look back and stare at us and our dogs from a safe distance, inquisitively. Our dogs knew well not to challenge them. Sadly, within a few years, the pack was wiped out by distemper. Domestic dogs could be inoculated but many wild dogs succumbed in epidemics.

Kinyatta Polo Club was next door to Naitolia on a farm owned by David Begg who was a large genial man with a knobbly face and wonderfully generous heart. His wife Lilian was similarly endowed in looks and spirit and the same attributes had passed to their daughters, so a visit to them was not to be missed. Lunch started with a great roast, fallen upon by our family half-starved on Alison's meagre pickings, followed by an equally lavish tea after driving around the farm. A visit to the polo ground and ponies was a highlight with much chat of times past during the club's glory days when teams came all the way from Argentina and Australia to play in tournaments. Drinks back at the house were then required and when we finally gathered ourselves to leave, it was well after dark. At the boundary with Naitolia there was a gate and it was the duty of the youngest passenger in the car to open it, so Peter was the one and climbed out into the glare of headlights. It was a five-barred gate and heavy, needing a bit of a push. Peter, still small and slight in build, strained at this and when it opened, without warning from the surrounding darkness came a flash of movement as a leopard sprang from the shadows and went through the gate in front of him, giving him such a fright he did a great leap in the air. This looked comical to those of us watching from the car and made us laugh so much that he returned very disgruntled, and refused to get out again. For years afterwards he continued to remind us of this incident and our lack of sympathy. 'It was the second time I nearly got eaten by a leopard,' he complained. 'Just because I'm the youngest and smallest I'm the one who gets to be disposable.'

'That's your fate when you're a runt,' Simon teased, but it was affectionate teasing and Peter knew that Simon loved him more than anything else in the world.

One morning when Alison and the others went off to Gilgil to buy groceries at Multi-Line stores and I stayed behind to help organise lunch, Cen invited me to join him for mid-morning coffee on the veranda, and indicated that he had something he wanted to tell me. When we had settled ourselves, without preamble he launched into a discussion of money. This surprised me as he never normally spoke of family finances in my presence. I was even more surprised when he said he wanted me to know that all his money was tied up in a trust in the Bahamas where no one could touch it until after his death. This, he explained, was to avoid any compulsory seizure of assets by the Kenya government that he feared might happen in the future and also, most importantly he emphasised, the rate of growth of the fund was calculated to deliver a million pounds to his estate when he died. He had estimated how many years he had left and the final amount was based on this assumption. It was his wish and intention, he went on to say, that Alison should receive this sum on his death, presuming that he predeceased her. She would have enough then to live on for as long as she needed it, and when she died it would pass to his heirs. He asked if I understood what he was saying and I said it seemed very sensible, not knowing how else to reply or why he was telling me this, instead of Adam. Later when I told Adam what had been said, he was bemused, knowing nothing about these arrangements. 'That's an awful lot of money. Who's going to look after Mum's finances when the kitty passes to her? Did he say anything about that? Mum hasn't a clue about money. Pa has always looked after that side of things.'

'You can ask him, tactfully, explaining that it's important for you to know how Mum is to be looked after if he isn't here anymore.'

'I'll have to catch him at the right moment or he'll clam up. If he thought you were the one to be told, then he probably expects you to pass it on to me.'

'That's a very odd way to go about it.'

'I have a very odd family. Haven't you noticed?'

Jim was impatient for Adam to start work on the ranch and wanted him there by Christmas (this was 1978) in just six weeks' time, so there was little opportunity to go round visiting Kenya friends. Many of them had stayed on, some still farming, and others with proceeds from selling their farms had bought houses and land in Nairobi. All were leading the same gracious lives as if nothing had changed, which made me nostalgic and sad to have left and disrupted the family with so many moves, exposing them to unforeseen dangers in Rhodesia. Kenya was still peaceful after fifteen years of independence, but population numbers had exploded and Kenyans were hungry for land and jobs. Indigenous forests were disappearing to provide cleared ground for small-holdings on which a family could subsist, using the forest timber to build houses and supply firewood for cooking, and for charcoal production which had become a big industry.

I wanted to show the children some of the places that had been special for me in my childhood. The lush Bahati forest had been a favourite place for picnics in glades full of butterflies and birds while colobus monkeys watched from branches overhead, clutching their babies. When I took the children for a repeat of the picnic experience I was unable to find the forest – it had vanished with no sign of its existence left to mark the spot. All I could see were scarred hillsides, but the land was rich and would be brought into production, I consoled myself.

When it was time for me and the children to leave Naitolia and set off on our separate excursion, Adam drove us to Nairobi in his parents' old Peugeot pick-up. The children sat on suitcases in the open back, while Adam and I occupied the bench seat in front. We were both miserable at the thought of leaving a country that still held our hearts and would never be out of our minds wherever we put down new roots. It was a fraught journey as we passed all the emotive landmarks achingly familiar along the old Rift Valley road, and Adam complained the whole way about what he thought was a crazy plan to take the children to see glittering sights and decadence in Paris. He had never been to Paris himself and for that matter neither had I, but I did have a vision of its style and culture and great history, which we would not find replicated in America where we were now intending to spend the rest of our lives, far from our ancestral roots.

The UTA plane was full of excited small men who were French-speaking Comoro islanders, wearing sharp suits and expensive scent, on a spree to Paris. A party atmosphere was in progress as we boarded and took our seats like well-trained English people, noticing that no one else was seated as all stood in the aisle with drinks in their hands or strolled about chatting to the air hostesses, who seemed on very friendly terms with them. 'Why are they kissing the hostesses all the time?' Simon whispered, intrigued, since this kind of behaviour between whites and blacks in public in Rhodesia would be thought scandalous.

'They probably do this trip regularly so they all know each other,' I suggested.

'They seem to know each other a lot better than you would expect.'

'They're French. This is the way French people express themselves. They're not all stiff-necked like the English. It's good for you to see different cultures, so you get a wider view of the world after living in Rhodesia which is a closed country and society.'

When we were due to take off there was the usual announcement about seat belts which seemed to assume that all passengers were sitting down, but very few took any notice despite the hostesses encouraging them into their seats. The plane actually took off with some of the men still standing in the aisle, hastily swallowing their drinks before these slopped over with the steep incline as we rose into the air.

Our first stop was the Congo to pick up more people on business trips or jaunts to Paris, so the route took us due west from Nairobi on a course which felt like flying over the sea when we reached Lake Victoria: a vast body of water filling the horizon up to the mighty Ruwenzori mountains. On the other side a great land mass of jungle passed below as we entered the mysterious wild reaches of the Congo, before landing abruptly at a very unassuming airport. When we came to a stop, soldiers with automatic weapons ran from the airport building and surrounded the plane, rousing Simon and Peter to the expectation that something exciting might happen, while our French passengers showed no concern whatever and were impatient only to disembark for more drinks. After steps had been brought so we could file off, the soldiers reassembled themselves as an escort for passengers to the airport building. This was no more than a big shed with barred windows and very poor lighting, so that we were temporarily blinded from the glare outside as we shuffled in, urged on by the soldiers' guns. 'Why are they being so *kali* (strict) with us?' I asked one of the hostesses.

'Look over there,' she said, indicating something I had not noticed while my eyes were adjusting to the gloom as we came in. At one end of the shed there were elephant tusks piled to the roof, hundreds of them. 'It's contraband,' she explained. 'The soldiers are jumpy because they are guarding it, and they're suspicious of anyone landing here, despite knowing we are only here to re-fuel.'

We were kept at the opposite end of the shed, well away from the tusks, and were warned that anyone taking photos would be arrested. Lukewarm Coca-Cola was served and the hostess said it would be better not to visit *les toilettes* but to wait until we were back on the plane. The heat and humidity were almost unbearable as we waited, herded into the cramped space with no fans or clean water. It felt like a prison, and the guards with their guns felt menacing. I understood now why the Frenchmen used alcohol as a prophylactic when stopping off in the Congo. Another benefit of this liberal intake no doubt relieved the tedium of a very long flight so they were well prepared for the many stops in obscure French-speaking outposts as we droned onwards. Our eventual arrival at Charles de Gaulle airport was late that night, and I was glad to have booked a room at one of the airport hotels so we could fall into cool beds and sleep for a few hours.

What I had not realised in advance was that this airport is twenty-two miles outside Paris. We can get a taxi, I confidently told the children next morning after a breakfast of croissants which was a new experience for them. The hotel ordered a taxi and I asked the driver in my O-level French to drop us off near the Eiffel Tower, having planned a grand vista from the top. Along the route taken by the taxi I expected to see some splendid buildings as we neared the city, and was disappointed when nothing but a wasteland of grey tenements lined the road for mile after mile, with washing hanging from windows and no brightness anywhere.

'Are you sure we are in France?' Louise asked. I translated this remark for the driver who sat in silence, hunched in his seat. I thought it might make him laugh and break the monotony, but he just grunted and drove on grimly through the wilderness of slum blocks. I watched the fare meter climb steadily and after an hour had passed with no sign of Paris landmarks appearing, I asked the driver how much longer it would be until we arrived. He mumbled, '*Bientot*, *Bientot,*' and continued driving steadily along the same fast road.

'I think we're being kidnapped,' Louise said, sounding genuinely alarmed. 'This might not be a proper taxi. The driver isn't being at all friendly. He might be a kidnapper.'

'The hotel booked this taxi for us, so it must be all right.' I tried to sound reassuring, while beginning to feel uneasy myself.

'I'm going to sing hymns to make us safe,' Louise announced, and began singing 'Onward Christian Soldiers,' very loudly. The boys joined in at full volume and the driver suddenly became animated, sitting up in his seat, visibly agitated as the sudden chorus of noise erupted from the back of his cab with sounds of Christian militancy. I could see him muttering and swearing as he peered ahead at the road, before pulling the wheel to turn off at the next exit. Within minutes we had entered a different world of avenues with trees and cafes and shops, and then some of the majestic buildings I had been waiting to see rose up ahead with the Eiffel Tower discernible at last. I decided not to argue about the fare when the driver dropped us off. Handing over a stack of francs to him, I said it would be interesting for the hotel to hear about our experience. He shrugged and glared at me, but he'd brought us as near to the Eiffel Tower as it was possible to get, and nothing was going to spoil things now.

We first had ice creams at a café to provide recovery and stamina to climb the tower, and were then relieved to find lifts to each view-point where the sight of this grand city presented a wondrous new world to the children after the dry savannahs of Africa. Aware of limited time to explore the wealth of visual and historic treasures spread before us, we found a bus which toured the main districts and sights, including Montmartre. I had a particular desire to see and feel the sensations of that quarter, wanting to compare it with London's Soho where many fond and free-living memories existed for me. The bus was a touristy option but why should that matter: we were tourists and I was discovering that my school French was leading us down blind alleys and we spent too much time getting lost. The tour rescued us and had an English-speaking guide who even showed us where to get lunch with crepes, so the day passed happily in a multitude of blurred impressions before it was time to find a taxi back to the hotel. There were taxis cruising on every street and I promised the children we would find a safe one this time. Not only did it prove to be safe and quick, it cost half of what we had paid that morning.

The next day everyone was tired and the boys wanted nothing more than to watch cartoons on television while Louise sketched views from the window. She had become a compulsive artist, seizing every spare moment to draw and paint. Even my shopping lists were illustrated, reminding me of Ros at the same age, which led to a career in art. Fa had taken up watercolours since retiring but no one else in the family had shown any talent, except Spindle who found expression for his thoughts in drawing and painting abstract designs which were often arresting in his use of colour and firm lines for dramatic effect. He was encouraged by art classes at the Suffolk hospital where he now lived as a permanent fixture, resigned to this fate since at the age of thirty-five there was little chance of the cure he had hoped could be found. 'Before it's too late for me,' he used to say wistfully.

Fa and Babs were on a cruise when we arrived in England a day later, so our first call was to Muz who met us off the train when it pulled in to the tiny platform at Marks Tey which was the nearest station to where she lived with Andy in their fifteenth-century cottage. She seemed distracted and diminished in some way since the last time I'd seen her three years before, and was in a fluster a short while later as we stood in the poky hall of the cottage with our suitcases. 'Andy,' she called through to the sitting room, 'come and help carry the bags.' There was no response so we walked through to the sitting room where Andy, without rising from his chair, raised a hand in greeting. 'Leave the bags by the stairs,' he said. 'They can be seen to later.' He looked at us standing there uncertainly. 'So you've arrived then,' he added, and turned back to his book.

The cottage was cold and the welcome only slightly less so as Muz seemed emotionally shut off in some way that was difficult to figure out. Ros had noticed this too and warned me that her behaviour had turned rather odd. She had started charging them B&B rates if they went to stay, complaining that she couldn't afford accommodation for so many now they had two children. I was sceptical about this as such considerations had never arisen with her before, but when we were due to leave, as Ros predicted, she presented me with a written bill for the nights we had stayed and food provided. What made it worse was the amount, which was a lot more than standard B&B rates. I protested, but Muz was adamant and pleaded poverty which was hardly evident in a new model Austin parked outside the back door. 'It's the only thing that gives Andy pleasure,' Muz explained, 'apart from his books of course.'

After reluctantly handing over the cash to Muz I had little left for snacks on the train or other expenses while travelling, but we did have return tickets to London and I could find a place to exchange travellers' cheques I told myself, while feeling anxious about running out of money. When not at home, I usually made sure to have reserves on hand somewhere. Living with Adam had taught me this. We were due to meet at Howleigh, Adam having already arrived there from Kenya so he could spend extra time with the aunts who adored him. He would get very spoilt by them which I felt compensated for the rather detached relationship he had with his parents, though they were mellowing as they grew older in the way that often happens as sharp edges soften with age.

The aunts would heap affection on the children too, especially Simon who was given special distinction as Adam's heir. If neither Adam nor Cen was present at a meal, Simon would be put at the head of the table, waited on by the aunts with the particular attention they reserved for the male head of each generation. This included buttering toast for them at breakfast and spreading marmalade on top lest it be too enervating to do it themselves, ignoring sniggers from the rest of us when it was Simon's turn to receive these ministrations.

Our decision to emigrate to America was viewed with bemusement at Howleigh. 'You don't have to become Americans as well, do you?' Aunt Diana asked, as if this might be disloyal in a family with a long line of good Welsh blood.

'It's the only way to get a permanent job and make a new home for ourselves,' Adam explained. 'In due course we will become American citizens but nothing will change the way we are inside. We will be starting a new line of American Hills,' he said, expecting this thought to amuse her, but it raised another concerning point. 'It won't change family values and the way you speak, surely?'

'No, but the children will develop accents, inevitably. To fit in.' I interrupted with a note of caution: 'Nothing is totally certain until Adam has seen the specialist in Cambridge to confirm that he is fit enough to go.'

After Howleigh, our next stop was with Ros and Gary at their new house on a Surrey estate full of young professional couples like themselves with children. We could leave ours with them while we went to Cambridge to see Dr Hazelwood, who had been recommended as the best in his field of rheumatology. Adam was much better since he'd given up running, so we were confident that the consultation would prove to be a mere formality, and were glad to find Dr Hazelwood reassuring. After examining Adam, and the paperwork we had brought with us from Rhodesia, he declared himself satisfied. 'The best place in the world for you is Florida with its warm climate,' he told us. 'No active disease is shown in Adam's current blood tests, so the recent flare-up was a warning, that's all. My advice is to go ahead and have a great life in the famous sunshine state.'

This was the best news and within a few days we were on our way. Ros and Gary delivered us with numerous suitcases and bags to Heathrow for the flight to Miami, and from there it was a short hop by American Eagle across to Fort Myers on the gulf coast. After spending the night in a motel, Jim came the next morning with a large truck and took us to be introduced to our new home. This was a trailer parked just off the road at the entrance to the ranch development that he was in charge of, next to a paddock with horses. My first sight of the trailer, looking like a big holiday caravan tucked into a small glade of trees, enchanted me, and Louise said it was just like *Little House on the Prairie*. When the boys saw the horses they were converts too, so it was an auspicious arrival. The trailer was bigger than I expected and Jim explained that it was two trailers joined together, side by side, called a 'double-wide'. 'Haven't you seen one of these before?' he asked, surprised.

'No. Nothing like this exists in England. What the English call a caravan is just that – a van on wheels, with barely room to turn around inside.'

'Wait till you see inside this one,' he said. It had a back door as well as a front door and even a bay window in the sitting room. Jim wanted me to see the kitchen first. This was modern and spacious and had a dishwasher, which was something I had never seen before. 'The trailer is hooked to mains water and electricity so it's all ready to go. But not in any kind of touring sense,' he added. 'You may have noticed that it's tied down with cables so it doesn't get lifted off by hurricanes. We do get those but they have usually blown themselves out before they arrive this far inland.' We continued our tour of the trailer which was luxurious and fully furnished with a sitting/dining room; ensuite master bedroom with a king-size bed;

a children's room with separate bathroom and, next to it, amazingly, a laundry room. This had two machines, one for washing and one for drying, with a linen cupboard built into the wall. I had never seen such a marvel as a machine for drying clothes. 'It's a tumble dryer,' Jim explained. 'The clothes fly around in hot air and when they come out they are ready for folding, so you don't even have to iron most of them.'

'I think I've landed in paradise,' I laughed, quite overwhelmed. The children were running in and out exclaiming at each discovery and deciding which beds they would have. I could see an immediate problem with all three of them sharing one room after Louise was used to having her own. She was fourteen and it was something we would have to sort out, but she was tactfully avoiding the issue while Jim was with us.

The boys wanted to know who the horses belonged to. 'Some are cow ponies for your dad and some for the cowboys, but most of them have their own. You'll be meeting the boys soon enough. They will be round each morning to muster with your dad before work.'

Jim had moved his family to a rented house on ten acres along the same road where several other families formed a small community on fenced land with horses and barns. Jim's wife wanted to have close neighbours so their children had others to play with and share school runs. I was hoping that we could join the runs, but Jim's children were at private schools which we could not afford, so ours would have to go to state schools and I knew one of my first tasks would be to register places for them in time for the new term starting after Christmas.

We were living in a district that was at the extreme end of the school bus route. The bus driver lived further down our road with the bus parked in front of her house and could pick up our children at 6.30 each morning on the start of her run. Such an early start was going to be a jolt to our English sensibilities and we soon learnt that American ways of working were a great deal more robust than those we were used to, even with our dairy farm conditioning. The only holiday over Christmas, Jim told us, is Christmas Day itself, instead of the prolonged shut-down of businesses extending into the new year, customary in British society.

On that first day we were given a welcome dinner at Jim's house and the children all sang carols together in a room filled with candlelight and good cheer, so we felt we were among friends and it was a happy start to our new life. The next day Jim took us to buy a car, 'We're going car shopping,' he said merrily, 'then I'll leave you at Winn Dixie to get groceries.'

Buying a car seemed no more complicated than choosing any other goods in this extraordinary country where the necessities of life were readily procurable and processes streamlined, so that time and effort was saved for more important activities. 'We work hard and play hard,' someone had said to me during our visit to America a few months before.

At the car showroom Jim helped us pick out an electric blue Ford Mercury which he said would be my car while Adam was to have one of the ranch trucks. There was an office annexe at Jim's house with a secretary and Adam's work base would be there, conveniently close to hand. Someone was coming the next morning to advise on feed-lot designs, Jim said, so Adam could get on with these. His energy and drive was impressive, but Adam had his own style of working and I hoped Jim would give him enough flexibility to apply this in his own way.

Driving the new car felt like driving a tank; though its width and length were modest by American standards, it was a giant compared with European models, and didn't have normal gears operated by a clutch either. Getting used to automatic gears took only moments but what Adam called, 'driving on the wrong side of the road', needed more practice, especially at roundabouts and intersections. We had to take a test to get Florida driving licences but meanwhile could use visitor licences, and be aware that state troopers patrolled the roads watching for anyone committing an offence.

I got caught almost immediately for exceeding the fifty mph speed limit on one of the highways that sped through Florida's flat palmetto countryside. It seemed entirely perverse for an American car manufacturer like Ford to produce a car with a splendid V8 engine restricted to this futile limit. It was almost impossible to maintain such a low speed for mile after mile on these long straight roads, and frustrating to own a powerful car without being able to step on the gas. The state trooper's car cruised up behind me flashing its lights to indicate that I should pull over. I had no idea what I had done wrong until the young officer with important-looking badges sauntered across to my window, said he was booking me for speeding, and must first see my licence. I began to apologise when, at the sound of my voice, he smiled disarmingly and it was almost as if our roles had been reversed when he started apologising.

'I'm sure sorry, Mam,' he said, drawling the words in a charming Southern burr. 'You must be English by your accent. We are sure glad to have you come visit here. The restriction on these highways can be a real dumb thing, but it's the law.' He reached through the window to shake my hand. 'Take no mind of being stopped, but you be careful how you go from here now. And Mam – have a good day.' He gave me another dazzling smile and walked back to his car, leaving me a bit stunned but relieved.

Each day brought new surprises and when I went to register school places for the children, expecting to be asked about their grades, it was a very different experience to find the main focus was on their emotional and psychological development rather than academic level. 'How well adjusted are they? Do they have behavioural issues? Are they socialised? How do they interact with their peers? What instrument does each one play?' I had not anticipated such questions and when I looked blank, the teachers realised that I was out of my depth and quickly assured me that the children would enter classes for their age group, and assessment would come later.

Another surprise was that they would be at three different schools: Louise at Punta Gorda Junior High, Simon at Middle School and Peter at Elementary. This was going to make school runs complicated and time consuming if I took them by car. We decided to give the bus a try despite the very long trip with numerous detours and stops along the way. It took more than an hour to arrive at Punta Gorda, but children from far out were given breakfast at school and this appealed greatly to ours because pancakes with syrup were served, along with bacon, eggs and hash browns. 'It will be *lekker* having school breakfasts,' Simon said, 'then you Mum will be saved doing breakfast for us.'

'You won't be able to say "*lekker*" anymore,' Louise told him, 'because no one will know what it means. And there's lots of other things you can't say. I heard Jim telling Dad he mustn't say "Christ" or "Jesus", or even "Crikey", or anything to do with the Bible or God, because it's blasphemy here in the South.'

'What do they say instead when they're mad about something?'

'I heard Sheryl, Jim's secretary, say "shoot" when she dropped some papers. It sounded like a swear word. I think it means something rude.'

'Is it a swear word, Mum?'

'I don't know. But Dad will probably know. He'll need to have some choice new words if the others are banned.'

'What about children? Are they allowed to say "shoot"?'

'Not if it's rude.'

'Why are only grown-ups allowed to say rude things?' Simon was a determined questioner of right and wrong where justice was concerned. 'Children need something to say when they're annoyed just as much as grown-ups. I'm going to hang around listening to the cowboys when they are here and see what words they use.'

'You'll be worse than Dad.'

'I'll be better than Dad.'

Several hundred acres of good grazing land had already been cleared and stocked by the time we arrived, with cowboys employed to work the beef herds and breeding cows. The cows were a motley collection but hardy and this was a prime consideration in tough conditions as many had calves at foot. Every morning early, a truck towing a horse trailer arrived with cowboys looking as if they had come off a film set, ready to meet up with Adam and go to work. Adam's horse was loaded with the others and he went off in his own truck, waving goodbye to the children who would be waiting for the school bus. The driver, Ms Chancy, lived in a clapboard house like others down our road, some of them not much more than shacks with the traditional porch and swing in front. She had strict rules for her passengers. 'We have to sit where Ms Chancy tells us,' Simon complained, 'and because we're new she puts us in the front instead of back where the big boys are smoking and having fun telling jokes and stuff.'

'They're smoking weed,' Louise said. 'Jim warned us about them. He said be wary of some kids who ride the school bus because some are dope heads. Ms Clancy might be trying to keep us away from them.'

'I hope so,' I told them. 'I've never been all that happy about putting you on the bus. There are some seriously deprived families living around here, so far out of town. They look as if they're struggling and they all have fierce dogs, which puts me off going to call on them as neighbours.'

'The kids call them "Crackers". That's what they call people living out here in the backwoods. They think we're Crackers as well, living down this road.'

'Not with English accents.'

'My teacher makes me stand up in class reading out loud so everyone can hear me speaking what she calls "real English",' Peter said. 'It's embarrassing.'

'In my class,' Simon added, 'they say they're sure glad I'm English instead of one of those damned Yankees. Why do they hate Yankees so much?'

'It goes back to the Civil War when northerners and southerners were fighting each other. It left such bitterness some southerners are still fighting the war in their minds.

'There are fights in the recreation area when local Rednecks beat up the Yankee kids. But the teachers stop them.'

'It's only the boys who do those fights,' Louise put in, 'girls don't bother with them.'

'Boys in my class don't do it either,' Peter said, 'It's just the bigger boys. And another thing: everyone calls me "Pee-der". It's the way they say my name. Some of them call me Pete.'

'Well, that's good. "Pete" suits you,' I said. 'We can all call you Pete.' The name stuck and it did suit him due to his small size and being rather cute, but this endearing appeal was not something he wanted to cultivate. He was beginning to assert himself now he was nearly ten and a more determined personality was starting to emerge.

Adam surprised me one afternoon when he came home early with a pile of papers and rolled-up plans he was working on. 'I can't concentrate in the office. There's too much noise and activity with people coming in and out all the time.'

'What sort of people?'

'Employees of various sorts. Cowboys, people selling things, government advisers. The phone ringing, constantly. Sheryl running about and her fax machine clacking away. Then, worst of all, Jim's daughter practising her clarinet when she's not at school. The walls of the house and annexe are so thin everything resonates and it's chaos in there. Jim doesn't seem to notice.'

'You'll have to be like him, shutting out the distractions. When the children are back from school it will be just as bad in here with them running around and needing to do their homework on the table.'

'Jim is hassling me with these plans. We've got young stock coming in ready for the feed-lots so we have to get skates on, building the lots in time. The plans need to be finalised by tomorrow and I'm still working on what to put in.'

'I thought you already had plans modelled on those from the state government office.'

'They are just samples, showing different types of lots. I've got to decide which ones to use, and put in specifics and details.'

'That shouldn't be too difficult. It's right up your alley.'

'No, it isn't. Feed-lots are a specialised area.'

'Jim gave you a book all about them, so you would have everything worked out by the time we arrived.'

'*Tant pis.*'

'Darling, listen, you can't say that. This is America. Where nothing is too much trouble and things get done. We're part of that now. I'm juggling a whole raft of jobs myself since Jim put me onto hosting his investors when they come to visit. They're not casual visitors. You know that. They expect a full itinerary with every detail organised.'

'You're good at that sort of thing.'

'Remember, I have the domestic side of life at home to keep on track at the same time: shopping, cooking, laundry, feeding horses. Anyway, I'm not complaining. I enjoy meeting the investors, they're brilliant, and also very appreciative. I'm just pointing out that each of us has to stretch ourselves to meet expectations.'

When Jim suggested the hostess job to me at a generous rate for my time, it was too good to refuse. My first day as a hostess was memorable when I went to meet a small group of investors arriving by private plane at Punta Gorda airport. This was a tiny airport with a short runway and simple control tower above a small office building. I arrived well before the plane's ETA and was invited into the control room to be briefed on the current position of the plane. The controller called up the pilot: 'I have your hostess here. Guess what – she's English.'

'Put her on,' came the disembodied voice of the pilot. It was strangely exhilarating to hear his voice high in the air and talk to him, confirming that a welcome was waiting and all was in hand for their visit. When the plane landed and taxied to a stop, three men bounded out full of anticipation for their day on the ranch. On the way there in my car I brought them up to date with developments and invited questions, having gathered facts and stats beforehand and found out from Jim what they would want to know. It was a novel experience and rewarding because their enthusiasm was infectious and they were delightfully receptive. I told them about the car I was driving too, which amused them. 'How come you know so much about cars?' they asked.

'Because American cars are works of genius and I like cars, so I'm sharing this passion with you.'

'Gee, do you have other passions?'

'Cows, horses, the ranch itself – and America generally.' There was a pause and I felt I was getting out of my depth with this line of conversation, trying to be too clever in an effort to entertain them. So I switched to telling them about plans for the day ahead.

Jim would meet them at his office and take them on a helicopter tour of the ranch, with an 'executive picnic' included in the tour. There was a landing site at one of the hammocks where a log cabin had been built as a refreshment stop with an accessible road so supplies could be taken in. On this occasion the executive picnic was provided by a specialist catering company and I would join them at the hammock to assist with it. For hunting weekends, tents and camping facilities were set up at the site – then the hunters liked to be left alone, boy scout fashion. Wives and girlfriends were seldom included.

Development on the ranch increased as more roads were built and heavy machinery rolled in to drain the swamps, creating good arable land where crops could be planted. Swamp water was diverted into canals and the landscape started to change with areas pleasant for walking in the evenings after work and school. Early mornings could be cold with frost at that time of year and we were surprised to find icicles hanging from the trees one morning, but when the sun came out these melted and the air temperature rose, so that daytime and evenings were warm.

On one of these evenings when we were feeding the horses in their paddock behind the trailer, a small plane flew low overhead, its engine spluttering. This spooked the horses and we had to calm them while watching the plane disappear beyond the far palmetto scrub. The children were curious. 'Do you think it has crashed? Can we go and look?'

'No, it will be dark soon. We'll find out tomorrow.'

The next day after the children had left for school I called at Jim's office to see if he knew anything about the plane, and found the county sheriff already there on his way to investigate. He had brought a posse with him, all of them mounted on horseback since reports suggested the plane had come down in heavy scrub which would be difficult for vehicles to access. The sheriff said the plane was probably smuggling drugs and he needed to get there before the haul was retrieved by others who would be looking for the wreckage, so he was impatient to get going. The horses were restless and milling around outside Jim's office, which looked like a scene from the Wild West as the men were all armed and impressive in their uniforms as they rode off.

The children were enthralled with this story when they arrived back from school, by which time the plane wreck had been found by the sheriff's party, but they were too late: the smugglers had survived the crash and escaped with their loot despite being injured, as blood in the cockpit testified. The boys were eager to see this for themselves, especially any blood or other gruesome debris, such things holding a fascination for boys their age. They had an ally in a backwoods character called Abe who was in charge of one of the work gangs. He was a tough southerner and fervent Baptist, never seen without a Bible under his arm, which he would pull out and flourish at opportune moments to quote scripture in a booming voice. The rough nature of his work with the gangs in some of the most inhospitable areas of the ranch required a rugged vehicle, and Abe had a much-envied swamp buggy; an ideal form of transport to the crash site. Abe was glad to take the boys who were always happy to tag along with him on outlandish exploits and listen goggle-eyed to his sermons.

Later, arriving back soaked and muddy, they were in a fever of excitement at what they had seen. 'Everything was smashed, and there was blood, but it had dried. Abe said he could see tracks of a buggy that had come to pick up the bad men who were running drugs in the plane, so they got away and took all the drugs with them. That's why nothing was there when the sheriff arrived.'

'Florida has a big problem with drugs,' Adam commented. 'Due to being so close to South America, it's a short trip for a small plane or boat crossing the gulf. Abe thinks the plane that crashed was due to land not far from here and was short on fuel. He says these planes are often seen flying over the ranch.'

'Abe seems to know everything,' I remarked.

'He's a curious combination of pious Christian and extreme racist, with dubious connections. Remember that time he arrived at the trailer with his work gang.'

I was at home clearing up after the children had left for school that day when a truck full of workers pulled up outside and Abe came to the door. He was in a hurry as he jerked his thumb towards the truck and said to me in his rumbling voice: '*Mam, I done brung you some niggers. They's yours fer a few hours.'*

I looked at him blankly. What do you want them to do?'

'*Anythin'. Choppin'. Diggin'. Mendin' the fence. Just so's you keeps 'em at it, till I gets back.*'

'Where are you going?' I asked in a panic.

'*I got bisniss seeing summun a bit along.*' He went to the truck and thumped the side. Several men jumped out and stood in a bunch looking enquiringly at me as Abe got back in the cab and tore off down the road. Do I give them coffee? I wondered. Or water? While I was hesitating, the sound of another truck coming fast down the road made all of us look up. It was Adam. Thank God, I thought, I'm saved. He stopped in the road and came over to where I stood with the men, saying it was lucky that Abe had left his gang with me because they were needed urgently to help unblock a culvert. 'I'm getting a change of clothes because I'll get soaked,' he said, turning to go into the trailer, and that's when I noticed he was limping. I felt a tremor of anxiety, remembering previous times when he went lame, but I didn't say anything with the men standing there watching.

When Adam came home later he was still limping and his ankles were puffy. This was a new development as there had been no problems since we arrived three months earlier and the Florida climate had seemed ideal for him, much as Dr Hazelwood predicted. I looked at his hands which were also a bit puffy, and he admitted they were painful. He tried to make light of it, but the warning signs were too obvious to ignore. 'Has Jim noticed,' I asked.

'Yes, he wanted to know if I was OK, but I laughed it off. Said it was just the cold weather.'

Adam had been given a supply of Brufen tablets by Dr Hazelwood in case of flare-ups, so he started taking these and the effect was remarkable. We assumed any inflammation must be due to the unusually low temperatures for this time of year, but it was his puzzling ambivalence towards the job which worried me more. I was enjoying my own part-time hostess role, and despite some drawbacks I was taking to our new life in a big way and determined to make a success of it. The children were excited and captivated by all the many new experiences, and when we took them for a treat to Disneyworld their faith in the American dream was complete. I was enchanted by Disneyworld just as much as they were, but from a different angle as it was the phenomenal technology and whole concept that intrigued me. Adam would have preferred a day's hunting and I longed to lift his mood and move on from nostalgia for Africa to seize this new reality with all its bright prospects. 'How do you feel about being here, and the job generally?' I asked him when it became increasingly evident that he had reservations.

'I'm giving it a go,' he replied. ' I can't do more than that.'

Alice with Peter, Simon and Louise

Peter with friends at the farm

The Bean House

Going for a ride with dad

Children with calf at Rogate Farm

Florida trailer

Gasparilla shrimp boat

Flemings

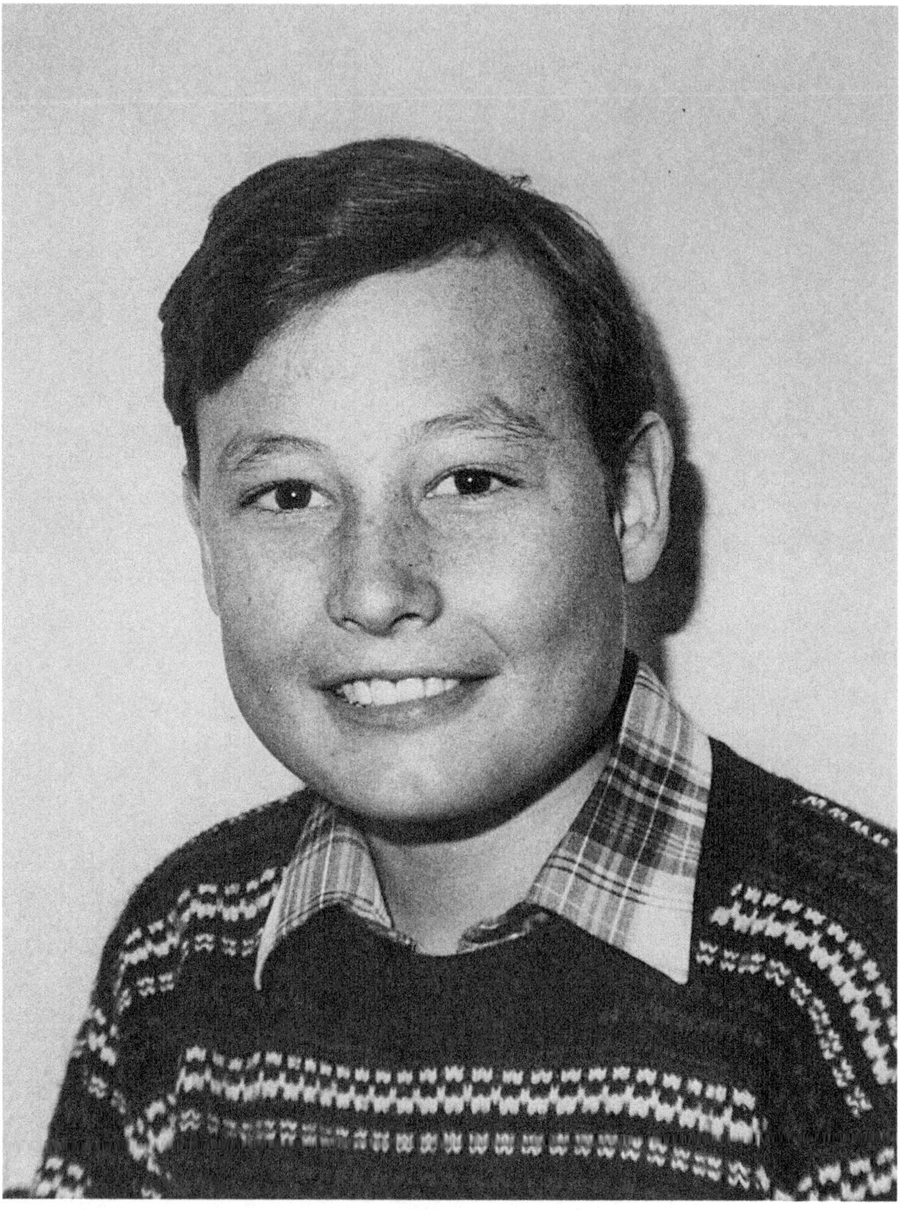

Simon

Charles and Wendy

Check House in 2003

Chapter 9

The savage winter of 1979 killed many trees and the damage to orange groves hit exports of Florida fruit and juice. Jimmy Carter was president and facing the biggest challenge of his time in office as the Iran hostage crisis remained unresolved, with nationwide outrage at this hostile act against American citizens. People were shocked by such defiance from a country which until recently had been thought of as an ally while the Shah was in power. A shiver went through the land which was not just the weather but a sudden sense of uncertainty.

Moments of concern for us were able to be forgotten as we ignored low temperatures to go and explore the many exquisite beaches within easy reach of our new home whenever Adam was free. Many of these were on offshore islands strung along the gulf coast like a necklace of jewel colours with roads of crushed shell beside turquoise water and palms rippling in a gentle breeze. While cold weather persisted inland, the warm sea of the gulf washed over miles of sand where the sun shone brightly all day and beach-side cafes offered fish sandwiches and fries. Best of all were the times when we went to meet shrimp boats as they came into the quay on Gasparilla Island after a day's trawling. We could get a bucket of shrimp (as big as prawns and deliciously crunchy) for $16 straight off the boats. On the way home whenever we had shrimp we stopped at Jim's house to share this treat. It took minutes to steam the shoal in a big pan before tipping them out onto a large platter in the middle of the table with everyone sitting round, shelling the shrimps and dipping them in mayonnaise as we went along.

The abundance of every kind of sea, plant and animal life in our new environment continued to surprise and thrill me. Everything about America seemed to present itself on a scale overflowing like a cornucopia. When I was shopping in the Arcadia Winn Dixie, people stopped to ask if I was lost when they saw me standing among the shelves mesmerised by the display. If I replied, yes, I was lost in wonder at such overwhelming choice, they would exclaim at my accent and want to shake my hand as if I were a rare species discovered far from its normal habitat. They wanted to know what I was doing in cowboy country, and when I said my husband was employed on a ranch and we lived there in a trailer, they were astonished. 'How come you living like that?' was the concerned response, thinking we must have fallen on hard times. It seemed to be a popular perception that respectable people did not live in the backwoods, and certainly did not live in trailers. They were mystified and I was too in trying to explain the anomaly, but also unsettled by the notions of some of those in a society that we were now part of.

Arcadia back then was thought of as a cowboy town and known for its famous rodeo. There were shops selling cowboy gear and cowgirl outfits with leather fringes and studded boots among saddles and tack and all the paraphernalia associated with horses and riders. The soothing smell of leather in these shops and friendliness of the country people working there, drew me to the town where I could buy groceries without having to go all the way to bigger and busier Punta Gorda.

The marvel of this new life in Florida however, I had to acknowledge, was not all joy and rapture. The rich diversity of flora and fauna included snakes everywhere and there were more of them on the ranch than I had ever seen in Africa. I had assumed we were safe in the trailer and was unsuspecting when I began to find them resting among clothes in drawers and cupboards. This was a refuge for them during cold weather so we had to learn to be careful, but I found it unnerving to be sharing my home with snakes. Outside too, we had to watch for them, and were often startled during tennis games on the court that Jim had built at his house when something black or mottled streaked across the court at odd moments, making us jump and miss the ball. Everyone laughed at the absurdity and all was accepted in the general spirit of eccentric happenings out in the Florida wilderness.

In normal times Adam would have responded with enthusiasm, but he was not his normal self since the pills he was taking for the flare-up of his rheumatoid arthritis stopped working after a while. One morning he needed help to get out of bed and clearly was not fit to go to work, though he tried to insist that he would be all right as soon as he got moving. I said I would go to the office and explain the situation to Jim.

It was a relief to have another adult to talk to about this problem as the deterioration in Adam's physical state of health was increasing. Jim said it was not just the physical setback that he was worried about, but possible psychological effects as well. 'Even before this happened he seemed uncomfortable about the job in ways that were difficult to understand. I'm baffled by this because he is well qualified and suited to the work. All the teams like him and will do their best for him. I'm prepared to take on as many extra hands as necessary to do all the physical work, so long as he can still go out on a horse and supervise. But I don't know if his heart is in it, and I need you to tell me how we can help.'

Jim's kindness and sympathy put me on the spot because I wanted to seize the offer of extra help, giving Adam a chance to recover, while at the same time doubting that he either could, or would, respond. We had been to see a doctor in Punta Gorda for advice and this had not been encouraging as blood tests showed active rheumatoid arthritis. We did have medical insurance but it didn't cover prolonged illness or drugs, and these were expensive. The doctor prescribed cortisone and we had great hopes for this as a miracle drug, but it seemed to make him worse instead of better, and the doctor then suggested that he should have a period of complete rest.

During this time, when he was at home with limited mobility, confined to an armchair and increasingly despondent, we faced the almost unthinkable prospect of having to leave and go back to England to get help from the NHS. It was a solution of desperation as we realised that we simply could not afford medical treatment for him in America. The doctor spelt it out for us at this stage when he stated: 'It is not going to cost thousands of dollars to get Adam back on his feet, it is going to cost hundreds of thousands of dollars.' This left us with no choice and was the most bitter of decisions to face after such a short time trying to make a new life for ourselves.

I had to tell Jim first, and then I had to tell the children. They had assumed that Adam would recover in the same way that he had done before, and refused to believe such dire news. 'We can't go – all our boxes are still on their way coming here,' Simon protested. 'We can't just go off like that and leave all our things behind. We don't even know where they will have got to by now. They might still be on a ship. Dad will get better. If we go to England we might get stuck there forever.'

'It would only be temporary, till Dad gets better. Whatever's best for him,' Louise said, always practical, and protective of Adam. 'Then we can come back if we want to.'

'Where can we live in England?' Peter (now called Pete) asked reasonably.

'We need to be close to good medical services,' I said, 'and good schools, especially for Louise who will go straight into O-levels. I'm going to contact Ros and discuss options with her. She's always sensible and will know what to do.'

My call to Ros so alarmed her that she sent an urgent message to Fa who was on a ship in the Mediterranean, and to my surprise he phoned me from the ship. He was dubious about Adam's prospects as there was no cure for rheumatoid arthritis and standard treatments were only aimed at initiating periods of remission. Gold injections and Penicillamine were the two drugs most commonly used to slow the progress of the disease, and Fa said we should get Adam started on a regime without delay. We would be welcome to stay with him and Babs at their house near Hereford when they returned from the cruise, he added, but this would not be for several weeks.

By now I had been in touch with Alison by letter and on hearing the news she immediately suggested we should go to Howleigh so the aunts could look after us. When Adam's sister Elizabeth heard about this, she insisted that we should go to them instead as they now lived in Dorset (having sold their farm in Ireland) in a house which was big enough for all of us, and we would be very welcome. She said they had an excellent doctor in Bridport only five miles away, and there was a good comprehensive school nearby at Lyme Regis so Louise and Simon could go there, while Charmouth Primary was conveniently close for Pete. This generous offer solved most of our immediate problems and we were glad to accept.

With all our household goods still on a ship somewhere at sea, there was very little packing up to do, using the same suitcases and assorted bags from a few months before. It seemed incomprehensible to be moving again, leaving so much promise behind this time, but the urgency and organisation of the move left me no chance to hesitate or grieve. I had to book flights, sell the car, pay bills and tie up a bewildering number of loose ends, while at the same time look after Adam who could barely stand or walk and could not wash or dress himself. When I saw him trying to lift a hand to his head to brush his hair, unable to perform even this simple movement, it was heart-breaking. Worst of all was the constant debilitating pain that affected all his joints, bringing with it a sense of hopelessness and frustration which inevitably impinged on the rest of us despite our valiant attempts to keep spirits up all round. Jim was unfailingly kind-hearted and did everything he could to help with all the details of leaving, such as organising a wheelchair and assistance for Adam throughout the journey to England. He and his family came to see us off on the very sad day of departure at Fort Myers airport, where we had arrived with boundless hope and optimism only a few months before. All of us were in tears as we hugged and held on until the last minute, not wanting to let go. Not wanting to go at all.

The reality of living under a cloud blanket in England after waking up to sun every day in Florida, met us with full force as we struggled through gloomy train stations on the long trip from London to Axminster, where Elizabeth and Peter rescued us. They had thoughtfully come with a wheelchair, which was a relief as Adam had lost all mobility after hours stuck in aircraft and train seats, and I was grateful for Peter's strong hands helping to guide and lift him. The children were numb with cold and shock at being suddenly transplanted into this unfamiliar territory, and had gone unusually quiet as they tried to smile and remember good manners; their faces stiff from holding back tears at the insecurity of our situation with Adam so incapacitated. They hardly knew Elizabeth and Peter who had been living in Ireland for the past ten years while we were in Rhodesia, and had moved to England for their only child, Michael, to go to an English public school. Another important reason for moving to England, Peter later explained, was for Michael to be absorbed into English cricket culture which was a family passion. Peter engaged me in a long and detailed conversation on the intricacies of bowling technique, and from then on I thought of him as The Bowler, with the family becoming known to us fondly as the Bowlers.

Michael was away at school when we arrived and this was a disappointment for the children, but he would be back for the holidays which was something to look forward to while they settled into this new strange life. Losing our home and coming to live in England with people who had never encountered such animated children as ours before was a huge shock to them. The house had radiators but we soon discovered that they produced very little heat and the house itself was damp and exposed to bitter winds on the north side of a steep hill. Elizabeth and Peter were not concerned about this as the site in their eyes made up for buying a frigid house perched precariously on a hillside. They were completely blind to any drawbacks while gazing with delight at views sweeping down to the Marshwood Vale and across to wooded hills beyond. They wanted us to love the location as much as they did, and genuinely wanted us to feel welcome and supported, while Elizabeth bravely attempted to cook sturdy meals for what was now a large and hungry family sharing their living space. I was a competent cook and enjoyed cooking, wanting to help, but Elizabeth was very proprietorial about her kitchen and made it clear from the start that she would allow my help only at the sink.

The first and most important call we needed to make was to the local doctors' surgery to get Adam registered and seen as an urgent case, thinking he might need admission to hospital for assessment. One of the doctors at the Bridport practice took charge, surprising us with his positive and authoritative approach to the management of rheumatoid arthritis which, after the Punta Gorda doctor's view of Adam's prospects, was reassuring and gave us confidence that he was now in good hands and the disease could be brought under control. The doctor prescribed gold injections and said I could give them to Adam as I was a nurse. When we collected the tiny phials of injectable gold together with syringes from the chemist, it felt miraculous to be living in a country where these were free and willingly supplied.

Other aspects of Adam's care were more tricky in a tall house with stairs, surrounded outside by steep slopes where no wheelchair had ventured before, while the guest bathroom had a bath but no shower. Getting into the bath was relatively straight forward for Adam with help, but when it came to getting out he needed lifting, and Peter was squeamish about any assistance that might seem uncomfortably intimate. 'You'll have to get the district nurse for anything like that, if you're having difficulty,' Peter said. Usually I was able lift Adam by stages to the edge of the bath where he could sit to be dried, but inevitably there came a time when he slipped from my hands and fell back into the water with a mighty splash, slopping a wave onto the floor. Each of us was seized with terror that the flood might seep down into the Bowlers' dining room with its valuable paintings and portraits, causing damage. This concern was far more pressing than despair at our predicament with Adam stuck in the bath, so mopping the floor with towels had to be a first priority. To my shame I felt tears adding more drips as I mopped, for the sense of helplessness at that moment seemed overwhelming in our wretched situation. Letting all the water out of the bath, and finding a dry towel to rub Adam down so that his skin was no longer slippery and he could be lifted more easily, saved the day. Later, to my lasting relief, no incriminating stain appeared below on the Bowlers' dining-room ceiling.

After getting Adam started on treatment, the next urgent issue was to enroll the children in local schools. One piece of good fortune in all the muddled happenings of the past few weeks was confirmation that our present address came within the zone for Woodroffe School at Lyme Regis. The school was rated outstanding and Louise and Simon would both go there, while Pete went to Charmouth Primary which was also highly recommended. This was on the same bus route so they could walk to the bus stop and go off together each morning. When this routine got underway it provided a measure of relief from the tension we could feel building up in the household as the Bowlers, despite their best endeavours, were beginning to crack under the strain of hosting our boisterous family. In Louise's words, written now from memory:

We were pretty madcap compared with English types and the Bowlers were alarmed by our loudness, the amount of space we took up, the amount we ate, and the way we tore around their garden like wild animals.

Her class at Woodroffe had already completed the first year of their O-level syllabus and Louise had to catch up on her own after school, sitting for hours at the kitchen table while Elizabeth scurried around her, chopping at lumps of frozen meat and crashing pots in a frenzy of supper preparation. She still refused any help from me and when I suggested, very tactfully, that it might be an idea to take meat or fish out of the freezer to defrost overnight so it was not still in a frozen state a couple of hours before supper was due, she flew into a rage. We all dreaded the outbursts of temper which she referred to as 'blowing her top', while strangely she seemed to take pride in these displays which left the rest of us terrified. Sometimes the force of her fury was exhausting and she flopped into the dog's basket, curling up with the dog who she said was her alter ego. Peter kept out of the way, retreating to his armchair in the sitting room and opening a newspaper to hide behind until calm returned. I could hear him muttering and swearing under his breath behind the paper, occasionally twitching it in irritation if the ranting continued beyond endurance levels. He was an affable man, not given to histrionics, and liked to discuss points of interest that had caught his attention while cloistered with the paper each day after breakfast. He was barely fifty but already settling into a life of contented retirement, with no obligations beyond walking the dog and tending a small vegetable patch exposed to the fierce north wind that shivered and blasted all green things on that side of the hill. The other side of the hill basked in sunlight with glorious views of cliffs and sea where I sent the children for long walks to give the Bowlers a break.

We needed a car, with a boot large enough to take Adam's wheelchair so that he could join us for walks once we were off the hill and onto a flat surface such as the seafront at Lyme Regis. The dear aunts, always wanting to help, said we could have Granny Hill's car which had been rotting away in one of their barns at Howleigh, but was still serviceable. It was a Hillman Minx of vintage status but the engine was in good condition with low mileage after sedate driving by Granny since the car was new. Its only visible defects were rust holes in the floor so we laid duck-boards over these to stop puddles splashing up from the road onto our feet as we sat trying to keep dry. Once we had the car, we could go to see friends and explore this very scenic and serene part of England that was offering such good medical care for Adam. He was already improving on the gold regime and had regained mental stamina, determined now to get back to full health and achieve his one objective, which was to return to Africa. 'We've landed in this benighted country out of dire necessity, that's all, nothing else, so as soon as I'm fit again we're going back to where we belong,' he said. 'It shouldn't take more than a year, and we'll just have to endure these agonies in the meanwhile, knowing that it's only temporary until we can escape.'

'What about the children's schools, and Louise due to take O-levels next year?' I asked.

'We'll sort something out. It will all be fine once we're headed home again.'

In one sentence he seemed to have summed up what had been in his mind all along. Even before we set off for America, despite his insistence at the time that it was what he wanted, I suspected that Africa held him by invisible ties so powerful that he could never feel at ease anywhere else. Africa was deep in my soul too, but we had children to educate and keep safe, so these practical considerations had to over-ride personal ones in my view, while in his it was the other way around. Maybe we could find an answer to this later on, I hoped, and for now concentrate all efforts on making life bearable and Adam well.

There were three bedrooms in the Bowler house: one for Elizabeth and Peter, one for Michael when he was home, and one guest room that Adam and I occupied. The children's rooms were in an annexe above the garage where a bathroom doubled as Elizabeth's laundry room. 'I couldn't possibly have a washing machine in the house,' she said. 'It wouldn't be hygienic.' I didn't enquire further into this aversion and was grateful for a washing machine in the children's quarters, while very much missing the miraculous tumble dryer at the trailer. Tumble dryers had not yet been discovered in England where housewives were devoted to washing lines. It was thought healthy for clothes and bed linen to hang sagging like flags on outside lines in the worst of weathers, often remaining damp when collected in. The smell of mould in the annexe, together with penetrating cold from its flimsy construction, was not a happy combination and the children complained so much that we decided to make a headquarters for all of us in the guest bedroom. The children could come there after school and stay until supper, doing their homework, listening to the radio or reading. After supper we went back there, leaving the Bowlers to watch TV in peace and this arrangement worked well, especially when Michael was home for the holidays and they were able to watch their favourite programmes together as a family, undisturbed by us. We had thought that Michael, an only child who was doted upon, would be a brat, but he was charming and unaffected. He enjoyed playing board games or scrambling about on the hillside with Louise and the boys, pleased to have cousins to enliven what otherwise might be rather dreary holidays with parents who behaved as if they were elderly, having formal tastes in entertaining and few contacts with younger people.

Pete had a school friend, Ian, who lived on a farm down the road and one weekend came to the house asking for Pete to go out and play. They went to run around in a wooded part of the garden well away from the house, but when Peter saw them he was incensed and came to find me. 'Did you tell Pete he could invite friends to come here?' Peter was almost choking with indignation. 'We can't have village children running around on our property. You must tell the child to go home, wherever that is.' I didn't argue and went to suggest that Ian took Pete to the farm.

Adam wanted to know what the fuss was about. I told him and asked, 'What does Peter mean when he objects to "village children"? He made it sound derogatory. All the houses up here are part of the village with the church and pub and post office down in the valley, so we're all village people. What's the difference?'

'The difference is that Ian's dad is a labourer on the farm. Not the kind of people that Peter likes to mix with.'

'What are we going to do? I can't live with such madness.'

'We're going to find our own place, darling. We're going to start looking for somewhere to rent *mara moja* (straight away), staying in the same zone for the schools. We don't have to go on relying on charity. We can have our own place now I'm back on my feet.'

This was welcome news and just in time, as I found out later when Peter asked to speak to me the next morning, alone. 'I need to talk to you about finances,' he began, and I thought how strange and surprising it was that he, like Cen, who never normally mentioned the subject of money, now chose to talk to me about it instead of Adam. His next statement was even more surprising. 'I should be a millionaire,' he said, 'but I'm just £100,000 short.' He stopped to light a cigarette, his hands shaking I noticed. His hands often shook, which he said was due to having polio as a child and I felt a wave of sympathy for him, seeing him not as a man cushioned by wealth and ease, but vulnerable to ill health and invisible personal struggles. I waited for him to continue. 'When you had nowhere else to go and we offered to take you in, I had an impression that the cost of supporting you as dependent relatives could be set against income tax. I checked with my accountant and he thought this was allowable, but now he says you don't meet the criteria for dependent relatives, so I can't claim, and your accommodation here is not an expense that we can go on meeting.

'Oh, I'm so sorry that you have been to all this trouble on our behalf,' I said, mortified that we had become a strain on their generosity. 'But it's all right, because we are going to look for somewhere to rent now that Adam is getting better and more independent. We will always be immensely grateful to you and Elizabeth for taking us in and looking after us. We don't want to be a burden, and you have been so kind.'

Peter, relieved and disarmed, beamed at me in the old way that I always found endearing. 'No trouble I assure you, but you will be glad to have your own home and somewhere to unpack your boxes when they arrive. We will help with anything you need, of course.'

The children shouted and jumped for joy when we told them, but we had to explain that it might take a while to find a place that we could afford, so any move would not be instant. 'We need to be close enough to the school for my rugby practice,' Simon pointed out. He and Pete had started rugby in their first year at primary school in Rhodesia and Simon was already in one of the Woodroffe teams. He was an ardent player and cross-country runner, dedicated to all forms of sport, but a slouch in the classroom, which was frustrating because he had a good brain; he just didn't like being indoors. He refused to wear shoes for running and ran barefoot which he said gave him an advantage. All three children went barefoot outside the house as well as inside when they were not at school. On weekends they took the bus to Bridport with their pocket money and told us that people stopped them in the street to ask if their parents were too poor to buy shoes for them. 'The rate at which you're growing that could well be true,' I said. 'What do you tell people?'

'We say we're poor but we like being barefoot, which is true.' When snow lay on the ground they still refused to wear shoes, but their feet were hardened and tough in all weathers. 'Someone in the street, who was very disapproving, gave me a lecture,' Simon reported. 'They said my parents could be arrested for neglect and they should be ashamed to send their children out like that. But I told them it's quite normal in Africa and that's where we come from. We didn't get to be Americans when we were there because we didn't stay long enough. I don't know whether we should say we're from Africa, or America, because that's the last place where we lived?' he asked, confused by all the moves.

'You can say you're from Africa because that's where you were born, and Dad too.'

'Can we go back to Florida when Dad is completely better? I liked being there and the ranch was miles more fun than anywhere else we've been to.'

'You can't do rugby in Florida.'

'I can ride and shoot and go fishing – that's three things instead of one.'

'We won't stay here any longer than we have to, that's certain. But we're lucky to have all this help for Dad, which you have to remember is the whole reason for being here.'

Within weeks we had moved to a rented house on the outskirts of Bridport close to West Bay, where the boys soon joined local fishermen at the pier, sitting for hours patiently watching their lines. Night fishing was a particularly engrossing occupation when they took themselves off after supper to link up with other hunched figures strung along the pier in darkness, occasionally grunting to each other. The boys were supposed to come home by nine o'clock during school holidays, but I was too tired by then to check their beds and suspected that they often stayed out much later waiting for bites in that mysterious communion of silent fishers. Compensation came in the catch they brought home if it was something edible, but too often it was a fat conger hauled home in a bucket. This could be eaten if heavily disguised in a stew, but no one had much enthusiasm for congers. Spider crabs were a treat and well worth the fiddle picking out their sweet delicate flesh, but best of all were mackerel, bream or pollock. Living close to the sea provided a natural playground for the boys where they could go off whenever they liked without supervision, and adults were relieved of bored children hanging around the house getting in the way.

Louise, who was now fifteen, bought herself a pair of black shoes with high spiky heels and a skimpy dress to go waitressing at a local hotel to earn her own money. The name of the hotel was Little Wytch and was as eerie and off-beat as its name suggested. When she started coming home with notes stuffed down the front of her dress we became alarmed and booked a table at the hotel one night, without telling her, to see what was going on. Louise was furious at our duplicity, 'spying on her' as she saw it, and wouldn't come near us the whole evening. We were served by the manager who was equally unfriendly, and the evening was not a success. Except that the memory of Louise teetering on stiletto heels while squeezed tightly into her tiny dress, simpering over the diners, remained with us ever after as a sure-fire tease and laugh.

Adam was well enough now to think about the kind of job he might ease himself into without too much physical strain, in preparation for more serious work prospects as he continued to make progress towards what mercifully looked like becoming almost a full recovery. He was walking and driving again and the desperate days when he couldn't wash or dress himself, became horrors of the past. Financial support during this time came from savings and those state benefits for which we were eligible. These included free school lunches for the children, which perversely identified them as scroungers so they were victimised by other children for this, in addition to further discrepancies marking them out from the herd such as Rhodesian accents. 'You don't need to take any notice of what people say; just ignore them, or smile at them which will not be the reaction they are expecting and will leave them confused. Unless you are actually physically attacked, you don't need to bother about any of this,' I told them, hoping it would deflect the hostility that I was surprised to find in an English school after Florida schools had been so friendly.

Living in these reduced circumstances was humiliating, but also a challenge in finding ways to economise and make the money stretch. Our rented house had one big asset – a Rayburn which was the beating heart of the home, always warm and ready for meals to be cooked as well as heating hot water and radiators. I could make bread in the Rayburn and put casseroles in the oven to simmer away for hours. Bridport was a traditional market town with a fishmonger and butcher, bakers and grocers, open all week with street stalls on market days. If I went to the butcher on a Saturday at midday, meat would be marked down and I could buy special offers. Mince is a staple for families on a budget but I always wanted to know what was in the mince and watch the butcher when he fed offcuts into his giant machine. He laughed at me for being so fussy but was tolerant of my interest and indulged me with good cuts. Braised in the Rayburn these enriched themselves and came out tender and dripping with gravy juices, ready to fill all the appetites waiting around the table. Elizabeth, when she was roasting a joint, poured good bastings from the tin into the dog's bowl, saying dogs need nourishment and we could have Bisto. This pained me as I hated losing precious scrapings for proper gravy, and children I thought needed nourishing just as much as dogs. Woodroffe School included cookery classes on the curriculum, for boys as well as girls, and when Simon brought home an apple pie that he had baked himself, it was the beginning of a keen interest in food. He had started keeping a journal to record details of fish that he caught and now any special menus or recipes were included.

Letters came from friends in Rhodesia, and others who were living in England often phoned with news so it was like a network keeping us in touch with events and people we cared about. I had a call after the children had left for school one day saying there had been an attack on Thornby Farm, next door to Rogate where we had lived with such fear of attack ourselves. My good friend Hazel and her husband had been killed, shot dead with AK47s in their house after the farm store had been raided. Their daughters were away at school so they were spared, but left as orphans along with a surviving brother. We were extremely shocked by the news, especially Louise who was a close friend of Eileen, one of the daughters. Who would look after the girls now, and what was to become of other Rhodesians like them who had few links outside the country, but also – what if we had been still there on Rogate – would the killers have come for us next? We tried to contact the Hornby family to ask about the girls and see if there was anything we could do to help, but no communication came back from them.

For the first time in many years the Craddock family were all back in England, scattered but communicating. Fa and Babs had found a bargain house on a new estate where the builder had run out of money and left unfinished houses for sale below cost, so this was irresistible to a skinflint like Fa. He and Babs relished the years spent foraging at the local tip for building materials and anything retrievable that could be used to 'finish off' the house.

Elaine and her family were in Gloucester, having returned from their mission in Ethiopia after Les had health problems. Elaine's well-being was another concern since complications during the birth of her twins in Ethiopia resulted in chronic ill heath, but she was very stoic about this. Babs, observing the series of woes suffered so unfairly it seemed by this missionary family, remarked at the time: 'They have one foot in heaven and the other on a banana skin.' Babs was perspicacious, always ready with a quip, which made her a good foil for Fa.

Ros and her family had settled near Weybridge, and Muz was in Suffolk with Andy where they lived like dormice under the eaves of their ancient cottage. We couldn't visit any of them because the Hillman Minx was too elderly for long journeys. Even a short trip to visit the aunts near Taunton was fraught with stops for its wheezing radiator to cool down. But the aunts solved this problem by coming to see us with picnics packed and ready for the beach with dogs and rugs and all the usual paraphernalia. They wanted us to meet the daughter of one of their many Hill cousins who had married a dashing young man with Kenya connections, so this couple was invited to join us at one of the inimitable picnics.

The young man, Charles, after leaving Oxford with a law degree, instead of joining a law firm, joined a musical show as one of the singers on a tour of the world. The show had a humanitarian purpose and after a couple of tours he was sent on a new project with the same organisation. This was to Kenya where a movement called Harambee Africa was active in support for President Kenyatta's drive to unite the nation. The word '*harambee*' in Kiswahili loosely means 'pull together' and there was a tremendous spirit of purpose and joining of hands to push forward in the country at this time. Charles, now one of the voluntary workers in Harambee Africa, found himself mentoring young Kenyan Africans who were ambitious in their desire for further education and skills, to contribute to the national effort. Some of them were invited to study in other countries, so Charles coached them and helped them to get passports.

Later, returning to England, he took up articles with a firm of London lawyers and became a solicitor, but noticed after a while that his business clients were achieving a great deal more satisfaction in their careers than he was in his, so he decided to leave the law and start his own business. At the time of the aunts' picnic he was a retailer with a chain of kitchen shops, all doing well, and a project in the planning stage to buy and restore a large derelict house, which he and his wife were excited to tell us about. The contrast between their lives and ours was so stark it was comical, but they were charming and didn't make us feel like the poor relations that we undoubtedly were.

I didn't want to be poor, and my parents' extreme frugality which was part of their Christian ethic during the time I was growing up, made me even less inclined to accept poverty as a way of life. I was encouraged to explore money making ideas by my friends Joan and Stephen Hemsted at whose farm in Kenya I spent holidays as a child, escaping from my rigid family. Later on, they took my parents' place at my wedding after Fa decided that fares were too expensive and none of my own family would attend. Stephen wanted me to have financial security in my marriage and discussed different ways to enhance income among the ups and downs of farming.

He claimed that he made more money playing the stock market than growing coffee on his farm, and shared tips with me. In particular he told me to watch the price of gold, which he predicted would take a hike, and as soon as it started moving – jump in. During the seventies when we were in Rhodesia I watched the gold price, and later, after we had left, I watched the price ever more closely and began to feel a hunch growing towards the end of the decade. This grew stronger and I pressured Adam to buy gold with his Glanjoro money, but he held out, convinced that it was just one of my foolish notions. In the end he agreed and gave instructions to his broker to buy bullion simply for the sake of peace and because he thought gold might be a safe haven. Speculation was against all his instincts, more from fear of losing money than any moral qualms about gambling, so when my hunch said the price had peaked and we must sell, he refused. This moment of maximum stress coincided with the aunts' picnic soon after we moved to Bridport and were on the cusp of a new decade, moving into the eighties.

In a panic at losing the chance to make a tidy profit on the gold purchase I sent an SOS to Fa, imploring him to phone Adam and persuade him to sell immediately. Fa, who usually delighted in losing money because it helped to ease his conscience about having any, on this occasion recognised the expediency of our situation and put such a tight psychological armlock on Adam that he called the broker and the sale was done in moments. This resulted in a remarkable bonanza that pleased him immensely. The boost to his morale led to the decision that it was time to buy a new suit and take the London train from Axminster to the offices of a recruitment agency. 'I need the kind of job where I'm earning again, back in business, until I'm properly signed off by the NHS and we can get back to a normal life, where we belong. It could be anywhere, darling. Botswana has opportunities. Even the Republic (South Africa) is worth considering. Kenya or Tanzania of course. The world is open to us now I'm on the verge of becoming useful again.'

He no longer needed gold injections and the pain and weakness which had been so disabling were now under control with anti-inflammatory drugs, readily available without a prescription. His recovery had been impressive, much assisted by an absolute determination to beat the illness and beat a trail back to Africa.

When we heard that our seafaring boxes had arrived at last and were stacked in a shed at Southampton waiting for delivery instructions, the situation became almost farcical as we dithered between putting them in storage to await further despatch over the sea, or bring them to Bridport where unpacking would be only a temporary exercise. Simon was anxious about his butterfly collection languishing in one of the boxes. 'The specimens will get desiccated, left in a shed,' he complained. 'I need to check them. Some will need re-mounting.'

His interest in butterflies had developed when we were living in Salisbury where avenues of flowering trees attracted large numbers of butterflies to the city and gardens. In our small garden at Montagu Avenue we counted well over a hundred different species that fluttered in from the avenue, and Simon bought books on butterflies with his pocket money, learning how to trap and study them. I was not so thrilled about the traps when I found out how they were made after Simon asked me for an old mosquito net. He stretched pieces of this over wire frames to form the traps which were baited with a mixture of dog poo mashed with banana, smeared onto a tin lid in the bottom of each trap. These were hung like crude lanterns from tree branches in the garden, and even my washing line until I objected. The stinking bait attracted butterflies in gratifying numbers, including prized visitors like the rare luminous pearl charaxes. A generous adult friend who had encouraged Simon's interest, commissioned display trays with glass tops to be made for the specimens, and a few of these had been stacked with great care in our boxes. It was now more than a year since these had set off on their many long voyages trying to catch up with us. Pete pointed out that there were things of his in the boxes as well. 'All my rods and fishing gear. It will be like Christmas all over again when we unpack everything.'

The recruitment agency put Adam through assessment tests for his level of fitness and what kind of work was appropriate for him at this stage of his recovery, leading to what he might aim for when fully recovered. They were very thorough and professional, even arranging consultations with a psychologist. This surprised me, but it seemed sensible to have guidance on job suitability since Adam had not found a job that truly satisfied him since leaving Glanjoro. I wondered if I had somehow been at fault in not supporting him enough, or not giving the right kind of support. Now we were at another crossroads I wanted to be sure that we found the right track this time. Who better to advise me, I thought, than the psychologist who was already counselling Adam and knew the details of our story. I asked if he would see me and he agreed, with Adam's consent, so I made an appointment at his consulting room with some trepidation that I might be opening myself to criticism.

I didn't know what to expect or how to present my concern to him but as soon as I sat down and composed myself to begin explaining, he stopped me. He then started to tell me in the kindest possible way what I had come to say, as if he already knew. This was so unexpected, all I could do was sit there listening, and try not to let tears well up as his insight touched me with the reach of this unusual understanding. When he paused for me to respond, I asked how he could know all this about me when Adam was his client, not me. 'From the way your husband described his life growing up and the relationship with his parents, it was easy to see how this could affect later relationships, in particular when it came to you and the marriage,' he said. 'Adam is intelligent and self-aware. He has the ability to succeed in those things he sets out to achieve, but feels crippled, not by illness, but fear of failure which goes back to his childhood.

'Poor Adam.'

'Don't say that. He is not a victim.'

'What should I do?'

'Stop being his PA. Stop organising him and thinking for him.'

'I only do it as any wife would want to, especially because he has been so ill.'

'That is not what he needs. It is perpetuating a form of dependence, which is precisely the opposite of what he needs. He has to learn to fly solo. To overcome his fear of crashing. You have to let him go.'

'What do you mean?' I said in alarm. 'We're married. I can't let him go, just like that, to find himself, if that is what you mean.'

'Talk to him. Let him tell you.'

We talked. 'I don't know what the ruddy shrink was going on about,' Adam said, seeming to be genuinely puzzled. But you never knew with him because he was such a good actor. 'Anyway, it's beside the point,' he continued. 'Now that the other boffins in that outfit have found me a job by extracting an enormous fee for their efforts, we don't have to bother about any mumbo-jumbo.'

He had already been for an interview with a company supplying dairy farmers with bull semen collected from selected Holstein bulls. He would be, in effect, a travelling semen salesman, he told me, delighted with the implications. 'What a chat-up line! Think of it with all the girls at parties when they ask me what I do.'

'Where are all these parties happening?' I had not anticipated such opportunities among the Holsteins.

'On the road. Wherever I'm staying on my semen rounds.' He was back on form. I was glad to see him like this and, following the psychologist's advice to let him go, was not inclined to discourage any of this new enthusiasm. 'It's only temporary,' Adam went on. 'Just to get myself back in action and earning, then as soon as I'm fully fit again, we're off home to the Equator.'

The new job involved travelling around farms during the week and coming home at weekends. After his first week away when he arrived home on Friday evening in his new company car, we all ran out for a full inspection. It was a shiny caramel-coloured Vauxhall, and next to the battered Hillman which was now my car, it looked regal. 'Now we've got Dad's car we can go on expeditions,' Simon exclaimed in excitement.

'What kind of expeditions?' Louise was wary.

'Army places where they have tanks and guns and firing ranges.'

'We could watch them doing fighting exercises,' Pete suggested, seeing the possibilities.

'No one is allowed to go anywhere near the ranges when they're training,' Adam said. 'But there are museums where you can see tanks and guns and that sort of thing.'

'That sounds boring. We could go to a good fishing place instead,' Pete offered.

Louise gave up at that point. She had reached a stage of teenage irritability and detachment in which younger siblings, and parents too, had become a trial suffered with increasing levels of bad grace. To counteract this burden she joined a boy gang at school, preferring their company and conversation to some of the preoccupations of girls her age. Her inclusion by the boys was surprising but tolerated since their group consisted not of rough elements but amiable thinkers. They came round at weekends to drape themselves over furniture and carpets in the sitting room, their long legs spread out casually as they discussed whatever it was that young people found absorbing in the final year of the seventies.

Adam was tired after his first week with the Holstein breeders but it was normal tiredness and his arthritis remained calm. 'At this rate we will be out of here sooner than expected,' he said, 'so we'll keep our boxes on ice. Simon's butterflies will have to take their chances. After all, they can't fly away.'

'What about the children and schools?'

'They can board at Woodroffe. Pete is just about to join the others. They're all eligible. All of them can board.'

Woodroffe was one of the few comprehensive schools that took boarders, who were mainly from army families and others working abroad. Simon would jump at the chance of boarding, I thought, but was not so sure about Louise who was not likely to jump at anything suggested by parents in her current state of mind. When she was not flying out of the door in her Little Wytch outfit, she had taken to wearing grunge gear in cowpat colours that were not flattering. 'You haven't inherited Dad's good skin colour, or mine. Yours is pasty so you shouldn't be wearing pasty colours,' I advised her.

'Why would I want to be like you or Dad?' was her reply.

Both she and Simon were going off in their own ways, developing contrary ideas. Pete was the opposite, easy-going, following in the wake of each day's latest action as Simon led some new quest. He was a force of nature and the only way to live alongside that level of energy was to let him romp ahead while others trailed behind. It was on the rugby field that Simon was most fearless, and peculiarly impervious to the knocks and kicks of hard tackling or getting squashed in the scrum. Any player who remained prostrated on the ground after being injured would have a bucket of water thrown over them to numb the pain, and then be expected to get up and carry on. When there was a match I always went to cheer from the side lines, surprised that so few other parents turned up, and if they did, unlike Rhodesian parents, behaved with what I concluded was English restraint. One of the parents explained: 'It isn't really approved of to show partiality. Competitive sport is frowned upon by the left-wing educational establishment as too elitist. Society must not have winners or losers anymore. With that attitude our children's brains and bodies are going to turn into blancmanges.'

These remarks did not extend to the bucket treatment and a dousing with cold water did generally produce miraculous results in bringing back to life those inert figures lying on the field. On one occasion it didn't work after Simon collapsed while running with the ball, unmolested. The bucket treatment failed to revive him so he was carried off and bundled onto the back seat of the Hillman to be taken home. He was pale and breathless, but no injury was apparent and by the time we got home he felt better, so no more was thought about it.

Chapter 10

Adam was enjoying his job with the Holstein company and discovered during his travels that several old Kenya girlfriends lived along his route, having moved to English southern counties in the great exodus of settler families after Independence. They provided an unexpected bonus when he found he could lodge with them for nights on the road instead of rooms in seedy B&Bs or budget motels. Not all of the girlfriends were still married to their former partners and one in particular I suspected of rather more generous hospitality than simply putting clean sheets on the guest bed. Doing his washing for him was not something that occurred, however, and a bag of laundry always came home with him, with suits to be taken to the cleaners. Bridport dry cleaners were meticulous in checking pockets before sending suits to the machine, and despite my pre-checking they often found loose change or stray pieces of the usual detritus that men absentmindedly stuff into their pockets. The dry-cleaning lady became wise to Adam's scraps after one day finding the stubs of two theatre tickets in a pocket. 'Oh, here are your London theatre tickets,' she said, handing the stubs to me. 'You might want to keep them as souvenirs. It's such a treat going to the theatre, especially in London,' she remarked innocently.

'I wonder who he took? It wasn't me,' I replied.

'Oh, dear!' She looked mortified. 'I'm so sorry. It's my big mouth again. I never should have said anything. I hope it's not going to cause any trouble.'

'I'm going to kill him when I find out who he took instead of me,' I said in mock horror, but so convincingly that the woman looked as if she was going to faint. 'No, I'm only joking,' I added quickly. 'But I will find out, and when I come to collect the suit I'll tell you all about it, and we'll have a good laugh.'

'I hope it turns out to be a laughing matter and not a crying one,' she said anxiously. When Adam came home the next weekend I asked him about the tickets and he was completely blasé about them, readily admitting that he had taken his old friend Pippa to the theatre and then to dinner afterwards. She had been his first love and first choice for a wife, but had scorned him in favour of a diplomat. 'What about Pippa's husband?' I asked.

'He's away. He's always away. Pippa's a social animal and needs company. She went for a life in the diplomatic world for the parties and swanning around embassies, meeting glamorous people, but most of the time she's stuck at home wiping children's noses and sorting out nanny problems.

'Oh, poor thing,' I said, imagining how a repeat of this conversation was going to brighten the day of the dry-cleaning lady the next time I went in with jackets and suits. When I told her the story of Pippa, and Adam's explanation for the tickets, contrary to my expectation she did not find any of this at all reassuring or amusing. 'Well, it's a good thing you don't mind,' was all she would say.

The boys were becoming useful at running errands to the town when something was needed, and Simon, who was gregarious like Adam, enjoyed chatting to people he met in the street or in shops. He came home excited one day after standing next to a woman in a queue whose perfume drifted past his nose as he stood beside her. 'I asked her what perfume she was wearing because I would like to buy some for my mum. She said that was a very nice idea and the perfume is called "Judder". But when I went to Boots to get some they laughed and said I was having them on. Have you heard of that perfume, Mum?'

I thought about it. 'Are you sure you heard right because it sounds more like 'J'adore', which is French. Next time you go to Boots you could see if they've got it. I can write down the name for you, so you can see how it's spelt and learn something useful to say in French when you get a girlfriend.'

'Don't be silly, Mum. You've put me off now.'

Adam's enjoyment of his new job did not mean that it featured as anything more than a stepping stone to a different future that he mapped out in his mind as he drove around the country, and discussed when he came home at weekends. 'Pippa knows everyone in Kenya and what jobs are going. I might have a shot at a complete change this time, nothing to do with cattle. When I was under the shrink they analysed what I was good at. Well, what they thought I was good at. One of the things was radio, as in broadcasting, due to having the right sort of voice I suppose, which also flagged up auctioneering. I could do that in Kenya or any English-speaking country in Africa. What do you think?' he asked me.

'It depends how easy it would be to break into those areas as a newcomer, without previous experience, and how satisfying you would find it. What about working for a safari company? That is much more in your line. Not as a hunter or guide because that's too physical, but in their support team.'

'It would be crucifying having to watch lucky people going out hunting while I'm stuck in Nairobi or Arusha loading supplies.'

'We're in a different ball park now, darling. Hunting days are over, but it doesn't mean we can't join in the fun. Just being back in Africa will be enough, but first we have to think about the children and the effect on them if we're moving again.

'Once we know where we're going we can think about that. Meanwhile, I'll see if I can get time off to make the most of my new smart car for visiting friends and relations before we go.'

We had a long-standing invitation since the picnic with Charles and his wife, to visit them and see the ruined mansion they were restoring while living in a caravan in the grounds. Old houses held a fascination for me in sensing the history and aura of past generations with their stories of eventful lives, so I was looking forward to this. Our first view of the house at the end of an imposing drive was not encouraging as it glowered from broken windows under a collapsed roof, like someone who has fallen on hard times and just wants to be left alone, I thought. Far from presenting a workable project I felt a sense of despair as I stared back at the dismal façade, and when Charles and his wife came out to meet us there was nothing I could say to match their enthusiasm as they described plans for a grand resurrection. Proceeds from the sale of a previous restoration project together with income from the shops would pay for the work, they explained, while holiday flats to be built in one of the wings would provide future income.

Adam despised old houses as much as anything else that, to him, epitomised morbid Englishness. He shuddered at the sight of this scowling relic and made excuses to leave as soon as it was polite to do so, muttering in an aside to me that he couldn't bear to spend another minute in such a creepy place. 'In your next letter to Mum,' he said on the way back, 'you can entertain her with a grim description of this latest Hill family exploit. It will amuse her.'

Since our own debacle involving the dramas with Adam's illness and abrupt departure from America, Alison had kept up a flow of sympathetic letters, appreciating my efforts to maintain some form of order in the family during the past tortuous year. 'Your nursing has come in useful this time,' she admitted. She and Cen had missed their annual pilgrimage to the Royal Show due to various incidents of ill health as they succumbed to the bodily malfunctions of increasing age. 'It's so tiresome one of my hips got broken falling over the dogs and now the other one is complaining for no good reason, so I'll have to get that one fixed as well. But I must see Sis (Elizabeth) so we'll have to come over this year one way or another,' she wrote.

We had decided to pay for storage in Southampton for all the boxes, and re-direct them as soon as Adam's next job declared itself, telling ourselves that the expense would accelerate a decision on moving and we would soon be on our way. There was a caveat because we had not discussed plans with the children beyond an intention to go 'back home' to Africa which pleased the boys, but Louise was immersed in O-level revision and not in a mood to be unsettled by imminent upheaval. One thing at a time, I thought: when we know where the new job is going to be, then we can decide how to play it.

Simon was always very upbeat and fizzing with energy, so I was surprised when he came down for breakfast one morning saying he felt sick and didn't want anything to eat. 'You can't go to school without any breakfast,' I said. 'If you're really sick you better go back to bed and I'll send a note with Louise for your tutor.' He looked pale and said he had a headache, which was unusual for him. Headaches were virtually unknown in our family, except for Fa who suffered years of crippling migraine until he married Babs when somehow they magically disappeared, never to return. I thought a quiet day at home was all Simon needed, but when he was still lethargic the next day and said he had stomach ache as well as the headache and sickness, I took him to the doctor. Our GP knew us well by now. After the success of Adam's recovery, which had been remarkable and a triumph of medical care, I had complete faith in the doctor's verdict when he said that Simon probably had juvenile migraine. 'Children can get abdominal migraine as well as headaches,' he explained. 'But you mustn't let Simon miss school. He has to learn to live with migraine and not get beaten by it.'

Simon was not a child to be beaten by anything and manfully set off for school each time the headache and nausea came back, even when unable to manage so much as a piece of toast for breakfast. It went against my instincts to follow the doctor's advice about learning to live with migraine when he looked so white and haunted by sickness, and seemed wrong to insist that he mustn't miss school, but on another visit to the doctor the same advice was given. 'Do you think I'm being an anxious mother?' I asked, sensing that he was impatient with my concern. He didn't answer and just gave a little smile as if to spare me a reply.

At school Simon was allowed to lie down in the sickbay if he felt unwell during lessons, but when this started to raise queries with the school I took him back to the surgery. I told the doctor that his symptoms were getting worse and I was worried about him. 'That's the problem – worry,' the doctor said. 'All his symptoms are conversant with juvenile migraine. It's something you have to live with. There are drugs you could try but I wouldn't recommend them.' I was hoping the doctor would examine Simon this time and look more closely at him, but it was obvious that he was getting annoyed with my persistence, and Simon just wanted to get out of there, embarrassed about being seen as a fraud even though he was almost too weak to care.

Adam had promised he would take the boys to a fun fair at Weymouth that weekend and they were looking forward to it, so I hoped Simon would feel well enough for the rides. 'I don't know what's the matter with Simon,' Adam said when they got back. 'He almost collapsed at one point and I virtually had to carry him all the way back to the car. What do you think is going on? It doesn't look like any normal kind of illness.'

'If only Fa were here, he would know, but he's off on a cruise again. I'll take Simon back to the doctor on Monday and insist on a blood test this time.'

On Monday morning when Simon came down to breakfast he could barely hold his head up at the table, and was so pale that his skin looked transparent. I knew something had to be done immediately without waiting a moment longer. The nearest hospital casualty department was twenty miles away at Dorchester, while the doctors' surgery was much closer. Adam had left early and as soon as the others left for school I took Simon to the surgery and said it was an emergency. The receptionist replied that our GP was on holiday and we would have to wait until one of the other doctors was free. We took a seat and waited, and waited. I kept going back to the receptionist's window to remind her that we were still there, telling her that I would not leave until Simon was seen. This seemed only to annoy her, and when it was nearly midday, she told me most of the doctors had gone out on visits and there was only a locum still there. 'Please, I'm desperate. Can he see us?'

We were saved just then because the locum doctor came through to the waiting room, and when he saw Simon he asked the receptionist what he was doing there. 'He didn't have an appointment and all of you have been busy,' she said. Without a second glance he took us to his room, asking the receptionist to bring Simon's notes. After a few questions he helped Simon onto the couch for a quick examination, and was already preparing a syringe to take blood by the time the receptionist came in. I watched as blood was drawn into the syringe and noticed that it was not the usual dark red colour. I looked at the doctor and he looked at me without saying anything. He asked the receptionist to call a taxi to take the sample urgently to Dorchester Hospital. 'Now I want you to go home,' he said to me, 'and Simon should rest in bed with plenty to drink, anything he likes. I will come round to see you as soon as I get the blood results, which will be within the next couple of hours.'

It was a shock but a relief that something was being done at last and we were no longer being ignored. The doctor was as good as his word and came round after lunch. He came straight to the point. 'The counts are so skewed it set off alarms in haematology.' I didn't know if he meant that literally, but he went on. 'Simon needs immediate transfusing. They will be matching blood as we speak. It's a wonder he was able to walk into the surgery, or stand up at all, the state he's in.'

'The receptionist made us wait for hours and it was only pure luck we caught you at all,' I said.

'Yes, my apologies. I will look into that. Meanwhile we need to get Simon to Dorchester where they are waiting for him. If you can drive him that will be better than getting an ambulance because it means you can leave straight away. I'm giving you a letter for the consultant, Dr Johnston. You should get hold of your husband to meet you at the hospital.'

I didn't know how to get a message to Adam except through the Holstein office and he would most likely be on the road somewhere. But more urgently, I wanted to know what was wrong with Simon. 'What did the blood results show?' I asked.

'All we know at the moment is that the problem is in his bone marrow, affecting the normal production of blood cells. A marrow biopsy will show what is going on and that will be done as soon as you get to the hospital. They won't waste any time, I can assure you.'

'Is he going to be all right?'

'He will be in safe hands at Dorchester. Dr Johnston will be able to tell you much more than I can. You need to gather up a few things for Simon and get yourselves off, then I can tell them that you are on your way.'

I was relying on the old Hillman to get us there and prayed that it would not choose this moment to have a seizure, but it met the occasion splendidly and with unusual speed we made good time.

At the hospital, a team of doctors and nurses was waiting: the paediatric consultant Dr Johnston, his SHO (senior house officer), a pathologist (that's what he said he was) with an assistant, a junior doctor, the ward sister and a staff nurse. They were expecting Simon to be brought in on a trolley and were surprised when he walked in and greeted them politely in the unselfconscious way he thought was natural when meeting people. We were taken to a private room where a transfusion had already been set up, and Simon was helped into his pyjamas while the staff nurse went through the admission procedure with me. As soon as this was done, Dr Johnston took me into a side room and told me that a bone marrow biopsy was needed straight away, and I might like to wait somewhere else while this was being done; but Simon said he wanted me there with him. Although he was given a local anaesthetic it was a gruesome procedure to extract marrow from his sternum, but he was brave and afterwards went into a deep sleep, probably exhausted by the day's events. It did not occur to me that he was being monitored at that point in case he slipped into a coma, and that there was some doubt among the doctors whether he would survive the night.

I was thinking about Louise and Pete arriving back from school and being told the news by a friend of mine who was staying to look after them until I could get home. There were no mobile phones in 1980 and I went to look for a pay phone to get an urgent message to Adam as there had been no response to my earlier call from home. I wanted to call Ros as well, who was my anchor in any family crisis, and, importantly, call home to Louise and Pete who would be very worried by now. Pay phones in my experience tend to be hostile machines that gobble up coins without any guaranteed connection, and it was maddening to be caught like this in my calamitous situation being harassed by a pay phone. After a crazy amount of time struggling with it in the lobby of the children's ward, rummaging in my purse for spare coins, I was anxious to go back to Simon. The staff had been looking for me, Simon was still asleep, and Dr Johnston wanted to talk to me.

He had preliminary results from the biopsy. 'It's not good news,' he said. 'But you will have suspected as much. What were your suspicions?'

'It was obvious that he was severely anaemic, but I didn't know why, and didn't suspect the very high white count found by the lab.'

'No, that kind of result would be a surprise to anyone. But it fits with the marrow picture, which shows acute lymphoblastic leukaemia.'

'It can't be anything like that,' I said sharply, as if contradicting him, too shocked to properly take in what he was saying. 'Not so suddenly, it isn't possible.'

'Yes, unfortunately, and it's T-cell leukaemia, which makes it more difficult to deal with. That and his age, just entering puberty. I'm giving you the stark facts because there isn't time to be more diplomatic. Due to the very late presentation, the next twelve to twenty-four hours will be critical.' I wasn't expecting that and was too shattered to speak. He said gently, 'Would you like me to tell Simon? He keeps asking. He has already done a bit of self-diagnosing, reading about leukaemia in medical books that you have at home.'

'If he got as far as that all by himself, why didn't he say anything?'

'I asked him that question and he said he didn't want to worry you.' That's typical, I thought, remembering my old paediatric boss, Dr Zilberg saying, 'Children are clever and mothers are stupid.'

I was stricken with guilt at having failed to get the right help for Simon quickly enough, and felt it was my responsibility to tell him that what he suspected was true, while trying to find something positive in the circumstances to hold onto. 'I would rather tell him myself,' I said, 'so we can talk about it and get our heads around it. How could we have come to this – why was no one listening or helping?'

'Leukaemia is notoriously difficult to detect in the early stages when cells are building up inside the bone marrow. It is only when they tip over into the circulation that they are discovered.'

'Simon was anaemic and weak and losing weight long before that happened.'

'Not that long if you look at his notes, and now he's here, all the latest advances in treatment are available if he can get through this current crisis period. We are in touch with the teams at Westminster (hospital) and Great Ormond Street, and you will have the option to take him to either of those centres for treatment if he becomes well enough.'

'Thank you for all this. There are no words for how grateful we are, and if my husband was here he would say the same.'

When I went to see Simon, he was awake, sitting up in bed, smiling and hungry which had to be a good sign, I thought. The transfusion was obviously having an effect so that the deathly colour which had been creeping into his skin was now replaced with a rosy tinge, but he still looked desperately fragile; reduced to a wisp of the boy he had once been, though his spirit was undimmed. 'When will Dad be coming?' he asked.

'I haven't been able to get hold of him yet, despite leaving urgent messages at his office. I'm sure he will get here as soon as he can.'

'Don't wait for him. In case I'm stuck here for a bit, I need you to get more of my things from home and bring them tomorrow, if you can come.'

'The staff think I should stay with you overnight.'

'Why? Where would you sleep?'

'I think they have a folding-bed type of thing for mums or dads. It's just to keep you company. Other mums sometimes stay the night if they are worried.'

'Well, this is different. You don't need to be worried.'

'I'll have to check with the staff that it's all right for me to go home now you're looking better.' I went to talk to the nurses, who were reluctant to let me go at first, but I persuaded them with assurances that I would stay close to a phone.

Adam was at home when I got back, not having received any of the messages and knowing only what the children and friend had told him. As I went through the events of the day, he found it hard to believe that things could have got so bad, and the children went very quiet as a sense of unreality came over us. Adam's illness with all the subsequent effects and dislocation of our lives had been bad enough, but we had come through it and naturally thought nothing worse could happen, so there must somehow be a mistake. Pete was the one who broke the silence by asking, 'Can we go and see Simon tomorrow?'

'We'll have to see how he is, and tell the school what has happened,' I told him, glad to think about a practical suggestion for the next day.

'I don't want to go to school tomorrow, anyway,' he said. 'Everyone will be asking about Simon.' We all stayed up late that evening trying to process the enormity of this latest body blow. How could this have happened? What causes leukaemia? How could someone as strong and healthy as Simon get it? Later, when we all eventually went to bed I was unable to sleep, and phoned the ward several times for an update. The night staff were sympathetic and didn't mind at all, but the report was always the same: 'No change.'

In the morning I asked if the children could visit but was told only parents for the time being, so Louise and Pete decided they had better face school after all rather than stay at home without us. Adam had to cancel appointments at work and make a few calls before we went in his car to the hospital. This was a luxury for me after the Hillman, still doing service as our family car, kept on life-support, scraping through its MOT with a friendly garage man who was a Minx enthusiast. I was impatient and anxious to see how Simon was getting on after a long night of constant 'obs' (observations) carried out to monitor his condition, which he understood were necessary but complained it meant he couldn't get a proper sleep. Electronic monitoring devices were not yet available, so checking was done manually.

He was in bed, cushioned on pillows, looking wan but he tried to sit up when we went in, his face breaking into a smile as he saw Adam. I stood back to let Adam go and give him a hug, but instead of embracing him, he stood at the bedside and they shook hands which seemed strangely formal and unemotional in the circumstances. I think Adam simply couldn't allow himself to show his feelings in case we all went to pieces.

When the doctors came to do their rounds we were given a full briefing by the team and told that the present focus was on stabilising Simon's condition while he was too weak for treatment to start, but the overload of malignant cells in his blood remained at a dangerous level so this had to be weighed against other factors. We were given a candid assessment of the situation with all its options and Dr Johnston suggested that Simon himself could be involved in decisions. I thought this was very perceptive of him and entirely agreed, knowing that this is what Simon would want. I had talked to him about the diagnosis the previous evening before going home and he was philosophical. 'I'd already done a lot of thinking about it, long before we got to this stage,' he said.

'Why didn't you say anything?'

'Nothing was going to make our doctor change his mind until something else happened, so I had to wait for that to happen, which turned out to be a stroke of luck when the locum doctor took over and looked at it differently. But now we've got Dr Johnston, it couldn't be better.'

He was so grown up about it. For a boy his age (fourteen) to use this kind of logic to make sense of an utterly calamitous sequence of events was humbling, but it didn't make me feel any less guilty about my failure to force intervention sooner.

Adam was so stricken that he could barely speak. The hospital environment and discussions with doctors unnerved him. He was impatient to leave and go home so that we could be alone with our thoughts and support for each other. Simon sensed this. 'You don't have to stay if the doctors have talked to you. Now that Mum has brought my books and things I'll be all right. I seem to be falling asleep all the time so I don't need anyone to keep me company. You can come as much as you like, of course,' he added.

Apart from Ros, we had not been in touch with other members of the family and needed to alert them before word got around, but it was a painful process. Everyone was seized with the same disbelief that we felt, along with the same questions: how could this have happened to someone like Simon who was a rugby player and cross-country runner? It defied reason and left us feeling helpless. Fa was still away, and Muz was no help at times like this, having become so introspective that any event or activity outside her domestic orbit was too confusing for her to think about. Elizabeth and Peter had distanced themselves since we moved to Bridport and I was reluctant to call on them due to my embarrassment at being so much in their debt, but they were entirely sympathetic and full of concern as soon as we told them. 'You must contact Ma and Pa (Alison and Cen) straight away,' they said, 'before you get in touch with Howleigh.'

Alison was distraught by the news, writing: 'Poor dear Simon, how utterly dreadful for him, and for all of you. If there is anything you need, or anything I can do, please say.'

The aunts at Howleigh were similarly overwhelmed when they heard, to the extent that life in their household came to a standstill. 'We can't think about anything else, or do anything else, while we're waiting for news each day. We're having prayers said in church for darling Simon, and we're asking everyone we know to pray for him.' They wanted to visit but this was still restricted to parents.

We didn't know how long it might take him to build up enough strength to start treatment, or even if he would make it that far. Dr Johnston was wary about giving a prognosis but was impressed that Simon was showing such resilience. Adam was much less upbeat and I was worried about the effect this latest crushing blow might have on him. I had always put him first as head of the family, but Simon's needs were greater now than his, so that had to be my priority. Remembering what the psychologist had said about releasing Adam to go his own way.

My fear had always been that if anything happened to one of the children it would be Pete who was delicate as a small child and nervous, afraid to go to sleep at night because he had terrible nightmares. I was protective of him while allowing Simon to go his own way because he was fearless and independent. This led to accidents but Simon had always been physically and mentally tough, appearing least likely to be struck down. Louise had given us a fright with her kidney problem, needing complex surgery at the age of eleven, so we had been through that ordeal, and then Adam's illness. It seemed too cruel just as we were celebrating his recovery, to be confronted with a new and worse disaster, so suddenly, without any warning at all.

Going back to Africa was now reduced to a pipe dream, I thought, but Adam clung to possibilities. 'The Holstein job was never supposed to be more than a stop-gap,' he reminded me. 'We can't survive on the pay I'm getting, and whatever happens with Simon, I need to earn a living wage. I have been looking at contract work with companies that supply managers for agricultural projects internationally. Don't worry, I'm not abandoning you, especially not now, but I'm looking at options.'

'Where?'

'All over. Places like Egypt, Libya, Dubai. Even China.'

'How soon?'

'It depends on Simon, but in any case I wouldn't be away all the time. Some of these jobs come with regular breaks, fares home, expenses paid, the lot.'

'Won't it be lonely for you stuck on a project somewhere completely foreign, way out in the sticks?

'I can put up with that if I'm earning good money.'

'Good money isn't everything. Keeping the family together is everything. I can get a job. We could manage. What kind of life will we have if you go away?'

'I need to do this, darling. You know that. But for the time being, keeping Simon alive is all that matters.'

After the first few days when we spent more time at the hospital than at home, Simon's condition began to stabilise and Adam was able to go back to work. Once a week, Dr Johnston held a clinic at the children's ward for leukaemia patients and I was introduced to other parents in my situation, while Simon was taken to meet some of the children. They were in various stages of treatment, all much younger than he was, and some of the mothers I noticed were pregnant. I felt a pang on seeing this, realising that it might be instinctive to want to create a new life when an existing one was in danger. But I was forty-two, with a husband who was away a lot and planning to go away even more, so my chances of having another child were slender, even if Adam agreed.

Meeting the other parents was like joining a very small and peculiarly exclusive club, because leukaemia was such a rare disease, but it was not the kind of close-knit association anyone would want to join in a bond of sadness and trepidation with other members. Two of the other families were from the Bridport area while a small cluster of cases had come from a tiny village called Wool. This made us wonder if there could be risk factors at these localities but we were told the incidence of cases was too small to be significant. I didn't find the companionship of other parents very helpful as their anxiety and stories of children in the clinic who had died, were not uplifting when I wanted to be hopeful. Simon took the view that he was going to get better and nothing was going to stop him, so his story would be different from the others.

As soon as he was strong enough to start treatment he was given the standard chemotherapy drug used for leukaemia, Vincristine, which takes its name from the periwinkle plant, *Vinca*. In contradiction of such a benign appearance with cheerful blue or pink flowers, the periwinkle produces an alkaloid poison which usefully kills cancer cells, while causing less harm to healthy cells. In order to achieve this balance the dose has to be carefully calibrated and this was done with regular blood tests. Once

Simon was allowed home, we had to be at the hospital early on a clinic day for blood to be taken as a first step in the process. We then spent the rest of the day waiting to see doctors and going through treatment. The leukaemia clinic was held weekly, but in between times children could be re-admitted to the ward day or night if there was any change or anxiety, or we could phone for advice. It was a very reassuring and caring service and a very personal one. Concern for the children was so genuine I had seen doctors and nurses in tears when there was a setback, and when there was a death the loss was felt deeply by all.

Chemotherapy was aimed at initiating a remission of symptoms, with the hope that this could last for months or even years, but total recovery was recognised only after five years if there had been no relapse during that time. Simon endured weeks of toxic and debilitating chemotherapy with his usual fortitude and entered remission remarkably quickly, confident that the disease was beaten and normal life would now be resumed. It was like a miracle, as if he had never been ill, and the only difference was that he had lost all his hair and was still weak and easily tired. He was impatient to get back to school but the Education Department officer who was now involved since Simon had missed a whole term, arranged for a home tutor to come to the house each day. This was a retired teacher who was very chatty, and when I commented on this after hearing what I thought was great deal of talking going on during the lesson, she said that she was delighted to discover Simon was a Latin enthusiast and they were practising Latin conversation together. I hoped they might be doing maths as well but didn't like to be too nosy. It was an excellent service provided by the state on one hand, while another hand of the state took away his child benefit because, I was told, if he was not in school he didn't qualify. This seemed perverse when the reason was illness. I was beginning to learn about the British welfare system.

Just after Simon came home, our landlord decided to move back into his house and gave us notice to quit. I had a panic with Adam away on his Holstein rounds, while still looking at jobs abroad, so I would have to find somewhere by myself. Rents were high and properties hard to find because Bridport was a popular place to live, so I thought maybe we could get a council house in our current situation with Simon. I made an appointment with the Bridport housing officer and was shown into a large office in a rather grand building next to a public car park. The officer remained seated at his desk as I went in and waved me to sit down. When I explained what had happened to our family, he leaned forward and fixed me with a cold stare, saying: 'I know your sort. You live the life of Riley in some fancy place abroad, then you come back when it suits you to get free treatment on the NHS. And now you think you're entitled to a free house as well.' He sat back in his chair, glaring at me, and I felt my face go red as I summoned a reply to this stinging accusation.

'We are British, by birth and by right, and have paid National Insurance stamps all the time that we have lived in other countries. My family are not scroungers. It is only out of desperation that I have come to see you.'

'Whatever you say for yourself, we have nothing to offer. The list for housing is as long as your arm. People have been on it for years. The only way you could get council accommodation is by sitting in the road with your suitcases, holding an eviction notice from your landlord.'

'That sounds very uncivilised,' I said, 'but thank you for the information.' I stood up, not wanting to spend another moment in the presence of such a hateful man and feeling hot tears about to shame me further, I almost ran out of the door and past the startled receptionist in the hallway. My belief in British values was badly shaken. To be humiliated by a person in authority who was employed to assist or at least show sympathy to someone in my situation was bewildering. But as soon as I was outside in the cool spring air I felt better, and took a side road to the high street where I could look in the window of an estate agent. There were pictures of houses for rent and houses for sale, and, I thought, if I am to live in England with the children while Adam goes somewhere else, we could have our own house instead of renting. We can use some of the profit from the gold sale for a deposit, and we can afford a mortgage on the money which Adam will soon be earning. I'll have to persuade him when he comes home for the weekend, and have some house details to show him.

Aside from the housing officer and any others like him that I had yet to meet, Bridport people were delightful and the town itself was a hub of activity and friendliness spilling out of historic buildings. The high street had been designed for 'rope-walks', when ropes were made by teams of workers who walked up and down the street twisting fibre to make ropes that provided Bridport with a thriving industry.

Excited by the prospect of owning our own home at last, I went inside the shop to talk to an agent, which was cathartic, erasing my experience with the housing officer when the house agent welcomed my enquiry. I soon found that the kind of property I thought we could afford was the most basic of houses and the selection was limited, but I took some leaflets to show the children and get their views. 'It doesn't matter, Mum, if it's a shabby house because it will be our home and we will love it, even if snooty people don't want to come and visit,' Simon said, looking at the photos.

'We need to be near a bus stop for getting to school,' Louise suggested.

'And near to the sea for fishing,' Pete added.

'One of these houses is in Morcombelake, which is on the way to school, and it says it's next door to a farm with cows, so that would be nice,' Simon pointed out.

'Yes, that was the one I thought was more like our kind of place than a terraced house in town on a busy road with its front door right on the street,' I said.

'Can we go and look at the Morcombelake house?'

'We'll have to see what Dad says. He doesn't know about the idea of buying our own place yet.'

When he came home the next weekend, we showed him the leaflet with a photo of the house, which I had secretly been to see and was smitten despite the fact that it was more like a large caravan than a house. My attachment to the trailer we had lived in the previous year may have influenced my view, but Adam was not impressed. 'For Christ sake, it's a frigging prefab, not a proper house.'

'That's why it's cheap,' I said, hoping the low price would spark an interest.

'It's not that cheap.'

'You can't argue about £29,900 for a three-bedroom house with a garage and a garden, plus stupendous views over farmland to Golden Cap and the sea. It's unique. Anyway we like it, and we haven't got much time to find a new place. The people selling it want a quick sale because the husband is changing his job. Like you,' I added. 'Please come and see it. I know you'll feel differently once you see the location. It makes sense to buy a house for ourselves now we have to think what's best for Simon while he and the rest of us are stuck in England. Renting is just throwing money away instead of using it to pay a mortgage.'

'You haven't given me much time to think about it, but you're probably right. We've got a bit extra in the bank since doing so well with the gold price so I expect we can scrape up a deposit.'

'Will you come and see the house, then?'

'I don't need to. I won't be living in it. If it suits you and the children and you're happy with it, then you can tell the agent to go ahead, and when you need the money I'll get it sent over.'

'What do you mean, you won't be living in it?'

'I've got a new job. I was waiting to tell you about it after the contract is safely signed and sealed, but to all intents and purposes it's in the bag.'

'I do wish you wouldn't talk in clichés. What is this job, and more to the point – where is it?'

It's in Tanzania, on Mafia Island, south of Zanzibar, about a hundred miles by sea from Dar (Dar es Salaam). The main industry of the island is coconuts and most of them are grown by a company with large plantations, where they need a manager. It's a perfect job for me because the company also runs a herd of Jerseys. There is a decent manager's house, I've seen photos of it, and a Land Rover and motorbike for transport. The company has its own power station supplying electricity, so it's all quite civilised. You will be able to come for the kind of holidays that tourists pay a fortune for. I know you'll love it, and when Simon is well enough, all of you can come. The children will be in their element.'

'When do you start?'

'As soon as possible, I'm told, which should be only a matter of weeks from now.'

'I know it's good news and what you have been looking for, but we will miss you dreadfully. It doesn't feel right for the family to be split up, especially just now. I wish you didn't have to go.'

'I know, darling, but we have to be practical and this is the best way for the family to be properly supported. I've got another piece of good news for you: this will make you feel better about my departure. The

Holstein people are letting me keep the Vauxhall when I leave, for a small consideration, so you will be able to have it and drive around in style, scrapping the Hillman.'

'Oh great! That really is good news. Every time I set off for the hospital with Simon I worry about getting there without more bits falling off into the road, or the engine conking out altogether.'

'Quite so, sweetheart. You see, our run of bad luck has turned, and things will only get better from now on, with Simon on the mend.'

I felt more cautious but could never resist Adam's optimism when he was roused by a new idea or project. I thought he must be right about our luck turning when the purchase of the house went through without a hitch and we were able to move in with his help before he left for Tanzania. Our friends laughed when they came to visit and joked about us living in a '*pondokkie*', which was a Rhodesian word for a tacky house, but we didn't care, and anyway it wasn't true. The house was sturdy and sound, but it wasn't pretty, and did look as if it had been assembled from a kit consisting of concrete panels. None of this mattered to us because it stood on a site of unparalleled beauty on the sunny side of a hill facing the sea. The hill with its valley and surrounding countryside was National Trust land, with a footpath through fields and woods ending in a scramble down to the beach. All of this formed an immense natural playground for children of all ages, while on the other side of the valley, a steep climb led to Golden Cap and a coastal path that meandered all the way to Weymouth and beyond.

The move energised Simon, who was soon well enough to go back to school while still having regular checks at the hospital. Before his first day back, during morning assembly, the headmaster at Woodroffe spoke about Simon's illness and how the treatment had left him with no hair, so pupils were asked to show kindness and not tease him. This appeal had no effect whatever and Simon was followed around by boys shouting, 'Bald Eagle.' 'It didn't bother me,' Simon told us. 'I shouted back at them: "Better bald than dead." It seemed to shut them up as they didn't know what to say after that.' Within a few weeks his hair started to grow back and it was dark and curly this time, which, together with a tan acquired that summer and his teenage body beginning to fill out, attracted girls and other friends, so he always had an entourage.

It was difficult to judge how much the impact of Simon's illness and rehabilitation affected Pete as he was inevitably side-lined to some extent in the turmoil, but kept his feelings to himself. He had his own friends, in particular Ian who had been his first friend at Charmouth School. They had both moved on to Woodroffe and caught the same bus with the others as it puttered through several villages, picking up children along the way. At weekends Simon and Pete with Ian and other friends went exploring the woods below our house, making dens among the trees where there was a lonely ruined house said to be haunted, which added to the eerie sensations of the wild valley. In a glade, Simon was elated to discover a meadow full of butterflies, and took me to see them where they flocked among wild flowers open to the sun. 'When the chrysalises appear I'm going to collect some to keep safe in boxes at home over the winter, then I can watch new butterflies emerge when spring comes. It will be a surprise to see which kinds come out, and amazing to have them flying around my room. Then I'll open the window so they can all fly away.'

Our long overdue household boxes after travelling thousands of miles on sea voyages before being locked in storage for months, had now caught up with us and been unpacked. But some of the crates had gone missing, including some of those with much-loved books and Simon's precious butterfly collection in its hand-crafted cabinet. He was calm about it: 'I've stopped wanting to collect butterflies now,' he said. 'I want to watch them alive and free, spreading their wings and getting on with life.'

Chapter 11

After Adam left, I was surprised to find how quickly we settled into easy routines and appeared to be getting on quite well on our own with just the four of us at home. At first I felt guilty about this and thought I should be missing him more, but he had needed a lot of looking after over the years and it was something of a liberation to be free of that extra burden. I began to understand what the psychiatrist meant by letting him go and no longer acting as his PA. I had thought this kind of support was normal and it was a revelation that roles were changing now in the eighties when modern wives expected husbands to look after themselves while sharing housework and childcare. 'I'd rather have you in my arms than my arms in the sink,' Adam would say as he carried his plate from the table to the kitchen, turning to give me a hug on his way out as he left it there.

The only way to communicate once he arrived on Mafia Island was by letter and these could take up to a month to arrive. The island's telephone service relied on a switchboard manned by a single operator who was more often absent than present, and due to the cost of calls these were best saved for emergencies. I wrote long letters in ink on thin airmail paper and Adam replied with enticing descriptions of the island and life among the coconuts. He was happy again, back in familiar territory with people who spoke Kiswahili and whose patterns of thought and customs he understood. Growing coconuts was a new challenge he welcomed, but it was the Jersey herd that gave him most joy. Milk supplied from the dairy was an important addition to the meagre diet of islanders and butter from rich Jersey cream was an important export, flown to Dar es Salaam by aircraft with names like Twin Otter and Beaver. Coconut cargoes went to Dar and more distant ports by sea and were loaded onto dhows from the beach at low tide or, in the case of company goods, onto their small freighter. The images conjured from Adam's letters made us impatient to see the island for ourselves as soon as Simon was well enough and we could all go for a holiday.

The name and address of Adam's new employer was needed on a form at the bank and when I wrote *Mafia Coconuts Ltd, Mafia Island, Tanzania*, the girl on the counter thought I was trying to be funny. 'You can't have *Mafia* as a name,' she said. 'It wouldn't be accepted.' I explained that it was a Swahili word and if she looked on a map she would see the island with its name, but she remained sceptical, and after that always looked at me suspiciously when I went in to cash cheques or for any other reason.

The bank manager was also wary of me since I had opened a personal account for myself, separate from the joint account I shared with Adam, and a rather large transfer from another bank appeared in my account. The manager asked to see me about this and when I explained that it was a gift from a friend, he looked doubtful. 'Who is this friend?' he wanted to know. 'The bank has a responsibility to check sources of money coming into customer accounts.'

'You can check with the other bank that the money is from someone entirely respectable, working in finance.'

'Customer information between banks is confidential. You will have to give me the details yourself so that I can check them.'

There was no need to hide anything from the bank so I told him who the friend was and his eyebrows went up in surprise. Not because he had ever heard of this person, but the name of the financial institution and the position held was enough.

This was Lanner, who on hearing about Simon wanted to help in a way that could be done tactfully. It was an extremely generous amount of money and impossible not to be aware that it came with loving concern, not just for Simon but for me as well. Lanner was at the peak of his career, attended by success in every area of his life. He wrote in one of his letters that nothing pleases a man more than waking each day to a job he enjoys and a happy home. Wealth came naturally to him because he'd always had it, and was unstinting in his kindness to friends and charities alike. Our brief romance when we were much younger clearly still touched him but he had married well, had a matching pair of children and, as one of my friends remarked about all the people we knew who had gone up in the world, 'Even their dogs are the right sort of dogs and get taken for walks by servants.'

Charles and his wife were doing less well at their Georgian ruin, which was swallowing money in restoration work, while attempts to generate income from a plant nursery in the walled garden had come to nothing when the nursery developer pulled out. A scheme for holiday flats was allowed and these now opened in one of the wings with a restaurant in the same wing to cater for visitors. Charles's wife was an outstanding cook and inspired creator of new dishes so her inventive menus soon became famous among the clientele. This should have brought success, but the house and its grounds continued to demand onerous levels of investment. I wanted to help and offered to do this in practical ways such as filling in when they had staffing problems, which was often. Sometimes I weeded flowerbeds or waited at tables in the restaurant, which was always full and very busy. Problems were often overlooked by the manager and customers sometimes left without paying. This frustrated me as I ran around trying to fill gaps in the service, but I had my own pressures at home to attend to at the same time with two teenage boys vying for prominence and clashing with Louise.

The shock of his illness jolted Simon into awareness of life as precious and too easily lost, prompting him to greater efforts at school and, to our surprise, after only a short time he was moved up a class. He was not allowed to take part in sports and this was a major disappointment, but he was untroubled. 'I'm not going to get depressed about it,' he said. 'Instead of physical exercise I'm going to exercise my brain and study science subjects so I can be a doctor later on. I know that's definitely what I want to do after seeing how hospitals work.'

Louise, who found Simon's enthusiasms irritating, was especially irked by them since starting A-levels. There was limited room to escape now we were living in a small bungalow with plasterboard walls and her room was next to the kitchen where Radio 2 chatted all day from the windowsill. She retaliated with Radio 1, played loudly from her own room, insisting that the monotonous beat helped her to concentrate.

Ros came often, arriving with baskets and bags of food she had cooked herself or bought from smart supermarkets. She helped redesign the cramped space of our prefab and one weekend she and Louise demolished a wall between the kitchen and sitting/dining room, so we had an open-plan living area and this was transforming. She always remembered birthdays and had to remind me when these were due because I had a tendency to forget anniversaries of any kind, including my wedding date. Adam was better at remembering and ordering flowers which arrived as a surprise when I had forgotten the day, but he wasn't here anymore and Ros did her best to keep us up to the mark.

A letter had come from Fa announcing that he and Babs were coming for the weekend of my birthday so that we could have a proper family celebration. When Ros heard about it, she offered to come and help, anticipating the strains imposed by them when visiting. Fa's restless energy combined with Babs' incessant twittering caused jitters in any normally calm household, so Ros was coming as a buffer.

Rearranging rooms to provide enough beds for guests in our bijou house had become routine since we now lived in a prime tourist area. Friends and relations arrived to sun themselves on nearby beaches or lie out on our small green carpet of lawn where it faced Golden Cap and the sea. Fa was ecstatic the first time he saw the view when he and Babs came to visit, and before even accepting a cup of tea after their long drive he went striding off to climb six hundred feet to the top of the Cap.

On the weekend of my birthday they arrived with a large parcel they said was a special present for me but I must not look at it or try to guess what it was. They wanted it to be a complete surprise. This aroused my curiosity and Ros's suspicion because it was unusual for them to produce anything lavish. After the parcel was stowed (even more suspiciously needing to go in the fridge), Fa leapt out of the front door to go and conquer Golden Cap once more, and Babs retreated to bed as she always did soon after arriving. 'To recover from your father's driving,' she would say. 'He's either hot on the pedal one moment like Stirling Moss shooting along, or he's gone into a trance slumped in his seat thinking about something while the car crawls along and people are hooting at us.' Ros and I knew this well. We dreaded driving with him. He was clever and dextrous in so many ways – how could he be such a bad driver? We were familiar with the signs when he was feeling tense due to some random irritation or setback. He would sit close to the wheel, gripping it with both hands, knuckles white like organ stops, eyes fixed ahead with steely determination as if he were driving a tank into battle. We knew what came next when a series of thumps on the accelerator made the car go off in a streak while we cowered in our seats, knees drawn up to our faces (no seat belts then), waiting for something terrible to happen. Usually it didn't and the steam slowly drained out of Fa as his foot eased on the accelerator, but sometimes a squeal of brakes and violent swerving announced a near miss, and of course it was never his fault. At the other extreme he could be lost in contemplation on some cerebral theme, driving the car like a lawn mower, forgetting to turn off until someone shouted loudly enough to indicate that he had missed a turning, which again could never be attributed to any error on his part.

The mysterious parcel in the fridge was removed by Fa and Babs after lunch on my birthday and carried into the back porch. The porch was a small glass-walled appendage tacked onto the back door to protect it from rain and weather: a good place, they thought, to prepare the surprise for my birthday, away from prying eyes.

'You mustn't peek while we're doing this,' Babs said as the treasure was carried through from the kitchen. Ros and I could not contain ourselves and crept around the back of the house to peer into the porch while staying out of view. Inside, we could see them hunched over a large lump of something white and floppy, which Babs was moulding together with her hands while Fa wielded a big needle threaded with string to stitch portions of the mass together. They whispered and giggled like conspirators as the sewing proceeded, until after an hour or so the reconstructed lump was wrapped up again.

'Dinner tonight is entirely our treat,' Babs announced on returning from this effort and looking pleased with whatever it was that had been achieved.

'You won't have to do a thing. Ros can show us how the cooker works. We need to start the oven early and the kitchen will be out of bounds to all of you, including the children. You are completely free to go off and enjoy yourselves for as long as you like until this evening.'

If Fa was a bad driver, Babs was an even worse cook. Oblivious to any shortcoming, disastrous meals were served at her home, or ours when she took over, but nothing ever daunted her with Fa at her side, smiling indulgently. Any attempt at diversion when she was set on a course of action stood no chance, so Ros and I left her to preside over the birthday treat while we took the children for a cream tea in Chideock.

At dinner time we were summoned to the table and sat down expectantly as inviting aromas drifted from the kitchen, suggesting unusual success this time. A large platter was brought in ceremoniously by Fa and placed in the centre of the table to the accompaniment of excited clapping by Babs. 'Here it is!' she cried as all of us leaned forward in unison to see what it was. Silence followed, not knowing what to say while we gazed at an object which for a second I feared might be a pig's head wrapped in something wrinkled and crispy to disguise its shape. Ros was the first to speak. 'What is it?'

'Can't you see?' Babs responded eagerly. 'It's a turkey. A birthday turkey. We got it specially for today, as a celebration.'

'What's happened to it?' Ros said, not even trying to sound tactful.

Fa cleared his throat, which was always a warning that something unwelcome was about to be revealed. 'There is a turkey factory near to our village so we went to get one for Wendy's birthday, and found they had special offers on birds that had got caught in machinery while being processed. You can see how it made sense to get a special offer when there was nothing wrong with it otherwise.'

'Except it hasn't got any legs and only one wing,' Ros pointed out.

'Yes.' He paused, his moustache twitching at the implied criticism. 'The rest of the bird is intact, and there's nothing wrong with it, as I said.' He was getting rattled and Babs stepped in. 'Start carving,' she told him, 'then everyone will see how good it is inside.'

Ros leant to whisper in my ear. 'Do you think it might actually be road kill. I wouldn't put it past them.'

'Shush, don't let the children hear. We'll just have to pretend it's Christmas with a normal turkey, not something that looks as if dogs have got at it.'

Ros was my ally during mad times with our parents and when Muz said she was coming on a visit to see how Simon was getting on, I sent an SOS and Ros came straight away. There was another reason for her visit, since Muz was behaving in odd ways and we were worried about her state of mind. 'Do you think living with Andy is driving her crazy?' Ros wondered. 'No one could stay normal for very long banged up with him, inhaling his vapours as they shuffle around in the same cramped space together.'

'Muz hasn't been normal for years,' I said. 'Not since Babs came along and snatched Fa from under her nose. He was her anchor and she's been adrift ever since. She even refuses to sleep in our spare room or go anywhere near it due to the horror of imagining Babs in bed with Fa, so she has Louise's room, but I can understand that. More out of line is the way she's getting haywire notions like making us take our own food if we go to stay with her, and then charging B&B rates for the privilege. That's not normal. It's something new.'

Andy refused to come with Muz to our house despite the opportunity for an outing in his beloved Austin. 'Andy finds it too tiring nowadays,' Muz said, but we thought the real reason was inertia, unwilling to exert himself and save Muz a series of train journeys to get from Suffolk to Dorset. That she could undertake this journey alone we concluded was reassuring, and indicated a state of good health. She certainly seemed in fine spirits when she hopped off the train at Axminster and looked very well, evidently enjoying the escape from household ties at home.

'I've got a present for you,' she said when we arrived at the house and carried her bags in. Ros and I exchanged glances, remembering the dismembered turkey. From one of the bags Muz produced a bottle with a flourish. 'I've brought you some of my home-made elderberry wine. It's awfully good. Andy and I have a glass every evening.' This was surprising, since Muz was teetotal and we had never seen Andy lift a glass of anything stronger than tap water. I took the bottle from Muz to thank her and was about to speak when I noticed there was no more than an inch or two of something inside, which looked like dregs. 'There's hardly anything in the bottle!' I blurted out.

'Surely you wouldn't expect me to bring a full one,' Muz replied. 'If you don't like it, I'll have it back. But you could at least try it, you and Ros.'

'We'll keep it for supper then,' I told her, trying not to look at Ros who was about to explode. Whether this was just another instance of Craddock stinginess, or something else, we began to be seriously concerned about Muz and how safe it was for her to be marooned in Suffolk with only the moronic Andy to look out for her. When there was a chance to talk to Ros later on her own, I said Elaine should be told of these developments. 'So all three daughters are involved instead of just you and me.' Elaine and her family had moved to Scotland where she was writing Christian books and achieving success as a published author, while Les was doing well in a new career connected with gas technology. They were busy with their jobs and teenage children, and communication with the rest of us was sparse. 'She wouldn't want to talk about it if we tried to involve her,' Ros said. 'The last time Muz visited them she reported that it was awkward because nothing of consequence was ever discussed. Elaine doesn't like to discuss 'difficult' subjects and it's certain that Muz's aberrations would come into this category and be linked to the sin of divorce in her eyes. Nothing is going to change Elaine's view on this, so we'll just have to look out for Muz the best we can on our own,' Ros concluded.

Simon continued to get better and was looking so well that I had to keep reminding myself of Dr Johnston's advice to remain cautious and not get our hopes up too much. Simon scoffed at this. 'I'm fine now,' he said, 'just waiting to be cleared for flying and then we can go to Mafia and see Dad.' We were all waiting impatiently for clearance to go, longing to see the island and be a family again. Each time I took Simon to the leukaemia clinic we waited nervously for the results of tests, hoping these would be good enough to risk travelling to a place with only the most basic medical facilities. It was a considerable risk because his immune system had been suppressed by chemotherapy and he would have little defence against the many diseases that might lurk on a tropical island.

An injection of gamma-globulin could temporarily boost his immunity for the trip and the medical team said he could have this when we were ready to go.

On clinic days Simon had to miss school as we set off early for the hospital and spent the whole day interminably waiting for test results before seeing consultants, so we seldom got home before tea time. Louise and Pete were used to looking after themselves, arriving back from school with no one at home, getting their own meals and clearing up. Simon and I took sandwiches and drinks for our long day at the hospital, and something to read to pass the time. On one of these days, reading a newspaper 'Lonely Hearts' column I saw the following message: *Middle-aged widower would like to meet educated lady for travelling and theatre, cinema and good food.* This is just what I need I thought. He's lonely, and I'm lonely. I can be a companion. It doesn't imply any commitment. I'll write to the box number in the paper and see who this is.

Within days I had a reply and could tell from the handwriting that this was a sensible man who was intelligent and caring. He said he had his own business, was recently widowed and missed his wife very much, to the extent that his secretary felt he needed cheering up and put the ad in the paper without telling him. He was now sifting through the replies and if I was not put off by his letter, perhaps I would like to telephone him, he suggested, giving me his number. I had to think about taking this next step, but was intrigued so I reached out and phoned. His name was Robert and he sounded 'normal', but this was no guarantee of respectability as my children quickly pointed out. They strongly disapproved of this association with a complete stranger. 'How do you know he isn't a kidnapper,' they said, 'or just after your money?'

'What money?' I laughed. 'No one is going to kidnap someone my age, and he can check out my address and see that we live in a shack so I'm not likely to have anything worth stealing.'

'Anyway you're still married to Dad. You can't go off on dates with other men.'

'He wants to meet me at his club in London where there will be other people, so it won't be like a date. In any case Dad often took Pippa and other old girlfriends on dates to the theatre and out to dinner when he was doing his rounds with the Holsteins, so I don't see how this is any different. It doesn't mean being unfaithful to each other.'

'If you go to meet this man at his club, you must leave all the details with us, so that if you disappear we can tell the police,' they said.

Ros and Gary lived near London so I arranged to stay the night with them after meeting Robert, intending to leave his club in time to get a train and then a taxi to their house. The children could look after themselves for a night and Louise was old enough at seventeen to be left in charge. All three of them liked to be left on their own unsupervised and trusted to be sensible and independent. They were more concerned about me than I was about them, and sent me off with strict instructions about phoning from the nearest public box after meeting Robert.

When I arrived at the club my first impression was disconcerting as I looked at the shiny cars parked outside including a silver Rolls and thought this kind of place is going to be too smart for me. Hesitating on the pavement I felt suddenly uncomfortable in my very ordinary dress and coat, and hoped Robert would turn out to be a genuine sort of person and not flashy. His instructions were to tell the concierge that I was meeting him there and a receptionist would take me to be introduced, which sounded a bit formal, but reassuring. This went to plan as I was taken inside and led through a series of rather grand rooms to the one where Robert was sitting. He rose with a smile to shake my hand as we were introduced, but he was so different from any image I might have had of him that it was a shock at first to meet him in person. He looked like an ageing pop star with black floppy hair and was wearing a rather camp black velvet suit, but he had a kind face and his handshake was firm and warm.

He was around mid-sixties I thought, a bit more than middle-aged and certainly eccentric in his style of dress, but I liked that. He won't be boring, I thought, and his desire to put me at ease in these unusual circumstances was comforting as we sat with drinks before dinner. Menus were brought and when we went through to the dining room it felt unreal to be sitting at a table for two with a new and congenial companion who was both amusing and well-informed. He said he'd had more than fifty replies to the newspaper advertisement but very few had accepted an invitation to meet for dinner and, of these, none had been suitable. I was alarmed. 'What do you mean – not suitable, what was wrong with them?'

'Most had stories of failed relationships or money lost through careless investments, and how they'd had a bad deal in life. Each one was more depressing than the last, which was not what my secretary promised by putting me up to this.' We laughed and I suggested a toast. 'Let's be optimists,' I said, and we raised our glasses to perpetual optimism, which led Robert to tell me how he started his business.

During National Service after leaving school he noticed that many spare parts for vehicles and machinery were imported from other countries, which surprised him because he thought these should be produced in Britain. He decided to manufacture a small range himself and produced samples that he showed to the army procurement officer with an offer to supply them at competitive prices. His offer was accepted and when he left the army he rented a factory, employed workers, and began production in earnest. Within a short time he built his own factory and switched to making steel blades for earth-moving equipment, which was more profitable because blades needed regular replacing. 'As of now,' he said, 'we are exporting to countries all over the world and still expanding, but everything depends on getting steel at the right price and staying competitive.'

I loved to hear this kind of success story and hoped it was all true and that he would take me to see his factory. 'Next time,' he said encouragingly, 'I would like to show you where I live, which is near Sandown Racecourse. I enjoy racing and it would be an honour if you accompanied me on a weekend.' It was all beginning to sound rather otherworldly and I felt cautious as we went on chatting and more wine was poured for me while Robert was drinking only soda water. I needed to remind myself not to get carried away, and allow enough time to catch my train. When I looked at my watch and explained that I was spending the night with my sister near Weybridge and must not miss the train, Robert said, surprised, 'I didn't know that your sister lived so close to where I live. I can give you a lift to her place. It will be on my way.'

I considered this before replying. I didn't really know him. I would be accepting a lift in a strange car, at night, in an area I didn't know at all. But it was clear that Robert was respected by staff at the club and he was well known there, so it seemed reasonable to conclude that accepting a lift from him would not only be safe but sensible as well. 'If you're sure it's no trouble that would be very kind,' I said. We collected my coat and overnight case from the hall porter who accompanied us outside and then did a very astonishing thing. He went to the passenger door of the silver Rolls which was still parked by the kerb and opened it. I stood on the pavement uncertainly, looking at Robert. He took my hand and said, 'Please don't be put off by the Rolls. I find it easier to drive at night than my other car. It practically drives itself – it almost knows its way home by now like a wise old horse. I hope you will find it comfortable.'

The porter continued to wait patiently for me to get in and any more hesitation would have looked foolish as well as ungrateful, so I slipped in, and the soothing smell of good leather reminded me of Fa's Jaguar and happy times in Malta. I settled down to enjoy the ride and Robert was right, the car seemed to drive itself as it hummed along velvety smooth with the marvel of its suspension, his hands light on the wheel as he leant back in his seat with audible sighs of pleasure. In a surprisingly short time we arrived at Ros and Gary's house on a small estate of maisonettes as if the car had been following radar. Robert carried my case to their door and thanked me with a quick kiss on each cheek, but before I had time to thank him in return, he had gone before the door opened.

'Did you really come in that Rolls?' Ros asked as she peered down the road to catch a glimpse of it disappearing. 'What happened?' They wanted to know all about the evening when I got inside, so I told them the whole story, which now sounded too surreal to be credible. 'Are you going to see him again?'

'I don't know. He left so quickly after dropping me off, nothing was suggested or arranged. I'll have to see what happens next. Whether he phones. Or whether I phone him. I need time to think about it. He's not at all what I expected. And the Rolls you saw, he's got two of them. One for driving in England and the other with left-hand drive for when he goes to France, where he has racing stables with a horse called Julius Caesar being trained for the next Derby.'

'Oh crumbs,' Ros said. 'Do you think it's true?'

'He also has his own plane, which he keeps at Gatwick for charity work, flying transplant organs for hospitals all over the place. He's passionate about this work and loves piloting his own plane, doing it all for free. The way he talks about it sounds so genuine and heartfelt, it's difficult to imagine he's making it up. Anyway, if we go on seeing each other I will be able to find out.'

'Do you want to go on seeing him?'

'I need to think about it, as I said. More particularly because he is quite an emotional guy. I'm sure he has more than a touch of Latin blood with all that black hair, even if it's dyed. He isn't just looking for someone to have dinner with and sit next to in the theatre. Whatever it says in the newspaper ad, it's obvious he needs a new wife or loving partner, not a part-time casual companion, which is all I could ever be.'

'But you liked him, didn't you?'

'What I liked was his vitality, his joy for life, his entrepreneurial spirit, his wide knowledge of all kinds of things and still wanting to discover more. I was drawn to that. It spoke to something inside me that would like to be the same.'

'What about Adam?'

'Yes, of course, he's my husband and I want to be with him. But we're living thousands of miles apart with no prospect of getting back together in any permanent sense if he refuses to live in England, while I have to be here.'

'Did you tell Robert that you're married?'

'Yes. I told him we were separated, which is true in all practical ways, and those practical ways make a marriage workable, or unworkable. Don't you agree?'

'Some married couples spend years apart for various reasons, including necessity, and still regard their marriages as rock solid.'

'Maybe I'm just being feeble, lacking the strength of character to sustain that connection. Or lacking faith in our parents' belief that physical contact is less important because spiritual bonds are stronger. It was total bunkum, allowing them to pack us off to distant schools with no shred of conscience. I don't believe in spiritual bonds replacing physical ones.'

'It was just an excuse to get rid of us.'

'You've become very cynical,' I said, and we laughed, which was our way of defusing painful memories.

The year had started with tension in the Falkland Islands, escalating to invasion of the islands by Argentina. Margaret Thatcher as Britain's Prime Minster took a tough line and despatched Royal Navy ships to the South Atlantic. It was the first time that Britain had been at war since the end of the Second World War and a shudder went through the country. At Woodroffe School, some of the boarders had fathers or mothers in the armed forces so there was anxiety for them, and fear of unknown consequences in this sudden conflict that no one had foreseen.

Simon had a friend in his class whose dad was in the Royal Marines and we waited to see if he would be deployed when others from his base joined the Falklands force. It was a time of waiting and not knowing what the next crisis might be. This applied just as much to our own situation with Simon, whose continuing reprieve relied on the results of weekly blood tests, as we waited and hoped he would stay well enough to spend the summer holidays in Mafia. 'I can't wait to see Dad and see what the island is like,' Simon kept saying. 'Dad says the fishing and snorkelling is tremendous. I know their hospital is primitive but we can stay in touch with the doctors here for advice, and we need to have faith that nothing bad will happen.' He was so upbeat and positive it was impossible to feel discouraged. All of us wanted to go to Mafia as much as he did.

Louise was learning to drive so the Vauxhall had 'L' plates fitted and I was the terrified instructor sitting beside her as she confidently pressed the pedals and surged off. The most unnerving moments came at corners where she either forgot or felt it unnecessary to slow down. We hurtled around these corners with centrifugal force throwing me about while Louise had the wheel to hold on to and thought nothing of it. Similarly, it should be obvious when seeing cyclists ahead, to slow down instead of doing a quick swerve at the last possible moment to avoid hitting them. After a few squeaky incidents Louise suggested that driving lessons with Uncle Peter might be less harrowing, and luckily he agreed. These proceeded with admirable calm and Louise remarked, 'The problem with you, Mum, teaching me, is that it's a case of fight or fright the whole time, while Uncle Peter never gets fussed.' She passed her test and then became useful as a taxi driver for her gang and the rest of us. A-levels were the next hurdle and it was frustrating because she wanted to do art combined with maths and English, but this was not allowed (maths had to go together with science subjects we were told), so she was forced to compromise. She was becoming a capable and assured young adult after long years of grungy teenage impertinence.

She wanted to meet Robert after he followed up our evening together with a series of phone calls, inviting me to his house for a weekend and, as soon as I could get away, a trip to Hawaii. I had enjoyed his company and found that we shared many similar views and concerns. His sense of social justice and citizenship in wanting to share his good fortune with others was encouraging, and made me want to hear more about the projects he had underway. When he told me how much tax he paid each year, it seemed a colossal sum, almost punitive, but he said he was glad to pay because it was his contribution to society and stable government. Most people try to limit their tax burden so it was refreshing to hear a different point of view and I looked forward to finding out more about him.

It was at least a month before I could go for the promised weekend and Robert said he would send his chauffeur, Ted, to meet me at Woking station. This was so far outside any normal experience for me, I felt apprehensive about what I was getting into but also elated to have found such an interesting new friend. On the train from Axminster I had been chatting to someone I knew in the same carriage and when we both got out at Woking, Robert's Rolls was there with Ted waiting. I caught a questioning look from the person I had been chatting to, but had no time to explain as I hopped in.

Robert's house was on a private estate of similar executive-style houses, all looking very trim and suburban. When the car drew up I automatically fumbled for the door handle before realising that Ted expected to come round and open the door for me, and when he did so, he gave me a kind smile instead of standing there inscrutably as I scrambled out. It was reassuring, and when Robert came out looking genuinely pleased to see me, I began to feel that everything might turn out all right. Ted took my case inside and handed it to Robert who said he would show me to my room first, so that I could unpack and settle in. The house felt like a film set, with expensive décor but no charm, and I began to feel less comfortable as we went upstairs. Most people would be impressed by this extravagant look, I thought, but would not love it. I lived in a tacky house but everyone loved it and visitors crowded in, oblivious to its deficiencies.

Robert opened a door and showed me into a bedroom suite panelled throughout in maple wood. The bed had a velvet canopy in pale gold to match and all the bedroom furniture was maple. 'From Heal's,' Robert said approvingly. 'My own suite is at the other end of the corridor so you will not be disturbed. I am a bad sleeper and very restless at night Make yourself at home and when you are ready, come downstairs. I will have champagne waiting.'

In any new place I always went first to a window, to look out and get a feel of where I was, and absorb the view. Even if it was a grimy backyard I was curious and wanted to see what was there. Other houses stood at a polite distance here, screened by their gardens with mature trees while Robert's garden, as expected, was formal with paths and hedges trimmed to a whisker. I unpacked, had a wash, and changed from my jeans into a dress I hoped was respectable enough for whatever came next.

When I was ready to go downstairs, I tried to remember which of the many identical maple panels with handles was the door to the room, but when I tried the one looking like a door, it opened into a closet. I went around trying the others but they all seemed to open into closets or cupboards, and I felt a sudden panic at the thought that I was trapped in a room with no exit door. This is ridiculous, I told myself, and sat down on the enormous bed to work out where the correct door must be. The children did warn me, I thought, looking round to see if there was a telephone in the room. I couldn't see one, increasing my nervousness, but then decided I was being melodramatic. The solution was obvious. All I needed to do was go round and try each door in turn. After a few tries, I got it, and got out, feeling relieved and foolish. Robert was downstairs in yet another panelled room waiting patiently to open the champagne.

He had the whole evening planned with dinner at a small unpretentious restaurant where everyone knew him, and I was introduced to them all without anyone seeming to think: Oh, here's another one.

'Tomorrow we're going to Harrods where I do my weekly food shopping,' Robert said during dinner. 'You can buy anything you like and we'll have lunch there. It's Ted's day off so I will be driving.' After a night of extreme comfort and restfulness, with breakfast laid ready by a housekeeper, we drove in the Rolls to London and Robert parked in a side street conveniently close to the illustrious building so we didn't have far to walk.

Shopping with him was like shopping with an eager child, full of exclamations and simple joy at each extravagant display. 'Please buy something,' he kept urging me. 'It will go on my account so you can choose anything you like. Shall we go and look at evening dresses?' I was wearing my jeans and they were not designer jeans. I knew I looked outré among the sharp shoppers in Harrods but Robert was wearing old clothes himself. I never did see the black velvet suit again and concluded that it must have been kept for first dates. I didn't want to buy anything, especially anything expensive or bought on his account so the next time he pointed to something he thought I might like, I told him he could buy me a coffee and, if he insisted, lunch too. He began to get the message that I was not attracted to all this glittery ostentation, and might even be repulsed by it, so he calmed down and was content to find a quiet table where we could sit and talk about all the subjects that interested us.

At home he had a small cinema consisting of sofas and armchairs facing a large screen where he could indulge his love of films and he wanted to show me what was so special about Hawaii, his favourite holiday place. He hoped this would encourage me go with him on his next visit, but I told him I could not leave Simon at this point in his illness. 'That's no problem. He can come with us,' Robert said, 'and your other children too. I'm a universal uncle where children are concerned. I love taking them to places they have never seen, and watch their faces. They find delight in the smallest things and need so little to make them happy. It's a humbling experience, and makes me happy too.' I told him that my first visit abroad with Simon had to be to Mafia Island to see Adam. But the next visit after that could be with him to Hawaii or anywhere else, and would be a huge treat for us.

Simon stayed well and spending the summer on Mafia became a reality. He was given an injection of gamma-globulin to boost his immunity against infection and all four of us flew to Dar es Salaam where Adam met us at the airport. He looked well, tanned and fit, and very much at home in the environment of steamy heat, which settled on the rest of us like a damp blanket as soon as we stepped off the plane and stood in a queue to show our passports. Adam had a Tanzanian assistant with him who held in one hand a bundle of bank notes. One or more of these was peeled off at intervals to ease our passage through various points, including the baggage claim area, for which we were grateful while other passengers were getting delayed. Adam introduced his assistant to us as an indispensable PA who was also his driver during visits to Dar, and I could see how essential it was to have someone like this to navigate the wildly confusing highways and byways of this swarming port city.

We were to spend the first night in a hotel and Adam apologised that it was not one of the best but a lot better than some. I just hoped it was clean and had running water and electricity. It had neither we discovered when we arrived at our rooms and went for a wash after trying to switch on the ceiling fans. The rooms were gloomy with stagnant air and there were puddles on the floor from leaks in the roof. 'Don't worry about that,' Adam said. 'It's only rain.' I turned my attention to the beds that were rumpled, unlike most hotel beds neatly made up and ready to get into. I looked closer and lifted up a sheet which clearly had not been changed since the previous occupants. 'Dammit, Adam, come and look at this. It's one thing having puddles on the floor, but I'm not sleeping in someone else's sheets. I need to check the children's room. We have to be careful with Simon. He's vulnerable to infection and it could be serious in his case. Just look at those sheets, stained with something disgusting.'

'Quite so, darling. I'll go and insist they bring clean ones.' When the new sheets arrived they were damp, but I was past caring after the long tiring flight. Once we had fed the children with fried chicken at a petrol station, we were glad to lie down and sleep in our rooms, having washed in buckets thoughtfully placed in the bathrooms.

We needed an early start the next day to buy provisions to take with us to Mafia where food was scarce, shops few, and nothing much was grown besides coconuts and cassava. 'The soil is too thin for crops,' Adam explained, 'but we do get some useful grass under the palms which is good for grazing. The cows like it and the trees provide shade. You're going to love seeing the Jerseys, darling, and the whole dairy operation. You'll be in your element again.'

I had asked Adam before we left home what he lived on, so we could be prepared, and he said, 'Fish, fish, and more fish. Lobsters by the sack-full. Oysters by the bucket-full. Scrawny chickens and eggs occasionally, but no bread, potatoes, salad or vegetables to go with them.' We had filled our suitcases with packets of Weetabix to ward off starvation, and toilet rolls as another essential after being warned that such luxuries were unobtainable on the island. 'What about rice and flour?' I had asked hopefully, thinking that it must be possible to import sacks of these, and with flour I could make bread.

'When a dhow is spotted coming in from the mainland, people go down to the beach to see what cargo is on board and sometimes there may be rice or flour, but maize meal is the main staple. It's what local people survive on, along with cassava, so we will be eating those too.'

Before catching the plane to Mafia that afternoon we stopped at the company office to pick up supplies already piled up ready to take with us. These included machinery parts and medicines, soap, bicycle tyres and anything else that could be stowed on the 18-seat Twin Otter plane that would take us across. Adam was loading all this into the company truck, and I had a bag of shopping with eggs in a box on top that I was keeping hold of while chatting to the Indian secretary in her office. The secretary suddenly stopped speaking when she saw the eggs and became hysterical. Other staff rushed in and explained to me that eggs are a strict taboo in her religion, so it was forbidden for her even to be in the same room with them. She fled and there was further alarm when it was realised that she had gone with the keys of the locked drawer holding our plane tickets. It was so hot in that stifling room I sank down in a chair to fan myself, still holding the eggs, while the children panicked that we would miss the plane and everyone else ran off to find the frantic girl. She was eventually found and the keys retrieved to everyone's relief. Adam put the tickets in his briefcase with our passports, and his trusty PA drove us to the airport where we climbed on board the Otter and were off at last.

The plane flew low over the Indian ocean where offshore coral reefs shone through bright water, and dhows leaned into the wind filling their sails as they carried their cargoes of goods and people in scenes unchanged for centuries. Mafia airport was a simple airfield where trees and scrub had been cleared to form a long rectangle marked out with piles of wreckage around its perimeter. When I remarked on this, Adam was laconic. 'There have been a few prangs in the past, nothing very recent as far as I'm aware, and when it happens the wreck gets dragged to the edge of the strip and everyone helps themselves to anything useful among the debris.' It wasn't a very encouraging explanation, and when we got closer I could see a dilapidated red fire engine racing up and down the side of the field as if trouble was expected. 'That's normal,' Adam said. 'It's the local fire brigade springing into action just in case. Tanzanian law says there has to be an emergency vehicle meeting every flight, but in reality the fire engine is the island taxi and as soon as passengers have disembarked, everyone piles onto it. Don't worry,' he continued, 'the company Land Rover is meeting us.'

It was a relief to be safely on the ground and the bumpy ride to Adam's house over rough tracks felt almost like a blessing. We drove through coconut plantations seeming to go on for miles until distant glimmers of blue appeared through the trees and there was the sea ahead, with Adam's house nearby. The house was basic with concrete walls and a tin roof, but it was spacious and several notches up from the bean-field house at Hartley in Rhodesia. It was also fully staffed, but no one spoke English and my Swahili was shaky after so many years away. The children as usual offered comments. 'Your Swahili isn't shaky. You never did learn to speak it properly like Dad.'

'In that case, how many of you have been swotting it up ready for coming here?'

'We can learn it while we're here, Mum, and you can practise yours.'

The journey had been tiring and Simon looked pale but was already assembling fishing gear ready to go off to the nearest beach or creek. No trip was ever complete without rods and reels and spare lines that accompanied us everywhere, stowed in a long rigid cylinder which was not always welcome on planes. The first piece of luggage to be opened was always, inevitably, the cylinder, checked by the boys to make sure its contents were intact. 'I'll take you to the best fishing places tomorrow,' Adam promised. 'Today is family time, all of us together at last and Simon back to his old self.'

Chapter 12

We were glad to have dry sheets and comfortable rooms waiting for us that night, ready to drop into our beds straight after a good supper of fried fish with cassava chips made by Adam's cook, Ali. It was a treat to be waited on and when we had finished eating, simply to walk away from the table which was cleared and the washing up done out of sight. Similarly at breakfast time the table was ready with Ali waiting to fry or scramble eggs for us. Bacon was ruled out because this was a Muslim island. The people were devout but few of the women were veiled and later among them I met a merry lot who stopped to chat. They were from the Makonde tribe whose women have black peg teeth made from ebony, each tooth removable as one of the women showed me. She plucked a black peg from her jaw and held it out for inspection, accompanied by hoots of laughter from the other women as she casually plugged it back in again. They were curious about my presence on the island and eager to talk, while the peculiarities of my Swahili amused them so much it made their peg teeth waggle in gusts of banter as they chattered on.

The islanders were friendly and alert to our arrival as Adam was the only white person living there, among a population of 20,000 Africans. They wanted to have a look at us and wherever we went we were objects of interest, always in a polite way with traditional customs observed, but we were foreigners and there was no expatriate social scene that we could join. The only hotel, built with aid money from Israel to encourage tourists, was an impressive facility and when we went to sample the menu, the Tanzanian manager apologised for having no food. 'We have only beer,' he explained, 'and no visitors come to stay due to this problem. It is very sad because the island has many unique attractions like coral reefs and ancient sites.' He looked very downcast as he went on to tell us that it was a hard job keeping his staff occupied in the absence of guests. 'That is another problem,' he said, 'as the hotel remains fully staffed despite having no customers. Wages for staff are paid to keep them employed, but having no work means they get bored and get into mischief.'

'What kind of mischief?' I asked, intrigued to hear what they might get up to.

'They bring their girlfriends into the visitor rooms and it gives a bad impression of the hotel,' he said. 'The inspectors don't like it, and then we get a low grade report.'

'Do you really get hotel inspectors coming to the island?' I was surprised to think any such service existed.

'They are employed by the tourism board of the government, so they come because they are being paid to do that job.' I didn't enquire further, feeling sorry for the manager who was doing his best in a situation much like ours, stranded on a remote island with few enlightened amenities despite prolific amounts of aid money coming in. Several aid programmes had been started by international agencies, he told us, but they didn't stay to monitor the schemes and train local people to ensure success. 'These agencies come with money to set up their projects and then they leave, thinking the job is finished,' he said.

One morning soon after we arrived and the children had run down to the sea as usual with rods and nets, I went to the harbour to see if anything edible might have arrived on a dhow. A small crowd had gathered on the beach for the same purpose and were clustered around a couple of vehicles sunk into the sand where a work-gang heaved on ropes to pull them out. I was told these were new Land Rovers that had come in on a boat the previous day as part of an aid consignment, but after being unloaded they had been left on the beach overnight as no one came to drive them away. During the night the tide had come in and flooded the engines with salt water so they were ruined. 'Inshallah,' everyone said as they watched the wrecks being dragged from the sand, attributing this calamity, like all others, to the will of God.

I was told a similar story at the hospital when I went to ask if I could be shown around, to assess what help might be available for Simon if he needed it. The Tanzanian doctor in charge was charming and welcoming when I said I was a registered nurse, and pleased to give me a tour while warning that it would not be like an English hospital. This became evident in the first ward we went to where they had beds but no mattresses or sheets, only thin grey blankets for patients to wrap around themselves. 'We have a serious problem here with anything that is easy to take away like mattresses, pillows, equipment, drugs, all too easily stolen. People are poor. The staff are paid too little. It is a big struggle for us. I will show you the operating theatre now and you will see more of our problem.'

The theatre was sparse but clean and had a neat line of latex gloves drying on the security bars of the open window. I tried not to think about flies and looked instead at a shiny new autoclave machine that caught my eye, and remarked on this.

'It is a very good machine donated by a Swedish charity but we have never used it,' the doctor said. 'The instructions are all in Swedish so we are unable to understand them and we are still waiting for a translation after two years, or for a Swedish person to come and help us.'

'How are you sterilising instruments?'

'We are just boiling them in a *sufuria* (saucepan),' he said.

'A good old-fashioned system,' I laughed and he did too.

'We are grateful to have electricity from the power station operated by your husband's company, otherwise what could we do?'

'I'm glad it's helping you, but I am shocked by the conditions you are faced with. I have nothing but admiration for you under these very difficult circumstances and it makes me wonder what types of surgery you are able to deal with. Do you have many emergencies?'

'Accidents, of course, and for women, caesarean section. For men it can be volvulus (twisted gut),' he replied. 'But anaesthetics are a problem. We use strong sedatives whenever possible.'

There were so many problems, and so many sad little funeral processions I had noticed since we arrived, winding their way through the plantations, often with very small stretchers or coffins carried at shoulder height on poles. I felt concern for this beleaguered doctor who was using whatever resources he could find to provide medical services under sometimes quite harrowing circumstances. Outside the hospital building a line of out-patients waited to be seen. Many were mothers with children and I asked about the most common illnesses. 'Malaria is the worst,' he said. 'Mortality is high, and then hookworm is a serious problem leading to severe anaemia in many cases and this can also be fatal, especially in combination with malnutrition. You can see it in some of the people waiting here: observe the pallor, and the emaciation.'

'There must be drugs for hookworm?'

'We are very short of drugs, as I said before, due to theft. We receive a consignment and then it disappears into markets where drugs get a high price.'

This was very depressing, in particular because these practices were ingrained in a culture with different ethical perspectives from our own, and hostile to change. The most useful thing I learnt from the hospital that day was to keep Simon well away from it. While he continued in good health there was no cause for alarm as he seemed just as fit and energetic as the others going off with Adam around the plantations every day, often stopping off at a beach to swim or explore along the coast, which kept them happily occupied.

I had a project in mind to grow vegetables and had brought seeds from England, but first needed to prepare the soil in a patch previously marked out for a garden. The main problem here I was told, was eel worm, and the only way to get rid of them was by sterilising the soil (which was mainly sand) before planting. This was done in a laborious process involving forty-gallon drums filled with soil, baked over a fire, then mixed with leaf mould and macerated coconut fibre to provide the right consistency. Plenty of natural fertiliser came from chicken manure which was readily available, and once all these procedures had been followed I was ready to plant my seeds and watch them grow. The humid heat encouraged rapid growth and green shoots sprang up so fast that we soon had emerging rows of onions and carrots and squash, but the runner beans which at first had shown promise speeding up their sticks, failed to set. 'You need long daylight hours to set the beans,' Adam said. 'Daylight here is too short.' It was disappointing, but most disappointing of all was when monkeys raided the new vegetables just as we had started picking them. Ali explained that it was inevitable. 'Inshallah,' he said, 'that is how it is with monkeys. They are very bad thieves. Everyone is hungry, even them.'

When the supplies we had brought from Dar began to run short I had real worries about feeding three large teenagers and two adults without the normal staples we took for granted at home. Bringing goods in by air was expensive and the company freighter only carried coconuts. I hadn't experienced real hunger such as this since the war and any mother with hungry children knows the sense of mounting anxiety when there is not enough to eat. Ali told me one morning that a big dhow had come in during the night and a crowd was already gathering on the beach to see what was being sold from the deck, so if I went down quickly I might find they had something like dates, or even rice if we were lucky. I got a lift from Adam to the harbour and joined a noisy throng of women bargaining prices with the dhow captain, but when I saw that the entire cargo consisted of nothing but lemons, my disappointment was intense. They were hard little yellow buttons of fruit, not worth a cent to me, but prized by local people. Ali used tamarind to flavour curries and other dishes and there were any number of tamarind trees on the island so it was a good substitute. But what I craved that day at the harbour were sacks of flour and rice and sugar, or even by some miracle a sack of potatoes, but no one had heard of potatoes.

I asked the dhow captain if he had anything else on board besides lemons and he called to one of his crew who was sitting on a tin trunk a little way off. I went over and the trunk was opened to reveal stacks of flat-bread and chapatis. They must have flour hidden away somewhere for themselves, I thought, but the sailor looked blank when I asked. After some haggling I was allowed to buy a few flat-breads and went to thank the captain. He wanted to chat and ask questions about England, which he had never seen but visualised as a place where banks overflowed with money that was handed out freely to citizens, who had no requirement to work and lived indulgent lives. This was a common impression among local people and any attempt to explain the social welfare system generally led to even greater astonishment at such liberal distribution of public money, as they saw it. The captain seemed genuinely eager to talk and hear about life outside his own world of coastal trading, which surprised me since Muslim men like him were usually reticent about engaging in conversation with women, but the captain was surprisingly open. This encouraged me to ask if he would take me on a trip in his dhow. He smiled deprecatingly. 'We do not take ladies. The ship is not a polite place for ladies,' he said with elaborate courtesy.

Among this island group was Chole which was famous for its ancient boatyard where dhows were still being built by local craftsmen with the same traditional tools they had used for hundreds of years, requiring no modern aids. The construction of every part of the hulls was of wood, using wooden rivets and fastenings. I wanted to see this and thought a trip to Chole would be a grand day out for all of us, to include snorkelling and a visit to the island's colony of 'flying foxes'. These were fruit bats the size and colour of ginger cats with black wings and behaviour that could be intimidating in its ferocity and raucousness when feasting on their favourite food of kapok fruit.

There was a daily ferry service to Chole on a large open boat and we turned up with bags of swimming gear and a picnic in time for the morning sailing. No bookings are taken for such trips and however many passengers arrive, all are accommodated regardless of safety considerations. We were slightly nervous about this as accidents happened quite often, but on this day there were fewer passengers than usual. The captain was displeased because it meant there would be less money from fares and this put him in a peevish mood. To make up for the loss he dismissed his crew so he didn't have to pay them, saying that the passengers could work as crew instead. Showing no deference to any of us he gave orders and Adam was delegated to man the main (lateen) sail with its great boom towering above our heads, while other passengers who were all local people, were allocated to varied tasks. When it came to my turn, the captain looked me over doubtfully and handed me a bag of oranges. 'You can look after these,' he said (in Swahili). 'I have counted them, and you will sit next to me at the steering so I can watch you don't eat any while we are on the sea.'

I was curious about these oranges and wanted to ask where he had got them, but his sullen manner did not invite questions. Younger passengers were given baling tins and we set off with Adam at the sail while I sat beside the captain at the tiller, holding the bag of oranges on my lap. He spoke not a word to me during the entire crossing, but kept his eye on Adam who was straining at the mainsheet, while shouting orders to him and the other amateur deckhands who had been so abruptly pressed into service. Luckily, with a following wind we hurtled across and after scrambling ashore, found ourselves in a tiny world: a microcosm suspended in time, intimate and charming. At the main boatyard, builders were busy securing weathered planks to the deck of a high-sided dhow. The rhythmic thud of their wooden hammers released puffs of dust into the sultry air of the yard as we watched and marvelled at the sight of the great hull they were shaping with skilled precision.

To the children's delight we found a kiosk selling Fanta and corn cobs roasted on a charcoal fire, which we added to the boiled eggs and cassava chips Ali had made for our picnic. We ate these sitting on a log under palms at the side of the beach while Simon described to us the life history of fruit bats. He was keeping a journal to record his experiences on the islands and became very elated at each new discovery. He looked tanned and well since losing the bloated effect of cortisone taken during treatment, and his hair, now thick with dark curls, matched his brown eyes. All the old enthusiasms and energy which were such a driving force in his personality had come back, and I noticed how these qualities now impacted on Pete who was trying to assert himself as a teenager.

Pete no longer felt so inclined to follow in Simon's wake, while Louise remained intensely irritated by any exhibition of revived jaunty behaviour by Simon. These were normal family dynamics, within which my own role as mother and wife had confusing elements since Adam did not think that living apart most of the time should make any difference to the way we felt about each other. His life had reverted to its familiar environment and patterns, giving him stability, but my life had changed and moved into different territory since being taken over by Simon's illness, and meeting Robert. Added to this, I still missed the steadying assurance of David's friendship since he too had moved on, with a new career out of the army.

Stray thoughts didn't last long on days out when there were things to see or do and there were plenty of these on Chole Island. We had been told to look out for the ruins of an old German fort, still visible among tangled undergrowth, a remnant of the First World War when German forces occupied these islands before surrendering to the British. Local people acted as guides, taking us on a short walk through the bush to what was left of the fort, its crumbling walls invaded by vines. Nearby was a tree where we were told the Germans hanged people who disobeyed their rules. Our guides saw no injustice in this; along with other islanders we met that day they spoke of the Germans with nostalgia, admiration and respect.

We had a different captain on our return and the boat was full to capacity with no space for passengers to move around, so Adam was spared manning the sail. It had been a memorable day but the legacy of Chole came back with us in the form of jiggers that had burrowed into our toes as we walked around in sandals. Jiggers are a type of flea found in the dusty sand of tropical places so that our exposed toes scuffling along island paths were easily invaded. Having attached themselves, the jiggers then burrow under the toenails of their unwitting hosts and lay eggs, which remain undiscovered until they start to hatch and an intense itching declares their presence. Ali knew all about this and what to do. The nests have to be dug out from underneath each toenail with the point of a knife or large needle, which in some circumstances might be classed as a form of torture were it not for the fact that the itching is a worse torment. The excavation of jiggers became routine after the Chole jiggers blazed a trail in our toes for Mafia Island jiggers to follow.

Insects of all kinds flourished in the lush paradise of these islands where few chemicals were used and thickets of wild bush provided a fertile habitat. Supper times for us were accompanied by an aerial circus of assorted bugs batting at the light bulb above our heads and dropping onto our plates, while Adam swore and uselessly swatted at them. During the night mosquitoes came in hordes to look for holes in our nets as we lay in bed trying to ignore the incessant whining that announces their arrival. If it suddenly stops, like the dreaded doodlebug bombs over London in the war, it means that one had landed. In the bathroom, spiders emerged from plugholes and scorpions scuttled into wet corners, hiding until disturbed; while outside in the dark, cicadas held their nightly orchestral rasping which for me was a soothing sound: the sound of African night.

At supper one evening all conversation centred on what to do about one of the Jersey bulls that had escaped from the herd and gone rogue, terrorising villagers by charging at them from pockets of bush where it had taken cover. Jersey bulls are notoriously fierce but this one according to the villagers, had gone *wazimu kabisa* (totally mad), and wanted to kill someone. 'I'll have to shoot it,' Adam said, 'but how to get close enough for a safe shot is going to be tricky.'

'You could lasso it, like you used to with cattle in Florida with the cowboys,' Pete suggested.

'That was on horseback, moving fast with running animals. We don't have any horses, or cowboys, here.'

'What about getting the vet over from Dar to dart it?' someone else suggested.

'Much too expensive. Anyway we want the bugger dead, not darted. When I've located where it's lurking, I can approach from a distance with my rifle in the same way as with buffalo when the blighters are in dense cover ready to charge, then get a close shot. It should work a treat, as long as the demented beast storms out and reveals itself full on.'

'What if it doesn't?'

'We'll annoy it by various means until it gets fed up and charges. One way or another it can't win.'

Word had spread of the plan by morning and Adam was called to the latest sighting. The boys were in a fever of excitement, checking Adam's rifle with him, counting the rounds as he slipped them into his pocket. An expectant crowd had already gathered by the time we arrived at the clearing where the bull had been seen grazing that morning before it strolled off into the undergrowth. This open area, normally used as a football pitch, now resembled an arena where a bull might appear if sufficiently provoked. Adam addressed the crowd on his intended strategy, with instructions on how to avoid any accidental outcomes by keeping well out of the way as he approached the bushy area that the bull was reported to have entered. There was a tense silence when he loaded his rifle and started walking slowly towards the point indicated, whistling in the way Kipsigis cattle herders call their animals. The bull could not fail to hear this sound and was likely to be irritated by it and come charging out, Adam surmised.

He was right, as within seconds an enraged black and tawny animal with sharp horns erupted from the bush and went straight for him. He raised his gun and a crack split the air, reverberating around our ears as the bull fell almost at his feet with just one shot to the head. Hardly had it fallen than knives were out as men from the crowd ran to cut its throat before it stopped twitching. The meat had to be halal for the feast that would follow. Adam had first choice of cuts as the undoubted hero of the drama and we all had steaks that night, but they were not the best of beef suppers – Florida steaks could not be outdone and Jersey bull beef was never going to match them.

The next day Simon was feverish and admitted that he had felt unwell for some days and had blood in his urine, but hadn't wanted to say anything because we were all enjoying ourselves so much. It was what I had been dreading. We had brought antibiotics and I started him on a course immediately, following instructions from Dr Johnston. He felt better quickly but the haematuria continued and we couldn't get blood tests done on the island to see what was going on. Our holiday was nearly over at this point and we had planned to go from Mafia to visit Cen and Alison in Kenya. There was a doctor at Naivasha, ten miles from their farm, who we hoped could give advice. This was Dr Reggie Bunney, Fa's old friend from the London Hospital where they had met as medical students. I would much rather have gone straight home for Simon to be under the care of specialists again, but he wanted desperately to see his grandparents and there was always the thought that opportunities like this were precious and should not be missed.

The responsibility to keep him well and the fear of sudden acute illness was hugely stressful as we left the island and flew via Dar es Salaam to Nairobi, where I had arranged a blood test for Simon at the main hospital before we drove to the highlands. The haematologist at the hospital was another old friend of Fa's and this gave us a connection which was reassuring, until he told me that in all his time working in Kenya he had never seen a case of leukaemia. He said he had no experience in this field but was willing to do a full blood count and see if we could discover anything that might be helpful. I was curious about the apparent lack of cases encountered and wondered why this was? Were people dying before they got to a doctor? Were they being misdiagnosed? Certainly, throughout the time that I lived in Kenya I had never heard of a case of leukaemia.

'It may be something to do with altitude, or environment,' the haematologist suggested. 'Or merely coincidental. It would be interesting to do a study. Your dad would have been the one to do that,' he said with a smile. 'He was always hot on any new line of research, shooting up to Makerere (Makerere University in Kampala, Uganda, famous at the time for its medical research). He is much missed among the rest of us who are left plodding on here.'

The blood results when they came through did not show anything too alarming, but these were simple tests and no substitute for the sophisticated ones Simon would get at home. It was an anxious time as we pressed on, leaving Nairobi by taxi to drive down into the Rift Valley. Passing Mount Longonot and Naivasha town, we turned off the main road and up into the hills above Gilgil where the farm stood on a ridge looking across the immense valley with its lakes and volcanoes. Cen and Alison were touchingly glad to see us, and especially Simon whose favourite pony had been brought to the house to greet him, which was a poignant moment as horse and boy nuzzled each other. Pete and Louise had their favourites too, and next day in the cool of the morning all were saddled and we went with Adam for a ride around the hills and plains where herds of zebra and gazelle grazed the short grass and a small family of giraffes browsed the trees. It was good to see the children out in this wild countryside after the cosiness of England, so I bottled my emotions and put out of mind Alison's bacteria-infested kitchen and other threats to Simon's compromised immune system.

We took him for a consultation with Reggie at his house on the lake shore, but it was more of a social visit than medical as Reggie was reluctant to offer any advice since he, like the Nairobi haematologist, had no up to date experience of leukaemia. The Bunney family lived in a wildlife paradise where a tame baby hippo accompanied us as we strolled beside the lake, while fish eagles flew overhead with their haunting cry and pelicans swam among the reed beds. The hippo was given a lunch of lucerne hay alongside us as we had ours outside on the lawn under yellow fever trees. Reggie's wife Mary was there, and his daughter Diana who lived with them and ran the household. Reggie told us that when he was a medical student at the London Hospital, he met Adam's Aunt Diana who was training to be a physiotherapist, and fell in love with her. 'She had the most beautiful blue eyes,' he said, 'the colour of cornflowers. I was smitten and wanted to marry her, but she was devoted to her home and parents. She was the youngest daughter and felt it was her duty to look after them. When I had my own daughter we called her Diana in honour of Diana Hill, Adam's dear aunt.' I wondered what Mary thought about this but she made no comment and I sensed that her role was very much a supporting one, of husband and daughter, in the manner of many women of that generation in much the same way that Aunt Diana had committed herself to her parents.

Our visit to Cen and Alison was short but it was a happy time for all of us and goodbyes were done in a rush at the end when we had to leave. I was anxious by then to be back in England so that Simon could be checked over by the team at Dorchester Hospital. He was still unwell but determined to keep going, while each day increased the risk that he might suddenly take a turn for the worse and I was on edge due to this uncertainty, but also because of my ambivalence about leaving Adam. It felt like being in a play where I was acting two different parts: one as a wife that Adam still wanted beside him, but only in Africa. The other as a single mother plugged into the needs of each child and the home, holding the family together while floundering in a void of loneliness, craving the day-to-day companionship and support of a capable adult partner.

There was Robert, but his wealth made me feel uncomfortable. So much money in that privileged environment was a world away from my own, but I could see that my indifference to it was appealing to him. He had been wary of gold-diggers since becoming single and his lonely hearts advertisement had been carefully phrased. It did feel an honour to be the only one remaining out of the fifty hopefuls, but I was wary too. I still hardly knew him. He had been patient and understanding during my absence and wanted to meet the children on our return, but my priority now was Simon.

When we got home tests were run at the hospital and despite all indications nothing too serious showed up that couldn't be corrected by a blood transfusion, so this was a relief. Transfusions always had a magical effect so that after receiving a unit of packed cells, in the space of a few hours Simon was restored to his old self, impatient to get back to his various projects, and especially, back to school. This time hardly any of the new term was missed and he was excited to be seeing his friends again and entertain them with stories of the holiday.

Louise left home to start her art foundation course at Bournemouth Art College, and Pete at thirteen was sculling around in the lower divisions of Woodroffe School with little evidence of achievement, but happy among his friends who were all similarly unmotivated. He and Simon were growing apart in their personalities, which may be a normal feature in teenage brothers as they develop independence, while Simon was racing ahead in his own life, leaving Pete behind. They each had their own friends and interests, but fishing was still top of the list and Simon was still an avid collector of anything relating to bugs or natural history.

Soon after coming home, while tidying his room, I felt a sharp sting on my leg, and then another sting, and looking down I saw a line of safari ants marching across the floor from an open suitcase. Simon had brought live ants home in a cardboard box packed in his suitcase and they had escaped, looking for food after chewing through the cardboard with their powerful jaws. This was not a moment to reach for insecticide spray as I knew well enough by now that Simon's bug menagerie was sacrosanct, so I left them to invade his room and looked forward to watching his reaction when he came home from school to face the horde. He must have captured a whole nest of ants for so many to have survived, and I hoped they would not spread through the rest of the house before he found a way to contain them. I was always careful when encountering any small box in his room knowing that if I opened it, one or more infuriated insects were likely to jump out and attach themselves to my hand or arm with baleful intent. Simon would accuse me of scaring them instead of appreciating that most creatures are harmless. He was just like Fa in this, as in the old days of swimming in Lake Baringo with crocodiles when they stared at me with unblinking yellow eyes on a level with mine in the water, Fa would shout: 'Don't frighten them. They're only coming up to have a look at you.'

Ros and I were surprised when Muz told us that she and Andy had decided to sell the cottage in Suffolk and move to Dorset. 'I've always wanted to live in Dorset,' Muz declared, which surprised us even more as she had never mentioned this before. She went on to say, 'Andy and I are driving over to look at houses around Dorchester and we can stay with Wendy while we are looking. We are quite set on the idea since deciding this is what we want to do.' She was adamant that no time was to be lost on this new quest, and Ros hurried down from Bath to help out as always whenever a parent came to stay.

The first alarm was when Muz and Andy failed to arrive on the day arranged, having taken a wrong turn and found themselves following signposts to Margate which was not supposed to be on their way. They stopped at a B&B for the night and phoned to explain what had happened, and that they now had detailed instructions on the correct route to Devon. They stuck to this and arrived the next day without incident, but getting lost was a worrying development. Andy blamed Muz and said she'd had the map upside down, which was plausible, but it seemed to have taken him a very long time to notice. After settling them into our new spare room (which had been Louise's room before she went to college), we took them to see an estate agent in Dorchester. Andy was asked by the agent what kind of house they had in mind, and their budget. 'I am looking for a gentleman's residence,' Andy replied, 'no more than £30,000.'

The agent remained poker-faced in front of this greasy-looking man who showed few gentlemanly attributes in either appearance or manner, and said that she would show them what was available, while Ros and I sat trying not to snigger and Muz sat smiling sweetly. It was not a surprise when the houses shown to them failed to meet expectations, but almost as an afterthought when we were due to go home, the agent mentioned a garage conversion and Andy's interest was ignited.

'It's in the garden of a village house,' she explained. 'The owners had a double garage which they didn't need, so they extended one half of it into a pleasant living space with two bedrooms, leaving the other half attached as a garage.' Andy immediately saw the potential as a worthy home for his Austin Princess, and an appointment was made for a viewing the next day. Ros went with them because I had to take Simon to the clinic.

The viewing was a triumph. 'The property suits us perfectly,' Andy said, his big sweaty face glowing. 'A proper garage for my Princess. And nothing wrong with the other accommodation either.'

I cornered Ros as soon as I could. 'A gentleman's residence then?' I enquired of her. Ros sighed. 'It's what the agent said – a garage with flat attached. There's a little strip of garden outside which poor Muz seized on as a bonus. She's trying to make the best of it. She really loved Phlegms.'

'Why was she so keen to leave, then?'

'She's got itchy feet for some reason. I think it's connected to her other strange behaviour. She feels unsettled and wants to be closer to the rest of us on this side of the country. I think it's a security thing.'

'They won't be very close on the other side of Dorchester.'

'It's a step closer. Anyway, let's go out and celebrate the purchase of a live-in garage. When people ask me where Muz is living now, I will have to say: "In half a garage".'

Somehow we didn't feel like laughing about it as we might once have done, but we did go out to celebrate at the Clock House pub just down the road in the next village. Because we hadn't booked, we were put in a back room where extra chairs and tables were kept, while a doddery woman of advanced age was extracted from the kitchen and pressed into service as our waitress. She was a wisp of a woman, wobbling on stick-thin legs as she took our order and staggered to the kitchen. 'Do you think she will remember to come back?' Ros muttered, and hardly had she spoken, than almost by reply the lights went out.

'It must be a power cut,' Muz suggested unnecessarily. Roars from the bar filtered through to us but there was no filtering of any assistance as we sat waiting for reconnection.

'Places like this always have emergency generators,' I reassured Muz who didn't need any extra events of this sort to bring on spasms of anxiety. As I said this, a shaft of light momentarily lit up the room, coming from a glass-panelled door almost hidden behind a stack of chairs at the back. I went to see if a handy 'Ladies' might be there, in case Muz needed one. The door led to an empty room with no useful signs, but my attention was caught by a dark shape in a far corner that seemed to be draped in some sort of cloak. As I stood there, wondering what it was, the strange object started to shake and tremble with groaning noises, followed by shrieks and then screaming. This was so unnerving I thought the poor huddled creature was being attacked and I must have walked in on a crime. I was stuck by the door, frozen to the spot, unsure what to do next, when it became clear that the screams were coming from a cage covered with a large black cloth, and inside the cage, I realised, there was a parrot seized with rage at being disturbed by my intrusion. Behind me in the room where all the others were sitting patiently in the dark, the shaky waitress had entered with a candle and tray of drinks. Unsteady as she was at the best of times, startled by the sudden screeching of the parrot she toppled over. The noise of smashing glass brought assistance at last, but it was all too much for Muz who felt chest pains coming on. 'Do let's get out of here,' she pleaded, 'before anything worse happens.'

Avoiding the bar we felt our way through the parrot's room where it was now swearing mournfully, and out to a rear car park. The brief flash of light seen earlier I realised must have come from the headlights of a car. We climbed back into ours with no supper. 'Another Craddock disaster,' Ros observed on the way home.

Plans were made for Muz and Andy's move to the garage flat, which had been named Sun Cottage. 'Because it's on the sunny side of the garage,' Muz told us. 'I love that name, it's a good omen.' Later when they had gone back to Suffolk to start packing up, Ros thought the move might help to restore Muz's balance of mind. 'Phlegms is a depressing house with such tiny windows, hardly any light gets in, so the move to a sunny place might bring out her own sunny side. I thought she seemed much better this time, after the nonsense of the empty wine bottle last time she came to stay.'

Since recovering from the infection or whatever it was that he had on holiday in the summer, Simon remained well and his check-ups at the clinic continued uneventfully after coming back. He was certain that he had been cured because he said being a Christian means believing what the Bible says when it promises that anything we ask for will be granted, if we have faith. He had plenty of that, he said, and had asked to be cured. It was a child's simple reasoning and we all wanted to believe it despite medical caution. I thought the doctors must be mistaken in their warnings when they could see how well he looked, and was developing normal signs of puberty as he proudly told them he was growing 'big balls'. But instead of being impressed they sent him for a scan. The scan showed testicular tumours which on further tests turned out to be malignant. This was a cruel blow, particularly as Simon loved babies and children and looked forward to having his own. He wanted to get married early he said, and was excited about potential girlfriends among girls in his class at school, some of whom were already going on dates. It was ironic for Simon to have developed a different type of cancer while his leukaemia was in remission, and brutal for him to be told that the surgery he needed would make him sterile, but there was no alternative.

Porters had gone on strike on the day of the operation, so I wheeled the trolley to the theatre with a nurse and it felt like taking him on a tumbril and nothing could get worse. There was no comfort later in hearing that the operation had been a success and the tumours removed, since one of his best hopes had now been dashed, but he remained philosophical. 'Girls won't want to marry me if I'm sterile,' he said, 'but there are other ways to have children, and anyway I can still be a doctor and look after children.'

Like all teenagers he felt pressure to keep pace with male peers who were all at a stage of rapid physical development, growing taller and more muscular with voices that had started to break, while none of these changes were happening to him. He was anxious about this and we had a long discussion with Dr Johnston who restored Simon's optimism by telling him that he could catch up later if he remained well. All indications for this were good since there had been no spread of the malignant tumours and no sign of the leukaemia returning, so life went on and we hoped Adam might come home for Christmas. Meanwhile Simon liked to be left in charge of the house with Pete, trusted to keep order during weekends when they invited friends for all the kinds of things teenage boys enjoy doing, so that I could go off to see Ros or Robert and have a break.

Charles and his wife had a new baby and we all went to see the tiny infant who had been born in a frail state and was later found to have Fallot's

Tetralogy, which luckily was able to be corrected with open-heart surgery when she was a year old. Simon was enchanted by the baby and enormously flattered when he was asked to be a godfather. It was an occasion when he could wear his suit, a hand-me-down from cousin Michael and treasured by Simon as, to him, wearing a suit symbolised adult maturity so he could feel that he was making progress towards that goal at last. It was also symbolic for him to have a godchild to care for if he was unable to have children of his own.

When the christening day arrived and Simon put on the suit, it looked baggy instead of fitting nicely as it had done before, and I realised with dismay that he must have lost weight. Soon after this, other dreaded symptoms began to appear and tests showed that the leukaemia had returned. I was talked through this by Dr Johnston and other doctors involved in Simon's care, comprehensively and with great sensitivity. It was a very emotional meeting with clear distress and even some tears from medical staff who felt personal disappointment at the relapse, despite their best efforts. I was touched by their empathy while discussing options for the next step: whether chemotherapy might induce another remission, which was likely to be no more than temporary, or try for a bone marrow transplant which was the best hope, but risky. Simon was mature enough to make his own decision so the meeting concluded that Dr Johnston would discuss alternatives with him.

Without hesitation, Simon opted for a transplant and the first stage was to test our immediate family members for a donor. I was the only one with the same blood group, but when tissue-matching for compatibility was done at Westminster Hospital, the cells rejected each other. This can happen even with close relatives but was an immense disappointment as nothing could have given me more happiness than success in donating bone marrow to save the life of my own child. The next hope was to see if the Anthony Nolan Register could find an unrelated donor.

Simon refused to believe that the relapse was anything but a temporary setback and remained convinced that he would get back into remission, but he was already very unwell and, worst of all to him, he was missing school. This caused severe frustration as he missed his friends as well. Visits to the hospital became more frequent and involved some very unpleasant procedures such as injection of drugs into his spine, in addition to the inevitable bone marrow biopsies that were always an ordeal. We took pyjamas in case he had to stay overnight, or for longer, depending on test results. Blood transfusions gave him a welcome energy boost and were essentially life-saving while we waited for a donor.

As soon as Robert heard what had happened he drove down to see what he could do to help. The sight of a Rolls parked in our road electrified neighbours who thought a celebrity had arrived in the village. A small crowd gathered, which included Simon himself as, roused by the excitement, he didn't want to miss the rare sight of Robert's Rolls basking at the kerb beside our modest row of village houses. Robert offered to take Simon for a spin with anyone else who volunteered and off they went, Simon in the front passenger seat grinning rapturously, a flush of colour returning to his cheeks.

When they came back we sat down with a cup of tea to discuss a plan that Robert had come to tell us about. This was for Simon to choose a place anywhere in the world he would like to visit, with Robert organising and paying for every detail, and of course coming with us. 'You will have a chariot,' he told Simon, 'which will be the best wheelchair I can find, with me as chief pusher and attendant. Everything will be provided. All you have to do is take your pick and your wish is my command.'

Mafia Island was the first choice but had to be ruled out as just not safe or suitable, which was disappointing, but Simon said he would love to go to Florida instead because he had great memories of our time there and had always wanted to go back. Robert was delighted with the choice, thinking it an inspired idea. 'All we need to do now is fix a date,' This had to be discussed with the doctors and with their agreement everything was arranged quite quickly. Louise was at college and Pete went to stay with one of his school friends, resigned by now to being bundled off or left on his own due to the vagaries of Simon's illness.

Robert wanted to book a luxury hotel on the beach in Florida where Simon could swim in the warm sea of the gulf, which Robert was convinced was health-giving, but Simon wanted to stay with Jim and his family and because it was Simon's choice, that is where we went. I wanted them to meet Robert, particularly because he was already suggesting marriage, even though he knew I wasn't free. In his opinion my marriage to Adam was a sham and I should make a new life for myself. Robert was a Catholic and did not approve of intimacy before marriage, which explained his forbearance beyond modest kissing, but it did not accord with my own view that any life-changing decision such as this needed to be based on full disclosure of all issues relating to it. We argued about this, but my most pressing issue was Simon, and Robert understood this.

He sent his chauffeur to collect us on the day we were due to leave for Florida so it was an easy drive to Heathrow where Robert was waiting with the 'chariot' and a porter to take our luggage. When Simon had been belted into this high-tech vehicle, Robert took off with it, dashing through the crowds as if they were schoolboys on a lark, doing wheelies and causing mayhem. Whatever he was wearing, Robert still looked like a floppy-haired pop star and was inclined to displays of flamboyance, which drew a more tolerant response from people displaced by the antics than otherwise might have happened. Every possible convenience and facility had been thought of and provided by him, so the flight was yet another indulgence and we emerged refreshed at Tampa, where Jim met us.

The trip took a different turn when we arrived at the ranch and Robert looked around, viewing the unfamiliar scene. The Florida wilderness which in our eyes was glorious in its natural state, to Robert's suburban eyes felt uncivilised, but he was too polite on first acquaintance to show any discomfort. He was quickly distracted when Jim's children ran to welcome him and jumped with joy at seeing us all. The next day Jim took us on a tour of new developments such as a network of canals to drain the swamps, where hundreds of acres of rich silt now formed valuable arable land. Alligators basked along the canal banks but Robert was not impressed with them, or the bumpy roads, or the steamy heat of the reclaimed scrub-lands. Simon however was much revived and excited by all the innovations and being with old friends again, in an element where he felt at home and energised.

Robert would feel more at home, I thought, with a trip to Disneyland or Busch Gardens and we were planning this during supper one evening, when a sudden interruption stopped all conversation. A long black snake was sliding across the floor and when Robert saw it he bolted for his room and slammed the door behind him. The snake didn't pause and, looking for an opening to escape, shot through into a corridor where doors led off to bedrooms. As luck would have it there was a gap under Robert's door and the snake went through in a flash as the rest of us watched in horror. Instantly a shout came from Robert and Jim ran in to rescue him. Robert had taken refuge on the bed where he was sitting with his feet drawn up, terrified and also outraged at finding himself in this situation. He refused to stay in the room while we looked for the snake, so Jim's wife took him to the kitchen for a cup of tea as the rest of us searched, but the snake had disappeared. There was no sign of it, despite combing every inch of floor and furniture.

Robert was given another room and the next day when we had almost forgotten about the incident and Robert was calm again, Jim suggested going to Sarasota for a lobster lunch. Robert went to get a new film for his camera and when he opened his suitcase, there was the snake. This was absolutely the final straw and Robert said in order to avoid a heart attack he would go to a hotel on one of the islands after lunch, and hoped I would join him. Simon could stay with Jim's family it was suggested, or come with us to the beach. Neither of us could resist the invitation, and Robert was right about the healing qualities of swimming in the gulf as we immersed ourselves in the sensations of that sublime coast for another few days, before we had to go home.

CHAPTER 13

There was news from the Nolan Register when we got home. Twelve potential donors had been found in different parts of the country and each one was willing to go to London to be tested for compatibility. It seemed extraordinary that so many unrelated people shared the same tissue type as Simon, which made the concept of a human family seem very real in this discovery, but tissue matching was a slow process. Simon needed to stay as well as possible while we waited for results, relying on drugs and blood transfusions and avoiding accidents. He lost his hair again so the NHS wig that had been supplied to him the first time round was retrieved and dusted off, with no more success than last time when he mostly preferred being bald. As a precaution he carried the wig around with him, hanging half-out of his pocket like a small furry animal, ready to be clapped onto his head if need arose.

He missed school and his friends and looked forward to visits from one friend in particular, Andrew Nuttall, who shared his passion for steam engines. They had their own model locomotives and Andrew brought his on the bus to our house to run it with Simon's, causing congestion as they puffed their way from room to room. The exertion and excitement brought back the old exuberant Simon and lifted his spirits so that he began to look for a project to keep himself occupied, while still hoping to be allowed back to school.

The number of potential donors and confirmation that he was on the waiting list for a transplant at Westminster Hospital kept our hopes up, despite being warned that not every child with a donor automatically goes on to have a transplant. A shortage of beds and funding meant these had to be rationed and doctors had to make heart-breaking decisions we were told, so it might be the child whose condition offered the best chance of success who would be chosen, rather than the next one on the list. 'What about the others?' I asked when I went to meet the doctor in charge at the Westminster unit.

'It is a truly tragic situation and too many children die before we can help them,' he said. 'Techniques and procedures are advancing so rapidly, they have overtaken the ability to deliver. The cost of just one transplant is massive, and success is by no means guaranteed. Sadly it is a fact of life, and death.'

This information made a deep impression on Simon who decided he must do something while he still could. Even if it was too late for him, he reasoned he could start a campaign to raise money for the unit at Westminster Hospital. The decision had an extraordinary effect, inspiring him with a sense of purpose and new energy he was seized with impatience to get started. 'The way to get this off the ground,' he said, 'is publicity in the press. We need to go and see if the editor of the local paper can help.'

It was a stroke of luck that the newspaper had a visionary editor who was an enthusiastic supporter of causes such as Simon's. He understood straight away what was needed, and was ready with advice and contacts and a photographer who took pictures to go with a story for the next edition of the paper. From the first day of meeting David Cozens, editor of the *Bridport News*, Simon's life took on new meaning and he became quite transformed with the impetus of ideas and plans to work on. When the story came out in David's paper, announcing 'The Simon Hill Leukaemia Fund', it was picked up on national news, resulting in a huge response from people wanting to donate. This caused our local bank manager some consternation as money started sprinting into his small bank without any formal warning when we set up an account in the name of the fund. Other branches of the same bank found themselves receiving donations for a fund they had never heard of, which led to our unfortunate manager being reprimanded by his head office for failing to provide relevant information. All of us had been caught off guard when the story went public with such a powerful response, so he was not the only one to feel overwhelmed. It was the second time he'd had to call me into his office to explain parachutes of money landing unexpectedly in his bank. At this rate it would not be long before we were able to present a respectable cheque to the hospital, and meanwhile Simon was becoming something of a celebrity as he appeared on TV and radio and was not at all shy about making speeches wherever he went.

After meeting Fern Britton, who was a young presenter at our regional TV station, Spotlight, she became a spirited supporter and joined us on a sponsored walk along the Dorset coastal path to Abbotsbury where the walk conveniently ended in a pub. Simon gave her a painting of the Dorset landscape as a memento, and kept a photo of her in a frame to revive his spirits when overcome by moments of weakness. It was remarkable that he was holding up so well most of the time with this unexpected run of better health, which surprised the doctors as much as the rest of us. They were keeping wary eyes on him and monitoring his blood picture closely in between those times when he went away to visit people who wanted to meet him.

One of these people was Spike Milligan, who at the time was appearing in a one-man show at the Bristol Hippodrome and sent tickets for us with an invitation to meet him in his dressing room before the show. It was slightly ironic just then to have money pelting into the fund account, while we as a family remained financially strained with a mortgage to pay and extra costs now for travelling and other expenses connected with running the fund. It would never have occurred to us to deduct expenses from fund money.

I booked a cheap B&B in Bristol near the station for Simon and myself and we took the train, changing at Taunton. Later, we had the luxury of a taxi to the Hippodrome and were shown to Spike's dressing room where his wife was helping him to get ready. She was an imposing woman, dressed all in black and very attentive to him while trying to get him to settle down and talk to us. He was restless, pacing around, complaining about noise from a loudspeaker on the wall which was piping tinny music into the small hot room. Distracted beyond endurance by the irritating sound, he pulled a chair to the wall, stood on it, and reached up to the loudspeaker with both hands, wrenching it off the wall. Simultaneously the lights fused and the theatre went dark. There were shouts from the auditorium where people were taking their seats, with a great deal of running about heard in corridors outside as we stood waiting to see what would happen next. Spike's wife, Shelagh, ever prepared for such events, produced a candle which she lit and placed on a table, telling Spike to come and sit down and talk to us. The candlelight soothed him and he leaned forward across the table to speak to Simon confidingly, with none of the edgy tension just displayed, except when I put in a comment and he told me to shut up – he had come to speak to the boy, not the mother. When the lights came on again there was urgency to get on with the show and we were hurried to our seats, leaving Spike with only minutes before he was called. After the drama of meeting its sole performer, the show was disappointing as Spike looked tired and lonely, propped on a bar stool all by himself in the emptiness of that enormous stage; a spotlight shining on him while he delivered a monologue of jokes and anecdotes that sounded just as tired as he was.

Before we went home the next day I wanted to show Simon the marvel of Clifton suspension bridge and share with him the sensation of floating in space while walking above a dreamy landscape. He loved to see and experience remarkable things, but my urgency to show him this one went too far. The exertion made him breathless and close to collapse as we ran for a bus to get back to the station in time for our train home, and I felt guilty about causing him extra stress with my own enthusiasms.

After outings or events like this when Simon somehow managed to muster enough energy and focus to keep going for a limited time, he would crash out afterwards and have to spend time in bed to recover, isolated in his room. What he needed was a day-bed, I decided, like a sort of chaise longue, beside the sitting-room window where it was sunny and he could watch birds on the table outside. When Elizabeth heard about the day-bed idea she offered to get one for us, which I accepted gratefully as kind and generous of her. I had a picture in my mind of something that would be cushioned and comfortable, but what she brought was an old sun lounger she said they never used anymore. Apologising that it was a bit wobbly she hoped it would do and left it in the porch, folded up like a camp bed. When we got it straightened out and Simon lowered himself onto the stretched canvas, the whole thing flipped over. Further attempts to position himself on it with greater care only emphasised this tendency, which in his case posed a hazard since falling off might cause a fatal bleed. After this, the lounger was left in place for display purposes only, to avoid offending Elizabeth, while we found that two armchairs pushed together facing each other could be pressed into service as a day-bed.

Intervals when Simon was well enough to be up and about were getting shorter with hopes still fixed on finding a donor, but when news came at last from Westminster that none of the tests had found a match, it was the end of those hopes. Simon, again, was philosophical. 'In a way I'm glad,' he said, 'because I was dreading the ordeal of a transplant, knowing it might not work, and if it doesn't work it's a horrible death from GVH (graft versus host disease). Also, I would be far away from home shut up in a sterile room at the hospital like a zombie.'

'Now we know that you haven't got to face this,' I told him, 'whatever happens you will be here with us, in your own room, with Dad coming for Christmas, so we've got that to look forward to.'

He had his sixteenth birthday in October and the aunts came over from Howleigh with a cake and presents and their hysterical spaniels, who tore around the house scrabbling and panting to get out so they could run wild through the countryside. In normal times these distractions would be exasperating but for Simon they were a welcome diversion in his depleted state. He was visibly fading now and frail, but still alert to anything that sparked his interest and determined to be well enough to enjoy Christmas with Adam and not 'give in' as he saw it. 'For me it isn't a matter of, "Where there's life, there's hope". It's more a matter of, "Where there's hope, there's life",' he maintained. 'It is very disappointing to miss the rest of your life, if that is what happens, but there must be more important things beyond what we can see, and that is where life and hope lie.'

He wanted to be confirmed into the church, to affirm his Christian faith, and receive communion. He loved our local church, St Candida's at Whitchurch Canonicorum, which he attended for matins when he was well enough, but it puzzled him that nothing much happened there on weekdays. 'Why does Christianity only happen on Sundays?' he wanted to know.

'The rest of the week the church is empty even though people could enjoy going there, meeting and being friendly together, and welcoming pilgrims to St Candida's tomb. Not many churches have such an important saint buried where people can easily visit and pray beside them, but few people seem to know about her. Anyway, that's where I want to get confirmed.'

When I asked the vicar about a private confirmation, he surprised me by refusing to have anything to do with it. 'Such an absurd Catholic notion,' he said. 'Thinking it's necessary to take the sacrament before dying, in order to achieve absolution. I won't do it, and I doubt the bishop will agree either,' he added with feeling.

His vehemence startled me and I replied with equal feeling that it had nothing to do with any Catholic nostrum. 'Simon wants to be confirmed as a simple act of faith and, in his situation, to have comfort in receiving the sacrament.'

'I see we have opposing views on this and must agree to differ,' he replied, ending the matter. It was a sad reminder to me of Muz's distress when she was denied communion after her divorce, often lamenting: 'It can't be right for the innocent party in a divorce to suffer a double blow in losing a beloved spouse, and then losing the sacrament as well, just when it is most sorely needed. '

Friends who heard of our quest for someone to arrange the confirmation, approached a bishop whom they knew and he readily agreed to officiate at one of the churches in Weymouth, where we were welcomed, and the small simple service took place with members of that congregation attending. It was a friendly modern open-plan church and we would have liked to join them more often, but Simon was devoted to our parish church despite the vicar's disapproval. After confirmation he was entitled to receive communion there and was not refused.

He asked to be buried in the churchyard and went to choose his own place, wanting it to be on the south side of the church where it would be closer to our house and the sea than on the north side. It was a brave thing for a sixteen-year-old boy to do when he should have been looking at bright opportunities ahead instead of a place in the ground. 'I want to do this before Dad gets here,' he said. 'It's not the kind of thing that Dad likes being involved in.'

Adam was coming home early for Christmas so that he and Simon could spend time together with a particular source of excitement in view, since they had been invited to join a shooting party on a friend's farm, with Pete invited as well. This was clearly an all-male occasion that I was glad to miss, as my usual experience of shooting parties meant being recruited with other wives as beaters or dog handlers, but that was in Kenya and I had not yet discovered whether customs were different in England.

We were all very aware that it was to be Simon's last Christmas, and he was determined to be well enough to enjoy every minute of Adam's company and any activities that might be on offer. He had been primed with a blood transfusion and drugs to boost his energy and was in high spirits, when only a few months before he had been too weak at times even to get out of bed. There had been a momentous day in the summer when the Royal Marines came back from the Falklands and drove in convoy through our village with flags flying, returning to their base at Lympstone. Everyone turned out to cheer and wave as they drove past, jubilant with the sense of victory and that they had come home safely. People took chairs to sit out on the pavement to watch the vehicles pass and I took a chair for Simon, but he didn't have enough strength to join us and it seemed he could not survive too much longer at that stage. Now here we were, coming up to Christmas 1982, and he was surprising all of us, including the doctors.

There was a dip in morale when another child at the leukaemia clinic died and this was Katie, who was friends with Simon. He wanted to go to her funeral and I tried to dissuade him, thinking it would be stressful, but he insisted and wanted Adam to come with us. It was a crowded time for me once Adam arrived in the run-up to Christmas, with many friends and relations invited for social visits, and appointments for Simon at the hospital to be fitted in as well. On the day of Katie's funeral I wanted to be sure we arrived in good time, which was always tricky with Adam because he was incorrigibly late for everything, and dismissive of any inconvenience caused. Simon and I were both dressed and ready to go when Adam had not yet changed into the suit I put ready on the bed for him, and was engaged in a long phone call, waving me away when I told him: 'Please, please, hurry'.

'We'll have to go without Dad,' I said to Simon. 'It would be such bad manners to arrive late.'

'You can't leave Dad behind; that would be even worse manners.' Simon replied. So we waited while Adam took his time and all of us arrived at the church just as the first hymn was being sung. The main body of the church was packed, with no seats free, so an usher escorted us all the way up the aisle to the choir stalls where we were given seats in the front row, facing Katie's coffin. The poignancy of that small coffin lying so close to us for the whole of the service until it was carried away, was almost unbearable for me, and I felt stricken for Simon who I thought must have found it even more of an ordeal. But afterwards when I commented on this, he said, 'No, you're wrong, Mum. For me it was an incredible privilege to spend the whole of that time alongside Katie, even closer to her than her own family who were further away in the front pew. It was an honour, and wouldn't have happened that way without Dad being late. There are reasons for the way things happen. You can see that, can't you?'

Elaine was writing her latest book in a series of Christian books and sent Simon a list of questions with a blank tape for him to reply. The questions were direct and explicit, probing how he felt about death so early in his life and how his Christian faith related to this. To me the questions were tough for someone his age, but again he took it on the chin and spoke on the tape as fully and frankly as he could despite the effort required for quite a long recording.

He had a check-up at the hospital a few days before Christmas when he was due for blood tests and adjustment of his drugs, which were now mainly palliative, and I was hoping that Adam would come with us. I thought he would want to be part of any discussion with doctors and I craved his support, but he couldn't bring himself to come, or meet the doctors. 'You can tell me about it afterwards,' he said, and I knew that he didn't want to hear anything too difficult, and was only able to get through the strain of this time if he maintained a certain detachment. Simon understood this, and that it was better to go by ourselves rather than worry about Adam's state of mind if he was with us.

When the blood results came through on that visit, Dr Johnston gave me a wry look and commented that it was a mystery what Simon was running on. 'Some of the counts are so low, most people would not be alive, let alone walking around,' he said.

'He doesn't want to miss a moment of Christmas with his dad, and all of us,' I explained. 'Somehow he has found a reserve tank and is running on it for as long as he can until it gives out.'

The shooting party was a highlight that had been anticipated with mounting excitement for weeks, and when he went off with Adam and Pete it was a triumph for him, but took all his strength and the rest of Christmas was more subdued. Adam had only a short time left after Christmas before returning to Mafia, and during these last few days Simon decided he wanted to learn to play Bridge. I had been to classes so could teach the others, it was assumed. My grasp of the essentials was elementary after failing to graduate from the class at the end of a whole year of instruction, due to being inept, so my teaching of the family led to a rogue form of the noble game being played. This caused much comedy and flagrant behaviour, making us all feel a lot better.

It seemed perverse for Adam to be leaving when Simon was clearly sinking and Adam's presence meant so much to him. We talked about this and whether Adam should get an extension of his holiday as compassionate leave, but then it would seem to Simon that he was waiting for him to die, imposing a sense of urgency. We thought if Adam left as planned, it would indicate to Simon that life was continuing as normal, and that would be reassuring for him. We agreed on this so Adam left a few days after Christmas, with much tightening of our hearts for being apart at this time. The lack of reliable communication with Mafia Island remained a problem that bothered me greatly, but it was Simon who did the cheering. 'Don't worry, Mum, we'll get through to Dad if we need to,' he said, giving me a hug as emphasis of his concern to spare me anxiety. While many boys of sixteen might be uncomfortable with open displays of affection, he was naturally warm-hearted, tender and caring.

Pete, soon to be fourteen, was becoming more detached and was visibly maturing as he overtook Simon in physical development, while Louise was far ahead now. It stung Simon to see them well and healthy with full lives ahead, in contrast to his own. 'It's hard to think of the family going on without me,' he said wistfully. 'I'm going to miss everything that happens.'

The change in him after Adam left was sudden and striking as the energy he had stored up for the visit drained away and he went down fast. I watched in dismay as he became thinner and smaller each day, until in the evenings when I helped him out of the bath, holding him in my arms wrapped in a towel, he felt like a tiny child again. But his eyes were bright and his spirit, still irrepressible, seemed almost as if it wanted to burst out of his body and fly away all by itself.

Petechiae (small patches of bruising) had appeared on his legs and arms which we both knew was a bad sign but he said this was to be expected. More of a problem was the pain that had started in his bones at this point due to the increasing volume of malignant cells in his bone marrow. This caused pressure inside his bones and was often worse at night when there was no service locally that we could call for help. There seemed to be a disconnect between the hospital and our GP surgery so that I was not able to access adequate pain-relieving drugs from either source, or any visiting nurse to help and give advice.

Simon was fearful of being admitted to hospital and not getting out again so we struggled on at home, becoming increasingly stressed and exhausted with fraught days and nights. He was too ill to attend the clinic and Dr Johnston suggested seeing us at the ward to discuss how to manage this stage. A blood test, as expected, showed the need for urgent transfusion which it was thought could give Simon a boost and some relief. Dr Johnston said this required a stay in hospital overnight so they could observe him and adjust his pain control. Simon didn't mind a night in the ward with staff who were his friends and looked forward to the reviving effects of a transfusion. He didn't want me to stay so I was able to leave him in good spirits, promising to come and take him home in the morning.

When I arrived next day, hoping to find him refreshed after a better night than we had recently been experiencing at home, I was met at the nurses' station by one of the staff nurses who told me there had been complications with the transfusion. Due to Simon's debilitated state, transfused blood had overloaded his system and caused problems resulting in some necrosis in his lower extremities. He had been sedated but was fully conscious and waiting for me to arrive. Dr Johnston was on his way, she said, with tears in her eyes, so I knew it was bad and we had come to the end.

Simon, however, had only one thought when he saw me. ‘Did you bring clean pyjamas, Mum? I’m going to have to stay in for now so I’m going to need some more, and other things too. I want to show you my legs. They’re covered in black patches. I think it’s gangrene. I want you to have a look and see what you think.’ He uncovered his legs and we both knew what it meant – there was no way back now. When I tried to speak, he interrupted, looking at me intently but with no alarm. ‘I’m cracking up. I know that. You need to phone Dad.’

‘I’ll never be able to get through to Mafia on the pay phone here. I’ll have to go home. But I can’t leave you like this.’

‘Yes, you can. Dr Johnston will come soon and give me another injection for the pain. If you go quickly you can phone Dad and get my pyjamas at the same time.’ The staff didn’t want me to go but Simon was insistent, and if it was to be the last thing I could do for him, I would do whatever that was and get a message to Adam. I wanted Simon to know that his father’s thoughts were with him, and I wanted the comfort of Adam’s thoughts for myself too.

By the time I got home, driving fast and desperately, the Mafia switchboard operator had gone for his afternoon siesta. The Dar es Salaam office should be able to get a message to Adam, I thought, so I phoned there and explained everything to the secretary, then bundled Simon’s pyjamas into a bag and did another high-speed dash back to the hospital.

‘Thank God you’re here,’ a nurse said, coming to the door of Simon’s room. ‘We should never have let you go. Soon after you left, he lost consciousness and he’s sinking now, but still with us.’ I went to sit beside him and took his hand, squeezing it. ‘It’s Mum,’ I said. ‘If you can feel me squeezing your hand, squeeze back.’ There was no response but I went on talking to him, telling him that I had got his pyjamas and left a message for Dad, hoping he could still hear me as many unconscious people still have good hearing even when incapable of speech. His eyes were open and there was a moment when he suddenly looked directly at me and his whole expression changed. He looked excited and amazed as if he had seen something extraordinary and was just about to tell me what it was. I moved forward to hear him. ‘Yes, what is it?’ I asked, startled by his expression and certain he was about to speak, but then it was as if a light had switched off in his eyes and the contrast was instant, he had gone. There was just his empty body lying there and I was still holding his hand as a nurse bent over to check for a heartbeat, and turned to me, unable to speak through tears. I couldn't cry because I had just seen something beyond tears. It was the look he had as he died, a look of absolute wonder, a transformation. When I told Dr Johnston about this he said it was an effect of the brain shutting down, releasing a burst of electrical impulses. I accepted that as a physiological explanation but he hadn't seen what I had seen, and whatever it was, Simon had died with a look of rapture that was unmistakable and unforgettable.

All I wanted now was Adam to come home and be with us for the funeral. Louise too. She had gone back to college after Christmas, refusing to believe that anything bad would happen to Simon. When she got the message to phone me urgently she went to the nearest phone box completely unaware. I was at home by then with a phone constantly ringing as the news went round, and Ros had come to help as always. She answered the phone when Louise called, and told her what had happened, which she couldn't take in and collapsed in the phone box, still holding the phone. 'No, no, he can't be dead,' she kept saying, bewildered.

'He was very ill at Christmas, just hanging on, wanting to spend as long as possible with your dad,' Ros said. 'You need to come home. You'll have to explain to your tutor what has happened, so you can be here for the funeral.' There was silence. 'Are you all right?' Ros could hear her scrambling to her feet, and then the phone clicked off.

'We'll have to go and get her,' Ros said. 'I'll go if you want to stay with Pete.' He had been very quiet when I told him and didn't want to talk. 'I'm OK, Mum. I'm just getting on with my things.'

Once Louise had been collected and we were home again, Ros always the organiser, set about picking up loose ends which had been left waiting to be noticed and dealt with. She cooked meals, answered the phone and the door, went shopping, soothed Muz's consternation at the news, and sent messages to Fa who was on a ship at sea.

Robert wanted to come at once and help in any way that he could, entirely unconcerned about meeting Adam while wanting only to help me with arrangements, and pay for anything that needed paying for. But Adam, I knew, would resent any intrusion and would resent Robert's flair and composure demonstrated in taking care of things at such a sensitive time. The two of them would collide and I couldn't let that happen, so once again, kind, loving, generous Robert was held off.

Adam sent a telegram with his travel plans so we could set a date for the funeral, but there was a snag when we realised this would clash with Elizabeth and Peter's silver wedding celebrations. A big party had been planned long in advance and the two events could not be held in the same week. Elizabeth and Peter very generously offered to postpone their silver wedding party but instead of cancelling the guests and caterers, they suggested that all could go ahead in a new guise as a wake after the funeral. This was an excellent solution so we accepted gratefully.

I had to borrow a black coat for the service as the only coat I possessed was a green tartan long-line jacket which made me look like a bookie's assistant. This was clearly unsuitable for an occasion when the press would be there with cameras, since Simon's death had been reported in some of the national newspapers. On a foolish point of honour I had resisted Robert's attempts to replace the vulgar jacket with something elegant and expensive from Harrods, and the borrowed black coat was heavy and shapeless, but I could hunch myself into it and feel less exposed while crumpled with grief in the ordeal ahead.

When we arrived at the church, it was overflowing and the front pew where we were supposed to sit was already occupied so everyone had to move up and let us squeeze in. There was much shuffling about as yet more people arrived, to the dismay of ushers and the organist who was waiting for his cue so the service could start. Simon's coffin stood in front by the choir stalls and scent from the massed flowers piled around it came to us in sweet drifts. The atmosphere was electric as the first hymn was announced and the roar of voices released from suppressed emotion in that vaulted space sounded tumultuous. All was exactly as it should be and felt to me like a benediction as the vicar who had opposed Simon's confirmation, now delivered a powerful address of tribute that needed no readings or verses to follow.

It was at the graveside that reality set in when I saw Simon's name on the coffin as it was being lowered. Someone pressed a posy of primroses into my hand to throw on top of the coffin, but I couldn't let go of them and send the sweetness of those tiny flowers to lie crushed under the ground when they could stay with me, alive and cheerful. I went on clutching them all the way to Peter and Elizabeth's house, their yellow faces bright against my black coat, and later kept them in water at home.

Pete was put in charge of handing round drinks at the wake and we had a rousing party with quantities of alcohol dispensed, which made everyone feel a lot better. At some point it was noticed that Pete had disappeared and there was no sign of him in the house, so a search party went out into the lane where cars had been parked. He was discovered passed-out in one of the cars, dead drunk, having drained the dregs of glasses as he collected them for washing and refilling. This incident lightened the mood of the occasion even more as he was carted home incapable of standing, and everyone thought it was entirely in the spirt of the occasion to get blotted after losing his brother at such a young age.

By the next day all I wanted was to keep Adam with me as long as possible, hoping that he might see how much we needed him, in particular Pete who was struggling with his emotions and not doing well at school. The family, diminished now without Simon, needed an anchor and that was Adam's role but he had become busy with things to do, he said, as he took the car and went off, telling me that he would explain later. It sounded hopeful that he might be exploring opportunities for a new job nearer home, I thought. Time was short with only a week left before he had to go back to Mafia. 'It's a bit tricky,' he said. 'I don't want to get your hopes up, so I'm not saying anything until I know that this plan can go ahead.'

The anticipation and suspense was a good antidote to post-funeral gloom as I felt carried along on a wave of optimism, but not enough to go into Simon's room which had been left with all his things, books and boxes and little treasures that were so important to him, untouched since his last day at home. If we were moving again, I would have to sort out the room, but that could wait for Adam's announcement.

When he came back from the mysterious visits a couple of days later, he was smiling and impatient to tell me the news. 'It's all fixed, you can come and join me now in Mafia. I've been to see the headmaster at Allhallows School and arranged for Pete to go there as a boarder straight away. I've already paid the first term's fees. He needs a proper education. Woodroffe isn't the place for him. The Allhallows head has recently come from Gordonstoun where he was Prince Andrew's housemaster. He'll get Pete sorted in short order. You'll have to get all the kit he needs from the outfitters in Exeter. Louise has flown the nest so she's independent and doesn't need you here, but I need you in Mafia. It's all fixed. What do you think, darling?'

This was so unexpected, I was left speechless and floundering for a reply. I longed for the chance to go back to Africa, but not like this. 'Have you told Pete?'

'No. I thought it best for you to tell him. He's been very quiet since Simon went, and he'll probably take it better from you.'

'I don't understand why didn't you discuss this with me, and him, before going ahead and getting it all sewn up without any hint to the rest of us.' I was perplexed. 'How is Pete supposed to cope with being sent away at the very time he needs family support the most?'

'For pity's sake, love, you're being melodramatic. We're in a different situation now. We need to do what's best for our one remaining son, and all of us, including you and me. If you are so sensitive about telling Pete, then I will. It's a tremendous opportunity for him, I'm sure he'll see it that way.'

When Pete was told the news, predictably, he was outraged and defiant: 'I'm not going to sodding Allhallows, or anywhere else. You can't force me. If you do, I'll get myself expelled.'

I tried to reason with him. 'There seems to be a problem with your GCSEs and it's vital that you do them. At Allhallows they will have the right support, which you are not getting at Woodroffe.' It was true. I had been to see his tutor to find out why he was taking only CSEs instead of GCSEs and was told that he wasn't up to the standard required. 'He isn't stupid,' I said. 'I don't believe he can't do GCSEs. We could get extra help for him.'

'He has to be seen by the educational psychologist to qualify for extra help.'

'Could you arrange an appointment? He can't be left to wallow around at the bottom of the class if there is an alternative.'

'It's usually children with behavioural problems who get sent to the psychologist, and Pete isn't one of those.'

'If the psychologist will see him, then I think it's worth a try.'

'I'll see what I can do and let you know.'

I didn't hear anything, but on one of the days when the psychologist was visiting the school, Pete was sent for and given various tests, returning home later in a furious mood. 'Why the hell was I sent to the shrink, Mum? It was so embarrassing. They said you had requested it. I was put in a room with all the dummies waiting to be seen. It was a nightmare. Just the same as what Dad went through with his shrink. I'm not like Dad. What's this all about?'

'I need to find out why you're not doing GCSEs, that's all.'

'I'm not doing them because I don't want to do them, that's all.'

'We'll see if the psychologist comes up with the same conclusion.'

Instead of a letter arriving with his advice, the psychologist asked to see me at the school and I went full of optimism that Pete would now get extra help, so was surprised to be received in a distinctly cool manner. Dispensing with the usual pleasantries he began abruptly, giving me a hard stare. 'There is nothing wrong with your son. He doesn't have a problem. You are the one with a problem. You are trying to push him in a direction of your choice, not his. You belong to a class of ambitious parents who set unrealistic goals for their children, with predictable results, the proof of which brings you here.'

I was completely taken aback and baffled by this undisguised antagonism, but thought the best course was to play along. 'What is your advice then?'

'Parents like you need to back off and let the child find his own way, which he will, in his own time. You may not like it, but you will be doing him a favour in the long run, and yourself, if you think about it.'

'Thank you, I'll bear that in mind,' I said without blinking.

He seemed pleased to have convinced me, as he thought, but it had the opposite effect and made me even more determined to find a way for Pete to do GCSEs. When Adam announced the move to Allhallows it offered a solution, but was done in haste with no sensitivity to the impact on Pete at this time because his main concern was getting me to Mafia. Expensive fees had been paid and binding arrangements made in the aftermath of Simon's death with no alternative offered, so I was left with the urgency of getting Pete equipped and handed over to Allhallows within days of Adam leaving.

At first Pete refused to cooperate and was angry and tight-lipped during the entire process, but we made a deal. I persuaded him to go along with the move and give it a fair shot, on the understanding that if he still found the new school unbearable after completing two terms, he could go back to Woodroffe and board there. It was a gamble, but these were rocky times.

After Adam and then Pete had gone, there was nobody left in the house except me and our little cat, Baby, who had kept company with Simon, sleeping on his bed during the long days and nights of his illness. I had Baby's company now which was consoling, but the house felt desolate without all the usual comings and goings that accompanied Simon's constant enthusiasms. He had made me promise to continue his Leukaemia Fund and this took a boost when press coverage of his death resulted in a surge of correspondence and enquiries. Every day brought a pile of letters, mainly of condolence, but touchingly, since the *Daily Mirror* had carried pictures of Simon, letters arrived from kind-hearted readers. I wanted to answer all of them, and this would give me something to do, I reasoned, and be a useful antidote to the crushing listlessness that seemed to be settling on me like a fuzzy fog. David Cozens, always the best of friends and catalyst in driving fund activities, came round to give me a pep talk. 'Come on, Wednesday (his pet name for me), we've got work to do. It's Simon's legacy. We can't let him down. Spotlight wants you on TV at the studios down in Plymouth. You'll have to put your best face on. Simon was always ace in front of cameras. You're going to have to take that slot now'.

'He was a performer. I'm not. I'm a back-room person. The one who makes the tea and washes up. Can't you do the interview?'

'Don't be daft. Do I have a pretty face? You're the only one who can do this. For Simon. Keeping his dream alive.'

The interview inevitably generated even more publicity and the workload grew, while I wanted to be with Adam far away in Mafia obscurity, but could not leave until satisfied that Pete had settled at school. Letters came from Adam urging me to hurry up, but Pete's housemaster advised caution and I understood why when a problem developed. Soon after starting at the school he was rusticated for two weeks (sent home as a punishment) for fighting and breaking up furniture. This was seriously abnormal behaviour in line with the threat to get himself expelled, but we had a deal and I reminded him about it.

'The deal is still on,' he said, 'and the headmaster has made another kind of deal with me, so I'm stuck with that one too.'

He told me what happened when he was called to the headmaster's study after the fight. 'It wasn't what I expected,' he said. 'The head sat me down and instead of a massive bollocking, he was very calm and constructive. He said the school wants to be proud of me and that I have a lot to offer them. I can do it, he said, and be proud of myself too. It was all positive, looking ahead, chin-up kind of stuff. He seemed to know that I had been in the Army Cadets and told me about the School Corps, which he thought I would enjoy, and could become a useful member. So the interview turned into a sort of morale-boosting exercise in the end, but only on his terms, making sure I got the message.'

'What now, then?'

'I'll have to give it my best shot, like you said.'

I had an appointment to see the headmaster when I took Pete back and expected to be told that any repeat of violent behaviour would not be tolerated a second time. What I didn't expect was to be told that the school could not accept responsibility for Pete's continuing attendance without at least one parent remaining in the country. While this was sensible and reasonable in line with my own wish to stay until Pete was settled and happy, I had hoped it would not take too long for this to happen, so it was a severe blow that I was now stuck in England indefinitely. Adam was incensed when he heard this, but there was nothing we could do about it and here I was, alone in an empty house, wondering what to do next.

Ros had her own home and calligraphy work to keep up with, and Fa was still away at sea. Elaine was preoccupied with her books and family, having had little time for connection with us during Simon's illness, and she hadn't come to the funeral. Muz had come by herself during that tense time, explaining that Andy didn't like funerals, and Ros arranged for her to stay in a B&B with them to spare me having to look after her on top of everything else. Muz had been extremely indignant about this, protesting that she was being left out as it was only right that she should be included in the household of principal mourners. Her disgruntled behaviour dominated proceedings and when we were having supper for close family at our house on the evening before the funeral, Muz refused to get out of the car after coming over with Ros from the B&B. 'I'm not going into Wendy's house if she is not letting me stay there with them,' Muz protested, and went on sitting in the car on that very cold January night. Supper was rushed through and plates taken out to her but she refused to eat anything, sticking to her guns in this perverse mood, which spoilt everything for the rest of us trying to take comfort from family unity in circumstances that were anyway very strained.

Robert didn't come to the funeral either and I missed him, but he had been sent on a cruise arranged by his secretary who remained ever hopeful that her rehabilitation efforts might result in a new partner for him. This latest effort teetered on the edge of disaster only a short time after the cruise ship left Southampton and Robert was taken to meet other 'singles'. He described later his horror at being surrounded by a mass of eager females, the only other single man having fled, leaving Robert to fend off the mob. After extricating himself, he went for some fresh air on deck where he noticed that the English coastline was still clearly visible, within swimming distance, he calculated. He was a strong swimmer and being desperate to escape was tempted to jump, but thought it safer to go to the captain and ask for a helicopter to take him off. His request was refused on the grounds that his discomfort in no way constituted an emergency, besides which there was no landing platform on the ship. The captain said he would have to wait until they reached the Azores where he could disembark and fly home. 'It was days and nights of hell before the Azores,' Robert reported, 'lurking in my cabin, hiding from the horde. I'm never going near a ship again, but my secretary only laughed when I told her about it.'

Pete responded positively to the headmaster's appeal and now seemed fully engaged in school activities, which was a great relief to me. He had rugby at weekends and coast-guard duty since joining the Rousdon Station with other young volunteers. Weekends, I found, are the worst time for people on their own when families are together and everyone is busy. I needed a job, that was the answer. Back to nursing. The absence of district-nurse support supplied from doctors' surgeries as it used to be, was a loss to the community I discovered when needing help with Simon in his last days. I went to talk to one of the local GPs about my idea for a private nursing service, which he welcomed and said he had several patients he would be glad to refer to me when I was ready to go. Before this could happen there were regulations to meet and equipment to put together with uniforms and paperwork: then I had my first patient and was never lonely again.

Like Muz, who found solace in being busy, this was a distraction for me from low times when I felt that my life had lost direction with no one at home anymore. Losing Simon was like losing part of my own body, but more than being busy I needed peace of mind while all the questions about his death remained unanswered. There was no resolution to make me feel better about this despite knowing he died in a state of wonder. Kind people recommended books and in one of these a single sentence has stayed with me, offering that peace: *What happens to you in your life is not important; what is important is how you respond to what happens to you*. With this prompting I made a positive decision to remember Simon always with happiness instead of sadness, and when talking about him, remember to smile and be animated, for his sake, as that is how he was.

Adam had used up all his leave so there was no chance of a visit from him and I was still hoping to join him if Pete's record at school allowed me to go, but meanwhile I now had a new sense of purpose and new interests. Simon's fund was at the centre of these and Robert wanted me to become more involved in charity work with him. He had come to accept that my loyalty to Adam meant we could never be more than close friends and he was magnanimous about this. A more understanding and generous friend would be hard to find and I genuinely loved him for these qualities, and for the extraordinary person that he was: a maverick of the most rare and benevolent kind.

The biggest surprise of the year arrived one morning when I woke early and, going to the window of my room, caught sight of a man standing at the end of the garden, with his back to me, looking at the view. I recognised that silhouette and the way he stood, the shape of his head and his hair, hands loose by his sides and the stillness of him as I watched and held my breath. He must have sensed my gaze as he turned and saw me at the window, and smiled. It was a smile that bridged tens of years and thousands of miles. It was Lanner.

The awkwardness that had crippled our previous encounter dissolved when I opened the door and we held each other for a long time before anything was said. 'Is it really you?' he asked, as last time it had been the same question, but this time we laughed, remembering how it had been then as strangers, knowing that everything now had changed. He had come to England for a conference and on impulse that day drove from London to Dorset to see how I was in the aftermath of Simon's death, wanting to visit the grave and hear about my life. It was the briefest of visits and we talked insatiably over two days as if we could never come to the end of all the things we wanted to tell each other, walking for miles across the rolling countryside of West Dorset, stopping at tiny pubs deep in the heart of golden-stone villages. We knew it was the shortest time together, but we had years of lost time to make up for.

Chapter 14

When Lanner had to leave, saying goodbye to him was another aching loss for me after the most tender of partings, but instead of feeling overwhelmed this time I felt strengthened by the renewed connection between us, with promises to write. This was sustaining but I could not look beyond letters. He wasn't free. Commitment to his family was absolute in the context of a successful career and marriage, which he emphasised was central to his entire existence, provoking me to muse on this ability to compartmentalise different areas of his life. It was something that men seemed able to do without a care and reminded me of Byron's lines:

Man's love is of man's life a thing apart,
'Tis woman's whole existence.

Not any more, I said to myself. Lingering in a state of limbo while I waited to join Adam would serve this statement just as dependence on letters from Lanner would bind me to the same fate, but I had a career and could earn my own money and be free to choose what happened next. Simon's fund would go forward as a tangible memorial with David Cozen's help, and all that remained was acceptance that my home was now a small green island instead of the wide, burnt, beloved plains of Africa. That loss was another sorrow, and despite finding a measure of peace in thinking about Simon, it did not erase all questions and the ever-present sense of guilt which I came to realise haunts those who have lost a child.

Whatever the cause of death, a loving parent perceives it as a failure of responsibility to keep that child safe and well. Questions persisted. Was Simon's leukaemia triggered by the stress of moving to England? He had been more affected by the move than any of us, having embraced life in Florida wholeheartedly. Was there anything we could have done or failed to do for him? Pete said that leaving America was the worst thing that had ever happened to our family, but he was emerging now from those dark times and taking on a whole new persona, confident and aspiring. Could he have felt eclipsed in previous times by Simon, whose death by tragic irony now freed him to shine?

During this year of 1983 there were increasingly urgent calls from Charles's wife to go and help her at the big house where she was feeling the strain of looking after three young children with scatty nannies who caused problems instead of easing them for her. One of the nannies had crashed the family car and gone off to recover, leaving them short-handed and needing help. I thought what they really needed was a holiday and offered to have the children to stay with me so everyone could get a break. This idea was accepted and I collected the children who sat in a row on the back seat of my car like little mice, unnaturally subdued, until they arrived and met Baby with her kittens who were ready for playtime. From that moment the house was filled with rough and tumble far from a nanny world of clean clothes and set routines, as the children ran barefoot and rolled down grassy slopes outside, discovering somersaults and how to make daisy chains. My nursing work was suspended while this little family enchanted me with their endearing ways after an initial reserve had been thrown off. I hoped we might have other carefree holidays together, which I suggested when I took them home and noticed how quiet and solemn they became when the big house swallowed them again.

It was soon after this that Babs and Fa said they were coming for a holiday and were renting a caravan on one of the beach-front sites, which would spare me having them to stay, they explained. This unusual thoughtfulness alerted Ros to come down in her role as buffer, suspecting more episodes of weirdness after that of the mangled turkey. When we were invited for a caravan supper she became even more suspicious. 'How are they going to do any kind of decent supper in a caravan?' she wanted to know. 'Why don't they take us to the Anchor (pub) where we can have lovely fish and chips only yards from the caravan park?'

'Because Fa might have to pay for it,' I suggested.

'It can be our treat or we can go Dutch,' Ros said, but when this was put to Fa he protested that they had already organised the supper and it was their treat for us in the comfort of their caravan, instead of sharing a smoky bar area with people drinking.

'We'll have to risk that they haven't been fishing in bins at the back of the Anchor, collecting rejects from the kitchen,' Ros said.

Whenever Fa was about to produce one of his unspeakable surprises he would put on the widest of smiles and become more animated than usual as the moment of revelation approached. This time after we had squashed ourselves into the tiny space provided for eating at a tray-sized table in a caravan hardly bigger than a bubble car, Fa ceremoniously placed a plastic dish in front of us with a squat brown object sitting in the middle of it. We stared at it, thinking we might have missed something, but there it was – a small round pork pie – a favourite delicacy of his along with kippers which mercifully this time were absent. Fa flourished a scalpel over the pie and with skilled precision cut it into four equal pieces which Babs then handed round, one for each of us. Ros and I exchanged glances, wondering if there might be a lettuce leaf or tomato coming next, or even possibly some chutney. Babs noticed the looks of enquiry. 'There weren't any salad items in the village shop. We were lucky to find this pie. Such a godsend. Tuck in.' I glanced at Ros trying not to snigger as we did our best, Craddock fashion, to pretend that the few dry morsels on our plates equalled a full dinner, while using the time between tiny mouthfuls to hold a conversation as if all this was normal.

'You'll stay for dessert, won't you?' Babs trilled in her little-girl voice as we finished and she noticed us wriggling and looking at the door. 'We've got Angel Delight. I was glad to find packets in the shop and it's easy to do, instant, and full of flavour.'

At least it isn't her egg-nog with raw eggs beaten into a slimy gloop with brandy having to be swallowed all in one like oysters, I thought, grinning at Ros who was thinking the same. When the Angel Delight arrived we had to drink it out of cups because it was more like sugary pink soup than a pudding, which did not deter Babs from thinking it strikingly delicious. 'I told you it would be full of flavour,' she twittered on happily as Fa beamed at her for her efforts. I could see Ros edging towards the door when she finished her cup and there was enough of a pause to enable a polite getaway. 'Won't you stay for some instant coffee?' we could hear Babs calling after us as we made a dash for it, across a field and into the Anchor for sustenance.

Spring had turned into summer and one day I woke to find the house full of butterflies. They were fluttering around every room in the sunlight of early morning as Simon's chrysalises had hatched all by themselves, with no attention from me despite promises that I would look after them. When the children were staying they had found the chrysalis boxes and taken the lids off to look inside, conveniently leaving these off so the newly hatched butterflies were able to emerge. It was a poignant moment for me as I opened the front door to let them fly out, as if Simon's spirit went with them to live on in the cycles of nature he had been so passionate about, watching and studying them in the valley below Golden Cap.

It seemed paradoxical that this love of wild things went hand in hand with a love of guns and shooting, but this did not seem unnatural to Simon, or to Adam who fostered these interests in both sons so they grew up with a sense of respect and responsibility towards all countryside pursuits. Guns were never treated casually and strict rules applied with an almost religious sense of duty. When Adam was not at home Simon had been in charge of the gun safe which was bolted to supports in the loft, and keys to the safe were kept by him in what he referred to as a secret place. The plan worked well while he was alive, but no one had thought to ask him about the secret place before he died, so when a policeman arrived to do the annual inspection which was a gun-licencing requirement, we had a problem. The policeman was very understanding when I explained the situation and agreed to come back when the keys were found. This meant sorting out Simon's room, which I had been putting off, but even the most detailed detective-style fingertip search uncovered no sign of gun-safe keys. They must be somewhere in the house, I thought, so every crevice and crack was explored. Furniture, cupboards and drawers were examined, with Pete helping, and me complaining: 'You should have known where the keys were. You should have found out from Simon long ago, so you could both look after the guns.'

'I did know once, but Simon kept changing the hiding place, saying it was safer that way.'

'What are we going to do, then?'

'You could try sending a sort of telepathic message to Simon wherever he is, to give us a clue about where the keys are. It might work.'

'Good idea. Weird, but worth a try.'

When I was on my own, I focused my thoughts on Simon and the keys and the message, which was like a little prayer. Nothing happened, but I wasn't expecting miracles. Then a few days later when I had forgotten about it, the keys arrived, with no indication how they got there, lying on the mat in the hall, still on their key ring. The mystery of their reappearance was never solved but I was able to invite the policeman to come back for his inspection. There was a 12- bore shot gun and two heavy rifles (a 350 Rigby and a 470 Gibbs) and when I took them out to show the constable, he asked me which was which. I suggested he look down the barrels to see which had a smooth bore and which had rifling. He did this and was interested to discover these different features, knowing nothing of such distinctions, which surprised me if he was supposed to be checking licences for different types of guns.

Robert was frustrated that my weekends were as busy as weekdays since I had started working; frustrated that we had been unable to save Simon; and frustrated that his horse had come last in the Derby. Adding to this was impatience with what he called, 'The Adam situation'. 'You need to get a divorce,' Robert insisted. 'You have to accept that he has gone off and left you, so, in effect, the marriage is at an end. My lawyer can handle the divorce. It can be quick, and amicable.'

'No, Robert, it isn't like that. I have no grounds for divorce. Adam hasn't left me. We're separated, that's all.'

'Take it from me, you will never get back with Adam. You can be very naïve at times. You're too trusting for your own good.' I wanted to say that

I had made vows but that would sound sanctimonious and too much like Muz playing the Christian card as an excuse for ignoring reality, which maybe I was now doing myself.

Lanner was coming back to England for a concert organised in honour of Simon to raise money for his fund, but it was no ordinary concert. As a tribute to Simon being only sixteen when he died, all the musicians chosen were young, and all were outstanding instrumentalists. There was oboist Nicholas Daniel, who was the current winner of Young Musician of the Year, two violinists and a cellist from the Yehudi Menuhin School of Music, choristers of the Wells Cathedral choir, a pianist who was flying over specially from New York, and a charismatic presenter who held it all together. A large portrait of Simon was displayed on the stage throughout the performance and this was very emotional for me, together with Lanner sitting next to me holding my hand. We went to visit Simon's grave the next day, standing together beside his headstone, needing no words to express our feelings in those quiet moments. He won't find it so easy to leave this time, I thought, slipping back to his family and safe life. I was becoming more resilient to sadness after so much recent immersion, but the connection between us was now so intense that when he left it felt like another bereavement.

On the day and time that his plane took off from Heathrow I stood outside the house looking across the valley, imagining that I might see the plane flying south, high in the air above me, which was mere fantasy but comforting. I didn't expect to hear or see any aircraft but in a sudden flash from a clear sky there came abruptly the sound and swoop of a single-engine plane, flying low over Golden Cap and the valley. It was a Spitfire, or possibly a Hurricane, I didn't know which but could see RAF roundels on the wings, and watched spellbound as it turned over the sea and came back to dip and soar in the valley a few times before disappearing inland. Lanner had done National Service as a fighter pilot and this display, whatever its intention, felt like a surprise departing gift for me, from him.

The move to Sun Cottage for Muz and Andy revived an urge in them to go exploring new areas of the road map, with Andy indulging robotic driving skills in the Austin Princess while Muz dithered over the maps. Ros called me in a panic one evening after a message had come from Anglesey in Wales where they were stranded, having set off on a drive to York and turned left by mistake at some point on the way. They eventually stopped at a roadside B&B where a Welsh lady took them in and contacted Ros whose number they gave her after arriving in an agitated state. 'I'll have to go and rescue them, I suppose,' she said. 'It doesn't sound as if they are likely to be able to find their own way back. They're not safe to go wandering off by themselves, but I think this experience has given them such a fright they will hardly do more in future than creep out of Sun Cot to visit poor Spindle.' He had moved with them from Suffolk and was now incarcerated in a mental hospital in Dorchester, which luckily was only a few miles away. 'He seems much happier in this new place,' Muz reported. 'They have art classes for the inmates so he is drawing and painting again, which he loves, and some of his pictures are displayed on the walls of the visitors' room so we can see them. This was the first good news for poor Spindle for many years and when I went to see him he showed me the pictures, which regretfully I found completely unfathomable, being mainly black and abstract. 'What are they?' I asked rather undiplomatically.

'Black holes and vortexes,' he told me, as if that was obvious.

'What are those dots in between the objects?'

'They are disseminated particles,' he said impatiently, as if that was obvious too. In moments of relative clarity like this he could become surprisingly articulate and use language picked up from Fa. It was not hard to see a reflection of his state of mind in the drawings, and how he might find release in this form of expression to illustrate the dark times when he was seized by mania.

After the end of her art foundation course in Bournemouth, Louise set off on a series of train journeys to look at universities offering a degree in graphic art, and much to our surprise enrolled herself at Wolverhampton. This choice was met with incredulity by all of us who expected her to follow Ros who had gone to classy Corsham near Bath. 'Why Wolves?' we wanted to know. She said it was the best place and had impressed her with its friendliness, while Corsham had not felt welcoming. The art department and teaching at Wolverhampton was of high quality and she made many lifelong friends there, but within a year the faculty had to close temporarily due to asbestos contamination detected in the fabric of the building. All the art students were bundled out in a panic and not allowed to take their portfolios with them, so these were lost, but students were then moved to a beautiful listed manor house to complete their degrees and Louise felt this more than compensated them for any loss.

The loss of her work was a setback, but worse was to follow during the harsh northern winter of snow and ice when there was an explosion at the house she shared with other students. It was a classic case of frozen pipes with a landlord who took a blow torch to them, inadvertently welding the metal together so that pressure built up in a back-boiler causing it to explode in a room full of students, including Louise. Those who caught the worst of the blast had severe burns and lacerations from pieces of hot metal flying around the room. Some of these hit the walls with such force, they remained stuck there like axe heads. Louise's watch was blown off her wrist and found later in the garden outside a shattered window. A neighbouring house was shaken and damaged, but amid the uproar someone had the presence of mind to pull the injured students outside and roll them in the snow while waiting for an ambulance.

By coincidence Adam was on leave when this happened so we were together for this new alarm, driving up to the Burns Unit at Birmingham Accident Hospital where we joined other shocked parents waiting for news as each young person came out of surgery. When Louise was wheeled out she was conscious and able to speak, but we didn't recognise her. Her face was bright orange like a pumpkin, puffed up with swollen flesh that had closed around her eyes. A deep gash across one cheek had been stitched among pits of soot still ingrained after the top layer of burnt skin had been scrubbed off. The first question we asked the surgeon was about her sight and he told us there were tiny fragments of metal in both her eyes, with one eye more affected than the other, so there might be some loss of sight in that one. The deep slash in her cheek caused by a flying piece of metal had exposed the bone but luckily missed vital nerves and would leave an interesting scar, he said, adding that this kind of scar used to be associated at one time with swords and duels. Louise was later very proud of the scar on account of this dubiously heroic connection.

Some students were more seriously hurt than others and the operations went on for hours while we waited with other parents for mutual support, until late in the evening when we were all hungry as well as stressed. 'Let's go for a curry,' I suggested. 'We're in Birmingham, the Balti capital. Plus we all need a drink.' This statement was received with dismay along the lines of: 'How can we go out drinking at a time like this when our children are lying here in dire straits?'

'They're in good hands, they just need a good sleep,' I told them. 'Come on, Adam and I are going. Is anyone else coming?' Only one parent stayed behind and we went to a pub first and then a Balti house, returning to the hospital later when all the children were in a ward safely out of danger, so we could leave them and go to a motel to have a good sleep ourselves.

Louise had an attentive boyfriend who had been the sensible one rolling the burn victims in the snow and now took charge of her while she stayed in hospital, and then moved to new accommodation which he arranged for them both. We were grateful to him even though in the process of this continuing care he quietly relieved her of most of her savings, but at the time of the accident his assistance meant that we were able to go back to Dorset so Adam could spend time with Pete during the Christmas holiday. Louise joined us when her burns had healed, with the boyfriend Eric, for part of the holiday before Adam left. Her eyes, remarkably, had recovered, and the only residual problem was caused by bright lights such as car headlights reflecting off metal fragments permanently embedded in her eyes. For her art work, by good fortune, she had normal sight.

While Adam was at home a call came from Charles's wife saying that she was leaving him and taking the children with her, because life had become impossible at the big house, and she would be grateful for Adam's assistance to move her furniture and possessions. He felt a cousinly duty to oblige and went with a van to drive several loads of household goods to a house she was renting two counties away. I tried to persuade her not to go, and instead be brave and stay to salvage what could be saved from selling the big house, and then move on with Charles to something more profitable. 'He carries his fortune in his head,' I told her. 'You can make another pile of money with him if you stick together. You've done it before. He won't stay down for long and you're a strong team. It will be so hard for you on your own with the children – don't go.' But nothing would make her change her mind, and she had a favour to ask of me. She hoped that Charles wouldn't do anything 'silly' after she left, having lost everything, including the children, and losing them would be the worst blow of all. She asked me to keep an eye on him and report back to her, but I was forty miles away and had enough cares of my own so it was difficult to see how I could do this. I promised to phone occasionally to see how he was, and perhaps invite him over for lunch or meet him somewhere. I was not sympathetic because I thought the whole project had been over-ambitious and too costly to keep under control.

After Adam went back to Mafia I was busy again at work and a few weeks passed before I remembered to give Charles a call. Despite all the calamities, I found him in good spirits with news that there was a buyer for the house and his brother had given him a bottle of champagne to celebrate. 'I'll come over with the bottle,' he said cheerfully. 'We can share it and drink to better times.' This sounded good, so I said I would cook supper to go with the bottle, and made a Greek dish with slow-cooked lamb which was always popular with guests. There was quite a lot of garlic in the recipe and I assumed everyone liked garlic, unaware that Charles had an aversion to it, but he was stoic and champagne helped to mask the effect, so the evening proceeded with surprising vitality.

Neither of us could have expected to discover that we shared many common interests. I had looked on him previously with some disdain, influenced by my colonial background which viewed buccaneering men of the colonies as superior to Englishmen like him who were seen as living soft and rather wet lives, in a country with few manly challenges. Apart from which, Charles was Adam's cousin's husband, and it was the cousin who was my friend, so she was the one deserving sympathy and support during the trials of the big house. I had agreed to the dinner evening simply as a means of keeping my promise to report back to her on Charles's welfare, so it was a new experience to find him easy company with an enthusiasm matching my own on a wide range of subjects. At times this was shadowed by moments of desolation for him when we talked about his children and the crushing sense of failure he felt at losing them, and his wife too whom he loved dearly. He took all the blame on himself with the guilt and loss seeming enough to cripple him but for his strength of character and determination not to be kept down. I admired this and realised that I might have been mistaken in my disregard for him. We became so immersed in conversation with the mellowing effect of champagne that hours went by without any sense of time, only giving way to some snatched moments of sleep before dawn as we shared a growing sense of confidence in each other's outlook. After a restoring cup of tea at daybreak, Charles went back to his empty house much revived with plans to meet again. He was acting as caretaker for the prospective buyers until they took over and had a meeting with them that morning. When he arrived, I heard later, they had been startled by the way he seemed suddenly reinvigorated. 'Something has happened,' they said. 'Do tell us.'

'Not yet,' was the reply. 'It is a very sudden and surprising happening that needs a bit of getting used to.'

One of the elderly patients on my nursing circuit had moved into a nursing home and I went to see how she was getting on. 'You must come and work here,' she said. 'They need nurses like you who can train the young ones how to do things properly. I've already talked to the matron and she needs another SRN.' It was an inviting prospect because I could work late shifts to fit in with morning work on the district, and combined with this I could find out how the whole system of private care homes worked from the inside. Looking after older people was a new interest for me in discovering an affinity with the generation that had come through two world wars, and was now living longer and finding that this was a problem instead of a blessing. Many of them were ending up in homes and not all of the homes were places of kindness and compassion, or even safe in some cases. I could have my own care home, I thought, and make it a happy place with good food, company and comfort, instead of the dreary regimes too often accepted as standard by the Department of Health and Social Security.

When Adam had been home on leave I told him about my idea, with a proposal to sell our present house and buy a run-down care home which we could transform into a bright and profitable business. I would be the matron and he could be the manager. It would start as a small home and build up gradually, with modest living quarters for ourselves. 'We can be a family again, with a family business instead of always working for other people. We can be together – that would be the best part.'

'You must be joking,' he said. 'Care homes are toxic. I'm not going to start a new career rounding up wheelchairs instead of cattle. Anyway I've been waiting to tell you that I've signed another three-year contract with Mafia Coconuts. You can come and join me now Pete is getting good reports from school. You don't want to get stuck in this benighted country and turn into a Pommie, do you?'

'I needed to do something after Simon died and I've got my own little business now which I am enjoying and building up. You've only just mentioned another three years in Mafia, not even discussing it with me first.'

'*Inshallah*. It's my job that pays the mortgage and other outgoings. I'm not giving it up for a miserable future under the pissing rain of merry England, in a place full of demented deaf people shuffling about with commodes and zimmers. It isn't me. You can see that, darling, can't you? It might be your vision of paradise but it certainly isn't mine. Do say you'll come to Mafia. You know it's the sensible thing to do for all our sakes.'

Adam's entreaty was founded on an outdated notion that my place should be with him to meet his needs and look after him, but I couldn't live like that anymore, putting him first while sublimating my own ambitions. I had thought about opportunities in Mafia, knowing there was an acute need for skilled assistance at the hospital and possibly at rural clinics too, if they existed. But I had been warned off by local officials, who told me that non-Tanzanians were not welcome to work (paid or unpaid) in any department run by the government, or to start private schemes.

It was beyond Adam's understanding to comprehend what seemed to him a completely baffling rejection of life among the wonders of a tropical island, with no onerous duties while having unlimited amounts of leisure. 'Most women would jump at it,' he claimed. 'You can spend all your time reading books, or even writing one if you allowed yourself to relax instead of being so antsy all the time. Your problem is contrariness.'

This time when he left I felt that our lives had reached a point of divergence, despite only recently clinging to each other in mutual despair during the anguish of Simon's death and then Louise's accident, when we became united in that need for support. Any family crisis involving children, and most especially the death of a child, must bring parents closer together I truly believed, but in our case this only lasted while Adam was at home, and each time he went back to Mafia we seemed further apart than ever.

It was at this moment of irresolution that the arrival of Charles and the champagne evening with its stimulating conversation changed everything in the most unexpected way, but with caution in consideration for his family on the chance that they might return to him. His most pressing need was a new business and new income, but all his money had gone into the big house and there was no equity left from its sale for a new start-up or going concern. This is where there could be an opportunity to combine his expertise with my slender resources and start a business together, we thought. When I told him about my care home idea, unlike Adam he was enthusiastic and could see the potential since older people needing this type of care were increasing in numbers demographically. I had some money saved up, and Robert, dear man that he was, promised to guarantee any loan that I needed when I told him about my plan, graciously accepting that this was the way I wanted to go.

The house I jointly owned with Adam would have to be sold and this was the most difficult part of the plan, because I would have to ask him for a divorce so that our assets could be divided. First, I had to talk to Louise and Pete about this because it was their home as well, but to my surprise they both thought it was well beyond time for me to blow the whistle. Adam, predictably, did not agree, and took it as a grave affront that divorce was even mentioned. I had no grounds, he pointed out, since there was no third party or suggestion of unreasonable behaviour. All that was necessary was for me to be in Mafia, with him, as soon as possible.

I went to see a divorce lawyer, aware that this was the second time in my marriage that I had done so, remembering ruefully the first time which was to evict a stripper from our house in Rhodesia after she had dazzled Adam into letting her live with us. This time it was going to be different and the lawyer set out exactly what was to be done and how to do it, but I wanted to stay on good terms with Adam and avoid a fight. The lawyer was scornful. 'There is no such thing as a friendly divorce,' he said. 'If you want to stay friends, stay married.'

When Fa and Babs heard about the divorce, Fa was sympathetic but Babs was scathing. 'You're bringing disgrace on the family, walking out on poor Adam who's slaving away for you, far from home in Mafia. It's very selfish, thinking only of yourself. Marriage should be for life, staying loyal to each other.'

'What about Fa, then?'

'That was different. He was in an impossible situation.' She continued a tirade which seemed to emanate from some deeply held resentment of me, triggered by news of the divorce. 'Your father didn't rush into divorce as you are doing without long and careful consideration. He lived with the misery of his marriage for thirty years before allowing himself the freedom to leave and experience the happiness he deserved, but had been denied for so long. This does not apply in your case. You have no justifiable reason for leaving Adam. You are not in love with someone else.'

You may be wrong about that, I thought, but did not say, to avoid further inflaming her.

The supper with Charles which changed everything had been, in its intention, doing a favour for a friend. Romance was the last thing on my mind. I didn't need romance, I had Lanner for that. Charles wasn't looking for any kind of emotional involvement either. He was a pragmatist, looking for new ideas, not expecting to get them from me but happy to share his champagne with someone who offered dinner in return. To find in conversation that we struck sparks off each other which went on to ignite a blaze of mutual attraction was a complete shock, as it was to others when they heard about it, including Charles's wife who was infuriated by this unwelcome outcome. It may have been some consolation that she now had grounds for divorce, but the same grounds held no comfort for Adam who wrote an impassioned letter saying he wanted reconciliation instead of divorce. It squeezed my heart to read his letter, a copy of which was sent to my lawyer for emphasis, provoking a pithy response. I didn't want to hurt him, but there was no going back. The prospect of a whole new life starting up a business with someone who was keen and committed, with the intellect to make it a success, was too good to forfeit.

'We'll have to get married when our divorces come through,' Charles said as if that was part of the business plan. 'The care home residents will feel uncomfortable if they are being looked after by a couple living in sin under the same roof. The DHSS might be sniffy about it too, which could affect our registration.'

'We can be business partners running it together,' I suggested.

'Dearest, I'm asking you to marry me.'

'Oh, yes, I see. It's a bit sudden, that's all. Yes, of course.'

Money was tight and my only supply came from the small pot held as capital in a bank account which I was guarding like Cerberus, while sending regular amounts of cash in registered envelopes to Charles's wife to help her during this tense time when none of us had an income. I had given up my nursing work when the house was sold and moved with Charles to an empty baker's shop in a small Somerset village as a base for explorations. From there we cast a wide net each day, driving to look at run-down properties which might conceivably transform themselves into a functioning care home.

I no longer had the sturdy Vauxhall that had seen me through so many testing times (it had been reclaimed by Adam) and now had a very basic little Renault. This had undergone its own transformation at the hands of Pete who was learning to drive and mashed the gears, disabling reverse and introducing other defective features, so we were left with a vehicle that could not be relied on to arrive anywhere or get home safely. Charles's estate wagon, salvaged from the dissolution of the big house, was in an even worse state, used only in extremis with much coaxing of its starter motor and other erratic components.

Our vision of a congenial home for older people was based on elements of the kind that we ourselves would like to have in our everyday environment. The house needed to be warm and welcoming with a distinct architectural style, extending to comfortable rooms looking onto a garden, preferably with a view of the sea, if such a place existed. The search continued for almost a year as I watched our meagre funds dwindling and our situation so reduced that we were living like refugees in the old shop, camped around a collection of assorted bags and suitcases. Between us we now had five children with varying needs to meet as best we could, while trying not to let our precarious state affect them unduly, in particular Charles's three children whose changed situation caused him immense concern.

After looking at a depressing number of unsuitable houses spread over several counties all the way to Gloucestershire and back, we spent a weekend with Ros in a state of despair, admitting to her that we were beat. Nothing affordable with any appeal as a potential care home had presented itself, except one property which was ideal but well above our budget and already under offer to someone else. We showed Ros the sales brochure with enticing details and photographs, expecting her to sympathise with our frustration that this rare jewel was out of reach, but she didn't see it this way.

'You can't let this one go,' she said firmly. 'It's a perfect find. Precisely what you have been looking for. And the price isn't bad either for the amount of accommodation in a historic house standing in its own grounds – just look at the position with gardens going down to the sea – how could anyone ask for more?'

'We know it's perfect, that's why we love it, but we can't afford the asking price which has already been offered by another couple, and accepted, but they are being slow to exchange contracts. The owner told us if we could exchange quickly he would ditch the others.'

'There you are. Go to the bank tomorrow and get them to agree a bigger loan than the one already approved. Then go to the owner, say you are in a position to proceed, and set a date for exchanging. It's your best chance. You've got to go for it.'

'She's right,' Charles said to me. 'But it's going to need supreme powers of persuasion at the bank because they are very sticky about adding extra sums onto a loan once the amount has been set. You'll need to use maximum charm to do this.'

He was not involved in dealings with the bank because the business was to be in my name as sole trader since I was the one putting up the money and taking responsibility for the loan. My local bank knew me through Simon's Fund as a good customer and had already agreed a business loan, but my request for an increase was refused, so I went to another bank further away in a more commercial district. I wanted to make the right kind of impression this time and look business-like for my appointment with the manager, but had no money for smart clothes. What I did have was my old Singer machine so I made myself a short skirt and plain blouse, which didn't look quite right as the skirt kept bunching up around my hips, but it had to do, as Muz would have said.

Charles coached me on the business plan and cash-flow forecast so that I had everything ready when we arrived at the bank. It was a tense moment as I left him waiting in the car and went inside clutching a folder. The bank was in a new building with lots of glass and no mahogany doors or reverential aura, and all the staff looked young. When I went into the manager's office and saw that he was one of the young ones too, with a modern haircut and diamond ring on his finger, I felt hopeful that he was a new type of manager with a new outlook on lending. He went through the plans and figures with me, which was like taking an oral exam despite his helpfulness. There was a pause, then, for what felt like a long time, before he said that what I proposed was risky for the bank because I had no track record and very little equity to offer. Despite this, my one big asset, he went on to say, was a creditable guarantor for the loan and on this basis he felt able to recommend approval. 'I feel that you are a capable person who can make a success of this project and I will be watching it with interest,' he added. 'A letter with terms will be with you shortly.' We shook hands and I was out of the door with almost indecent haste to tell Charles the news, and head to the nearest pub for a drink to our joint future, confident now that we were on our way.

Robert's guarantee was a key factor in approval for the loan, which could not have happened without his generosity and faith in me. He was excited about the business venture and wanted it to succeed, accepting that my future was now with someone else instead of him. It was a measure of the kind of man he was that after meeting Charles he gave us both his blessing.

The house we had found was a Grade II neo-Gothic villa, built in 1865 by Lady Pauline Trevelyan as her seaside retreat, initially known as Calverley Lodge and later renamed Check House. Pauline was a patroness of the pre-Raphaelite movement and particular friend of John Ruskin who visited the house often. William and Jane Morris, Christina Rossetti and John Millais, were all part of the artistic circle who influenced the design and construction of this very unusual house. Florence Nightingale was another friend who visited when she was staying with Pauline's neighbour, Lady Louisa Ashburton, who built her own house next door so that all of them could enjoy convivial times together at their seaside villas.

Pauline's house was designed to be extraordinary. Built of white stone blocks and knapped flints in a chequered design with bricks that were red and grey, even the roof slates were checked. More Gothic detail was added with arched trefoil windows and pierced barge boards so that the house had altogether an appearance which was both distinctive and eccentric. A glass-roofed veranda with decorative iron supports ran the length of the building's south aspect where it faced the sea and gardens, with a path to the beach. There were lawns and trees and shady nooks presenting views to the wide sweep of Lyme Bay with its undulating coastline of cliffs and coves. All this, to Charles and me, offered an ideal place for our imagined large family of older people to come and share contented days with us.

We waited nervously for a letter from the bank to confirm approval of the loan, and when it came we went to the owner of Check House to make a competing offer against the one already accepted from the slow purchasers. He introduced himself as Dennis and invited us in for a cup of tea, sat us down and looked us over. 'You're not married,' he said reproachfully. 'This is a respectable guest house with regular bookings. The guests will not like being taken over by an irregular couple such as yourselves.'

'We're engaged and intend to get married very soon,' Charles told him. 'We would honour your bookings and look after your people with the same high standard of service that you provide. Best of all, unlike your other purchasers, we are not part of a chain and have funds to proceed immediately.'

He looked at us then with more interest and his eyebrows started twitching. It didn't seem to matter anymore that we weren't married as he went on to say: 'If you can present my solicitor with a contract within ten days, you can have it.' With that he sprang from his chair and shook hands as if he really meant it.

Despite all Charles's setbacks with the previous big house, he still had very good contacts including a solicitor who rushed through the contract for us, but the timing was tight when we collected the document from him on the day of the deadline. It was a fifty-mile dash in my battered little car to reach Dennis's solicitor in time and we arrived with only minutes to spare, after literally running from the public car park with the contract in our hands. We were both so out of breath when we arrived that we could barely speak, but the contract spoke for itself and the exchange was done as if this was no more than a minor matter for the grey man behind the desk, instead of the momentous step forward that it was for us.

Dennis then became a man in a hurry to hand over the house with its guests, but not before we had been taught his routines. 'It's important that you stick to house rules,' he insisted, 'otherwise it will be mayhem. People will take advantage and the place will lose its reputation. I've spent years building it up and I don't want its good name ruined by rookies.'

We agreed to spend a weekend at the house under his instruction, with increasing reluctance when we arrived as he ran around in a frenzy exclaiming about things being late or out of place. His wife kept out of the way in the kitchen, calmly preparing evening dinner which was served promptly at 6.30 when guests had returned from spending the day out, having been shooed off the premises as soon as they finished breakfast. During the morning, Dennis gave us a tour of light and spacious rooms, the bedrooms rendered drab by him in 1950s style with creaky Lloyd Loom chairs and candlewick bedcovers smelling of moth-balls. It was a relief when he let us escape to explore the much more inviting grounds leading down to a promenade and the beach.

By the evening we were ready for dinner and joined others in the dining room where French windows opened to views of the sea reaching to a distant blue horizon. Dennis stood at the dining room door, watch in hand, and with a nod to waiting maids at the stroke of 6.30, starters were brought. We had been warned that only fifteen minutes was allowed for each course, so this explained the absence of conversation among diners as they concentrated on their plates. Dennis remained like a sentry at the door with his watch, maids hovering as they waited for his signal at precisely 6.45 when all the plates were whipped away, whether finished or not. The main course was meanwhile being passed through a hatch from the kitchen and put in front of us at a run by the girls and Dennis himself who was leaping around with them. I noticed other diners had knives and forks poised ready for speed-eating, obviously well primed, and the same process was repeated for dessert after which guests were ushered out and down the hall to the sitting room for coffee. 'Why the rush?' I asked Dennis as he marshalled us in a different direction towards the kitchen.

'Staff need to get off,' he said. 'Save wages. I'll show you how the clearing up is done, double quick.' He sprinted about in the kitchen where his wife and the maids were clashing pots and crockery, scrubbing and stacking ready for the next onslaught, too busy to notice as Charles and I bolted for the nearest exit.

'I don't think our regime is going to measure up,' Charles commented. 'How does Dennis get all these people to come back year after year as he claims, willing to be dragooned like idiots while actually paying good money for it.'

'He probably makes them put down a deposit for next year before they leave, and they're too terrified to refuse,' I suggested.

With contracts now exchanged and money pledged, Dennis was impatient to hand over, so a date was set and all we had to do was collect our few belongings from the baker's shop and get ready to start this extraordinary new adventure.

CHAPTER 15

When Muz heard about the move to Check House and our plans for it, she decided that she and Andy would like to come and live with us. Recent lapses such as getting lost in Wales had scared her. 'My brain seems to be full of holes these days,' she said, and thought the nursing home would offer a place of care and safety for them both going into the future. Andy said he didn't mind where he lived as long as he was allowed to have his Austin Princess with him. Sun Cottage would have to be sold which could take a few months, giving Charles and me time to organise ourselves and the new business.

On the day we moved into Check House there were ten guests staying, so we had no time to unpack or think about anything except producing dinner for them that evening. Dennis was in a hurry to leave after giving us final instructions, with a short speech about keeping up standards as he handed over the keys with a jaunty wave and no visible regrets.

Louise and her boyfriend Eric had come to help: Louise as a waitress and Eric as an extra pair of hands, while Charles cooked and I filled in as kitchen assistant and chamber maid. Charles had no qualms about taking over the kitchen and was completely unflappable as he tied on a large apron and worked the big Aga with its steaming pots and pans, so that a three-course-dinner appeared with no fuss or pantomime. We had already introduced ourselves to the guests when pre-dinner drinks were served, and prepared them to find that some of Dennis's rituals might not proceed in the same way as before. Instead of being alarmed they responded with enthusiasm and dinner became the main event of the day, served by Louise wearing the tight black dress and vertiginous heels saved from her previous waitressing days.

When autumn arrived with cooler evenings, Eric decided to light the fire in the drawing room as guests assembled for drinks before dinner. The fire was a mock-installation of painted plastic logs with artificial flames, and Eric thought the effect could be improved with some driftwood he collected and arranged in the fireplace with screwed up newspaper, lighting the pile with a match. The effect was dramatic as with loud popping noises the plastic logs melted and erupted like lava from a volcano before oozing from the grate with puffs of noxious black smoke. This spread in a choking cloud across the room, dispersing drinkers into the hall, holding onto their glasses. Later when the molten mass had cooled and solidified, it resisted all efforts at removal and had to be covered with a fender to disguise this latest lowering of Dennis's standards.

Income from guests was never going to meet monthly loan repayments, so it became a matter of extreme urgency to get registered as a care home and start taking permanent residents. We were allowed to take three people while unregistered, but being new to the district and having no contacts we needed a link and went to the local doctors' surgery to introduce ourselves. The senior partner was welcoming and affable while warning of the competition we faced from other homes, and the doctors' terms, which came as a complete surprise. He told us that we needed his signature on a DHSS form stating that the practice agreed to attend their patients at the home, even though these were NHS patients. There was an annual fee to be paid by us for this arrangement, and it was not a small fee, but we had no choice because we needed to work with the doctors. In practice the arrangement worked well as it included services such as a weekly doctor's round and advice which I valued in a new home with new residents, who soon arrived. This luckily coincided with the off-season for holiday guests when Dennis's bookings came to an end.

Our first people were a married couple, the wife arriving by ambulance on a stretcher from another care home where she had been living with her husband, who came with her. The manager of the home phoned in advance to tell me that the wife was poorly, and when I went out to the ambulance it was obvious that she was unconscious. Her husband Walter was very concerned for her. 'Do you think she's dying?' he asked.

'When she's safely inside I'll see how she is and call the doctor.' I took his hand. 'This must have come as rather a shock to you.'

'Yes, it was sudden and the doctor suggested we come here instead of sending Dolly to hospital. He said you are a trained nurse so you will know what to do.'

When the doctor arrived he examined Dolly and was content that she should remain with us and given palliative care. I nursed her day and night until she died, with breaks when Walter sat beside her, and the doctor visited frequently. Charles kept the household running and we were like a small family around Dolly as she and Walter had no children or relatives to come and be with them.

Soon after this another couple arrived, but this time it was the husband who was very sick and survived only a short time. He was given every care and the doctors were pleased because it avoided sending patients to hospital in their last days. This satisfaction was not shared by everyone as word spread that people died as soon as they arrived at Check House, but we still had Walter, and new widow Kath, as permanent residents. They joined forces in consoling each other and pride in being founder members of the care home, each of them in good health with reliable funds to meet on-going fees. This was reassuring but was far from enough to keep us solvent, and every time the phone rang I panicked that it was the bank wanting to know progress. Too much money was going out of the account with very little coming in, and when I went to bed at night, images of red figures appearing in the accounts floated in front of my eyes.

The hideous process of divorce had at last been completed and we both had ex-spouses who remained very displeased with us. Charles's ex-wife naturally expected the business to help provide support for her and the children and we were doing our best to keep up, while my own children were not yet independent and also needed help. Pete had to sleep in the attic when he was home because all our rooms were having fire precautions installed. Ceilings had to be 'fire-planked' and doors fireproofed, while the whole building was wired into alarm and call-bell systems. Walter and Kath generously observed that it made life more interesting than what happened in 'normal' homes, even when they had to move rooms and take meals in the kitchen with us.

Most important of all we needed District Council permission for change of use from a guest house to a care home and had applied for this as soon as we moved in. With no time to lose on further essentials, work proceeded on a lift between floors and specialised baths and equipment, and then remembered we needed to get married. Kath and Walter were charmed by the thought of a wedding in the house, and were included with close friends and family invited to lunch after the ceremony at Honiton Register Office. The office was temporarily housed in a Porta-cabin next to a public car park with no frills or any semblance of romance, but that was in keeping with our threadbare circumstances and my wedding dress which I found in a hippie shop.

Our application for change of use was due to be heard a week before the wedding and we went to the council meeting confident that no reasonable grounds could be found for refusal, unaware that other care home owners had ganged up and sent in objections. It was a complete shock when these were upheld and our request refused, so we came away with nothing except the loss of a big fee paid for the application. This was a killer blow and we had to face losing everything if there was no other solution to save our plans.

As a first step, the wedding lunch had to be cancelled – we couldn't afford to be celebrating with food and drink for thirty people – but we could still appear at the Porta-cabin and get married with a ring we'd bought for twelve pounds. Close relatives like Ros and Gary refused to be put off and came with a few loyal others and our combined children. Charles's three had to be collected by taxi from their home in Somerset because neither of our cars could be trusted to go that far.

On the morning of the wedding it was a new experience to have the house full of people, and children running up and down the main staircase which rose from a wide hall reaching the full length of the house: a feature we recognised on our first tour as being ideal for future wheelchairs and walking aids. Now it truly glowed with the presence of a large family. The staircase, of Beer stone, was curved and cantilevered with an iron-work balustrade of gilded lilies: a centrepiece much admired, reflecting the Arts and Crafts style which shaped the whole house.

After cooking breakfast for everyone and preparing lunch, I went to change into my wedding dress while Ros took her boys to buy confetti in the town, but by the time we were ready to leave for Honiton they had not returned. Charles left early with his children in one of our decrepit cars, and when Ros at last appeared with the confetti we all piled into hers, but it wouldn't start. Gary got out and opened the bonnet. 'Don't panic,' he said, 'it's only a loose connection.' After a few minutes watching him fiddle with wires I went to see if I could help, thinking I knew a bit about cars, but two heads under one bonnet don't necessarily combine to produce the right kind of spark.

I withdrew just as heavy clouds released a sudden shower and I stood there in the rain, uncertain whether to go inside and phone for a taxi as I felt a damp chill start to seep through my coat, while drips ran off my hair which stuck to my head like a wet helmet. It was one of those life moments of utter dejection when nothing could get worse it seemed than missing my own wedding, but then as so often happens at the lowest point of despair, serendipity smiles. The car spluttered into action, we shot off, and arrived at the Porta-cabin a few minutes late as is conventional for brides. The ceremony was low key which seemed entirely appropriate in the circumstances: the ring was put on my finger, photos were taken and confetti thrown. We all went back for a modest lunch which somehow managed to include champagne in the dining room at Check House, but with no celebration for our prospects since planning permission to go ahead had been lost and we were in a fix.

With no time, cash or inclination for a honeymoon we paused to consider options, and simultaneously hit on the same solution, waking up one morning and saying to each other, 'I've got it. We'll re-apply for planning – this time for a nursing home instead of residential. There will be no grounds for refusing because they can't use the same excuse as before.' This had been based on a misleading claim that it was not safe for elderly people to cross the road from our gate to a pavement on the other side, because we had no pavement on our side. It was a spurious argument because the gate was inset for safety, but grounds had to be found to satisfy objections from other home owners.

When we applied for nursing home permission it was granted almost immediately with no quibbles, but this made the other owners even more annoyed, because nursing gave us better scope in meeting demand with older people living longer and needing more specialised care. The downside was now having to recruit enough registered nurses for both day and night shifts. They were not easy to find, and expensive. This is why our first choice had been residential care with its less rigorous requirements, but there was no going back. I would have to do most of the SRN shifts myself and take on the role of matron since we could not afford to employ anyone else in that position, or very many SRNs at all. It soon came to us on the local grapevine that other nursing homes in the area had put up their pay rates to stop their valuable nurses being poached by us.

All we could do was press on and get registered now that all conversion work was done and everything in place for a fully functioning home. We had learnt lessons in how to present applications to local authorities and made sure this time that every small detail was in order. This satisfied the DHSS which was the organisation in charge of both health and social security at the time, so with our registration finally complete we were ready to go.

When enough staff had been recruited, including registered nurses after we agreed to pay them even higher rates than they were getting elsewhere, I worked twelve-hour shifts as the SRN in charge, with one day off a week. Walter and Kath presided over the social side of arrangements as old hands, greeting new arrivals and starting a residents' association so that everyone was involved. Charles was still cooking at the big Aga and we had breakfast each morning at 9 o'clock sitting around the kitchen table with all the staff who had come on shift at 7.30. Sadly this agreeable custom didn't last long as more patients arrived, with more staff, and George, an experienced chef with his assistant Stan, to organise proper catering.

Charles and I needed to move out to free up rooms for patients and also because his children didn't like coming to visit us in a nursing home, so we started looking for a flat nearby. My joy in becoming a stepmother to his children was an added bonus of the marriage as we had a bond already through those times together when I looked after them so their mother could have a break. They were enchanting children, each with their own distinct personality: Flora was self-contained, quiet and clever. Luke was always smiling, open-hearted, highly imaginative and gifted, while little Clementine was spontaneously affectionate and sweet-natured. When we moved to Check House I imagined playing in the garden with them, making dens among its many secret places and running down the path for walks on the beach. They did some of these things with Charles, but sadly for me the carefree happy hours we had enjoyed together in previous times had been replaced by uneasiness, since I was now the person with their father instead of their mother. She was angry with me, and this rubbed off on them.

Before going ahead with our plans the previous year, even at that late stage Charles had written to her with an offer to get back together again for the sake of the children, if she wanted to. It was a cliff-hanging moment for me on the verge of starting a new life with him, but I knew the chance had to be given to her before he was able to move on, so that he could feel he had done everything possible to try and keep the family together. It was a last ditch effort, swiftly rejected by her, with a reminder of his financial obligations. It didn't help that the nursing home was slow to make enough profit to share reasonably with her, and this became a source of contention, which was another burden sensed by the children. There was nothing I could do except help to save costs by working as many SRN shifts as physically possible, sometimes staying on to work the night shift after a full day if a night-nurse didn't turn up, or called in sick.

Charles was the home's manager, in charge of accounts and administration, fitted around daily shopping, gardening and an endless parade of mundane problems with drains, leaks and machinery. His office consisted of a desk with phone and chair on the upstairs landing open to the coming and going of staff and patients, where he was conveniently placed for them to stop and chat and no phone conversation could ever be private. One of the rooms opening onto the landing belonged to a new patient, Mary, who would emerge during the morning and stand outside her door, dressed for shopping with handbag and gloves as she looked anxiously up and down the landing. 'Can you see the bus coming?' she would ask Charles or anyone passing by.

'It's a bit early for the bus. Come down in the lift and have a cup of tea while you're waiting,' someone would suggest, and she was happily diverted.

Dementia specialists advised that instances of confusion should be countered and people brought back to reality, so that in Mary's case she should be reminded where she was and understand that no bus could be arriving outside her door. In practice this approach seemed only to emphasise a person's awareness of being confused which I thought was cruel. Another official instruction was to avoid attachments or show affection to patients, but some of the people when they arrived had not felt the touch of another person for years. One widow, brought to tears when she was given a hug by staff on arrival, said no one had hugged her for more than thirty years since her husband died. Many people were starved of affection and some just wanted to hold hands. When we introduced aromatherapy this was a natural form of contact and especially calming for those who felt anxious or agitated. During times when I was on night duty, making sure that people were comfortable and warm in bed with their pillows plumped up really did seem to help them sleep better. Some even liked to be tucked in and given a good night kiss. In the morning, the day staff would ask what drugs had been given when the report showed a quiet night.

The worst part of night duty on quiet nights is having to stay awake when everyone else is asleep, so those nights which were good for patients, were challenging for us unless we kept ourselves busy. We used to sort laundry and clothes, sewing those that needed mending and putting the piles into baskets marked with room numbers. The voluminous 'bloomers' and synthetic Crimplene garments worn by that generation were a source of wonder to us in an age when bikini pants and jeans were standard for the rest of us.

One of the innovations when we converted the house to a nursing home was a fully equipped laundry with industrial washing and drying machines, while on every floor there were modern sluices, electrically operated beds and marvellous aids like Parker baths and CQR (secure) chairs. These are like adult-size nests on wheels, lined with soft lambswool, for people too frail to use conventional wheelchairs, and perfect for snoozing as I discovered when I tried one myself. We found them invaluable.

When Social Services became the government department in charge of nursing homes, taking over from the Health Service in 1988, there was a big change. Our hard-won registration was replaced by something called accreditation which included tests we had to pass in order to meet new rules and regulations. One of the requirements was a mission statement which I thought should be based on principles of TLC, and submitted our own Philosophy of Care statement. All members of staff had a copy of the statement as a core policy to follow when they came to work at Check House. This was dismissed by the new regulators who introduced us to a whole new concept of care with its own language of service-users and stake-holders, due process and equality outcomes. We were told that our patients must in future be called 'clients' because this was the term used by Social Services, our new bosses. When we had our first inspection by a social worker, I explained that in nursing homes, registered nurses look after patients, not clients. Walter added his views on this to the inspector, with the result that we never did have 'clients'. In other respects the revolution that had taken off with Social Services now in charge of care, led to a number of re-branding exercises, with new titles each time for the regulating authority and new rules for us. Memories of the DHSS began to fade into obscurity as years went by with a lingering nostalgia among those of us who had known the benefits of integration with the NHS.

Louise with her art degree was now in London working for the BMA in their educational heath programme, illustrating books, leaflets and posters, but all she really wanted was to be back in Africa. She was my link with Adam, and told me a powerful story of a recent experience he'd had off the coast of Mafia Island. The company freighter that sailed regularly between the island and Dar es Salaam with cargoes of coconuts, was on one of these sailings when its engines failed, and the captain sent a radio message to Adam to come quickly in a fast boat with the company engineer. What made the situation more urgent was that the captain had taken on board a large number of illegal passengers and the ship was wallowing with this extra weight, while it drifted without power many miles from shore.

Adam put spare fuel and engine parts into a motor boat and set off with the engineer to locate the ship, but ran into dense mist out at sea, a freak occurrence that happens occasionally. They were unable to see anything further than a few feet in front, let alone a ship somewhere off in the distance, and without radar or directional aids they had to cut the motor and wait for the mist to clear. There was no indication when this might happen as a sea mist can lie on the water like a heavy cloud for any amount of time, and every hour that passed increased the danger that they themselves could become completely lost. It turned very cold as the mist closed in, leaving them adrift in a silent white world with no sound except the lapping of waves. They kept straining for a glimpse of the sun to give them a bearing but not even a glimmer appeared, and then Adam saw something which he thought at first must be an optical illusion after spending so long staring at nothing.

It was a blurred figure at the bow, dimly seen, who Adam sensed instantly was Simon by his shape and movement pointing in the direction they should take. Keeping him in view they started the engine and set off on the course indicated, sticking to it even after the image had disappeared. After some time pressing on in hope that what they had seen was not just a trick of the light, they emerged from the mist cloud, and the freighter was there ahead of them.

Adam told me this story himself later when we met as friends after the bitterness of the divorce was over and there was comfort for each of us in reflecting on the possibility that such phenomena really can happen. A further happy outcome was that, despite the divorce, his family stayed on good terms with me which was generous of them since they could have taken a poor view of Charles swapping one Hill wife for another, as it might have seemed. But everyone liked him, including Fa and Babs once she acknowledged that her objections were having no effect and I was moving on regardless.

Our rooms at Check House were filling up fast and Muz put pressure on their estate agent for a quick sale of Sun Cottage, so that she and Andy could move in with us while a room at the front of the house that she had chosen, was still free. This room was originally the butler's pantry with a window onto the driveway where in times past he could observe carriages or people on foot arriving, and remove his apron in time to man the front door. For Muz and Andy the room was ideal in a different way because there was parking outside the window where Andy could keep his Austin Princess safely within sight until a suitable garage was found. As things turned out this became unnecessary when Andy found pleasure in having the Princess permanently on view outside the window. He would take a duster each morning to polish her chrome and paintwork before installing Muz in the front seat and going for a drive around the Devon countryside, or to Dorchester to visit Spindle, without getting lost.

By the time they moved in with us Muz was becoming more anxious and restless, but these drives seemed to calm her, especially when they followed familiar routes with landmarks she could recognise that served as an anchor against feeling lost or disorientated. When she wasn't being soothed by a drive and was back among the flurries of nursing home life, she needed to be busy and found another anchor down in the basement laundry room where machines churned hour by hour, washing and drying great mounds of clothes and sheets and uniforms. Muz was completely at home with laundry since her happy discovery of twin-tubs which revolutionised the life of housewives, and now she had the very latest of miracle machines to attend in the company of willing assistants who were laundry-enthusiasts like her. Endless times a day she would heave a basket of clean linen up the steep basement stairs to distribute among rooms, then scurry back to the steamy depths of her own little empire. She was as happy as I'd seen her for years, despite frequent lapses into confusion when a previously simple task eluded her, or she had lost something. Then I would find her searching cupboards and drawers in a state of frantic exasperation. 'What are you looking for?' I would ask. 'Tell me so I can help.' And she would answer, 'Don't be silly. If I knew what it was, I wouldn't be looking for it.'

When all our rooms were full, this riled the matron of another home so much that she came to confront me. She arrived at the front door in full regalia of hospital uniform with silver buckle and lace-trimmed cap. I went to open the door when I heard the bell ring and prepared myself to greet her, but she swept past me imperiously. 'I've come to see the matron', she announced as she went on down the hall like a galleon. I ran behind, trying to explain that I was the matron, until she turned round abruptly. 'You don't look like a matron,' she said, and I realised that my American-style trousers and tunic worn for hands-on practicality didn't look very matronly. 'Where's your office, then?' she asked, before I had a chance to do any more explaining. Not wanting to disappoint her in that regard as well as my appearance, I showed her into my small but perfectly decent office, converted from one of the kitchen pantries.

She settled herself into a chair while looking around in an appraising way at my shelves of books and files before drawing herself up to the matter in hand, and was about to speak when the door opened and Muz scuttled in looking like a washer-woman. She sat down opposite the regal matron and looked suspiciously at her. The look was returned with equal suspicion as the matron exclaimed in a voice like Lady Bracknell: '*Who is this? What is she doing here?*'

'It's my mother,' I replied. 'She lives here.'

There was silence for a moment as the matron took this in before saying with satisfaction, thinking to have found me out, 'It's against regulations to for you to have relatives in the home. You ought to know that.'

I started to explain the particular circumstances in this case, but was interrupted by Muz making a show of blowing her nose very loudly and rudely after ferreting in her apron pocket and pulling out a large handkerchief. It was a vulgar display impossible to ignore as the matron looked on with increasing disgust when the handkerchief to our watching eyes was seen to be a not-very-clean pair of knickers. Muz stuffed them back into her pocket and stood up, going over to the matron. 'I don't know who you are,' she said to the woman, now stiffening in her chair, 'but I'm sure you will be very happy here. No one minds what you wear so you'll be all right looking like that. I've got work to do so I'll be off now. My daughter will look after you.' With that she padded out of the door and back to the basement.

The Bracknell matron had seen enough and made for the door herself, billowing down the hall as before until she reached the front door and turned, putting a hand on my arm in a surprising change of tone. 'As I said, you're not allowed to have relatives or EMIs (Elderly Mentally Infirm) under the terms of your registration, but I can send you some of my heavier nursing cases in exchange for your EMIs. Which my own registration category allows me to have,' she emphasised. With that she sailed away and I was left contemplating the thin line that existed between the different categories. There were those with moderate confusion who pottered about happily, experiencing no problems, but depending on the view of inspectors they could be classified as needing secure accommodation with locked doors in case they wandered. In an EMI home they would be locked up with others who might be violent or severely demented and this could be distressing and increase their confusion. We had several patients with varying degrees of confusion who would clearly suffer in an EMI home, and we did everything we could to keep them, with the doctors' support.

Apart from their medical and psychological needs which we had no difficulty in meeting with the assistance of very good CPNs (Community Psychiatric Nurses), we loved these people and they thrived in the family atmosphere of Check House. Mary had been a dance-band leader and was an energetic pianist, taking turns with Muz who had brought her piano with her and played all kinds of music every day. This was much enjoyed by residents and visitors who came and often stayed for meals. We didn't charge for extra meals and George loved cooking for large numbers, having come to us from the kitchens of a holiday camp he continued in the same mode at Check House as if everyone was on a permanent holiday. Some of them thought they were, and Edna who had come from hospital to convalesce, stayed on, saying each day: 'I'll just have one more day here, and then go home tomorrow.' Several years later she was still repeating the same daily statement, and really should have gone to a residential home because she didn't qualify for nursing, but she refused to move when the inspectors objected to her remaining in the wrong category of home. Mary was sociable and those who had lived alone like Edna enjoyed Mary's company and chat. 'I've had five husbands,' Mary liked telling people, 'but I was only married to two of them.' She would go on to entertain everyone with stories of her dance band, while strolling around, sometimes forgetting where she was.

The inspectors were perplexed by our system which refused to be institutional and didn't fit their rules. Having worked in homes where everyone had to be up, dressed and breakfasted by 8 am, requiring a 5 am start when frail people were pulled from their beds to be ready in time, I was determined that we would serve breakfast in bed for those who wanted it. Some people might also want to have a lie-in or a day in bed, and why not, I reasoned, with staff there to look after them. The inspectors did not approve of this. 'Why are these people in bed when they are not ill?' they wanted to know.

'They are old and tired, so they're having a rest,' I explained, but this was seen as a slack and easy-going style of management, allowing people to stay in their rooms instead of joining others in the day room. 'They need to be in the day room where staff can watch them,' the inspectors insisted. 'It's safer, and they've got the big TV there.'

'They don't want to be stuck in front of the big TV, being watched all the time. They like the privacy of their rooms, with their own TVs. They've all got call bells if they need anything.'

'They'll get pressure sores, lying around in bed.'

'Anyone at risk has a special mattress. I can show you.'

'It's your care plans and risk assessments that we need to see.'

Care plans, the pinnacle of accountability for inspectors, recorded in detail every requirement for each patient so that nothing was forgotten and care was systemised. Like most bureaucratic exercises these drifted towards becoming an end in themselves and the process of continuous updating left less time for actual hands-on care. It seemed that as long as a plan was written up, and signed for, what happened outside the office in real care for real people was less important than paper statements.

One of the most onerous rules related to doors on people's rooms. Fire regulations demanded these were kept closed at all times with heavy metal automatic closures, resulting in people being shut in their rooms feeling isolated and trapped. We tried to get round this by propping doors open with wedges but this meant uninvited people could wander in, so the problem was solved with 'garden gates' on open doorways. The gates became unexpectedly popular as the idea caught on and rooms felt more friendly while keeping a sense of privacy. This gave particular pleasure to those with mild confusion who enjoyed standing at their garden gate to watch people passing by, without being caught up in outside activity. Others would stop for a chat over the gate and this innovation was so successful in creating a community spirit, everyone welcomed it, except the authorities, so it could not be allowed to continue. Open doorways were ruled to be a fire hazard and garden gates completely out of order for the same reason, so they had to be scrapped and people put back behind doors, or in chairs in the day room.

Everyone in the home at this time had a story to tell, including a few who remembered seeing Queen Victoria when they were children and described her as a small dumpy woman, which disappointed them when they were expecting to see the queenly figure of their imagination. We had First World War nurses who were sturdy and battle-hardened like war horses impelled to keep going until they fell, but in the case of the nurses always with a brandy flask at hand. Then there was Rena from Yorkshire whose fiancé Billy had died in that war and when she came to us, still grieving for him, she brought her trousseau intact in its chest to be kept safely under her bed. A photo of him stood on a side table with fresh flowers to be picked in his memory each day. But surprisingly she told me, 'When I was forty, I thought Billy didn't want me to be on my own anymore, so I decided to marry the next man who came round the corner.' She put on her best coat and hat (she was a very stylish dresser) and went on the bus to Harrogate. When she arrived at the main street, she got off the bus and waited by the corner where an unsuspecting man appeared just as she had imagined, and didn't protest when she asked if she might accompany him. 'I was married to Mr Heaton for the next many years with no bother, and Billy was always there too,' she told me with satisfaction.

Only about half the patients paid their own fees while others were funded by social services at a lower rate, but no one knew which was which, not even the staff, and everyone was treated the same. Several patients came from the small village of Beer, deep in a valley open to the sea with sides so steep that many of the older ones had never ventured far from home. Getting a ride to Honiton or Exeter was a major excursion and our marvellous gardener Johnny, born in Beer, had been to London once and talked of it as a highlight of his life. Beer people were characters and the story went that a ship from the Spanish Armada had been wrecked offshore in 1588 and the sailors, rescued by villagers, never left. If the story is true, this introduction of new blood I imagined could be still evident in some of the features of these exceptional people.

Fanny was one of them, from a family of fishermen she was round as a barrel and very exact in her opinions and what she wanted. She liked to have jam sandwiches every evening for supper: 'Lots of jam and not much bread,' she would tell George when he went to get the supper orders. He was indulgent and provided whatever was asked for, but was disappointed at the conservative choices of most people as, having lived through straitened times, they preferred plain food and were not adventurous. Walter's residents' association held meetings and when menus were discussed he reported that everyone wanted roasts, or fish and chips, never what they called 'Any of that foreign muck' which was spaghetti or rice. Puddings were so popular that some people skipped the main course, waiting for syrup sponge or jam roly-poly, with lots of custard.

Staff were served the same food during their breaks and we now had a staff room where they could eat in peace and take rests. I worked alongside the care teams with an in-house training programme for nursing assistants, but it was frustrating that there was no recognised qualification for them to work towards with higher pay and status at the end of it. After a few years, NVQ (National Vocational Qualification) was introduced, which was a big step forward and very welcome. I went on the first course run in Exeter for NVQ assessors when our hard-working assistants could at last become qualified and recognised for their skill and dedication.

This was good but I was beginning to feel overwhelmed with so much to do, and it was a stroke of good fortune when a very experienced and warm-hearted registered nurse arrived to take over as my deputy. This was capability Kathy who stayed with us through good times and bad for the next many years, and whose unfailing loyalty and sense of humour was a steadying influence during the inevitable blips when such qualities were most needed. Everyone loved Kathy. She was (and still is) the embodiment of good nursing, and if she had a lamp she would be carrying it as an emblem of all that is most true and worthwhile in the calling to be a nurse.

Check House was solvent, but it was a time of very high interest rates and I pressed the bank to reduce the percentage we paid above base rate. The young diamond-wearing manager was still there and had been following our progress, so I was hopeful of success when I went to see him with our latest figures. He was sanguine, and said on these results he could give me what he called: 'A very fine rate of two and a quarter percent over base'. The base rate for banks was still 15 percent which seemed to me phenomenally high and I expected a reasonable reduction on the 3 percent over base which we had been paying. The new rate offered by the bank manager amounted to a surprisingly meagre saving that I was disappointed to have to accept and go back to Charles with this news. We wanted to increase payments for his family and were under fierce pressure on that front, causing a great deal of stress, which didn't help.

What did help was powerful support from the local community and our great staff who appreciated what we were doing, and within a year we had full occupancy, and a waiting list. This went beyond all expectation but created a problem when we didn't have a vacancy for sixteen months, due to everyone keeping well and no one moving out. The waiting list grew and grew, while people who were on it got frustrated, or died while waiting. There was nothing for it but to build more rooms and this is what we did, but planning permission to extend a Grade II listed house was complex, and meanwhile I had to negotiate another big loan. It was three years before the new building, named the Rossetti Wing, opened in 1991 with ten single rooms and two double rooms, all ensuite. The inspectors were sceptical about demand for these rooms, despite the waiting list, and told us their office had bets on how soon we were likely to fill up. Their discouraging attitude came through to us in all kinds of ways and was difficult to understand, when all we wanted to do was provide a kind, comfortable and professional service for older people who clearly needed it.

During one of our first summers we had wheelchair races on the upper lawn organised by Walter. He appointed himself chief steward in charge of those residents with chairs who wanted to take part, with staff doing the pushing. Other residents and visitors gathered on the veranda where they had seats to cheer the races and afterwards tea was served outside to everyone. Despite its popularity there was only one season of racing because it was seen as dangerous by the authorities and banned, which may not have been entirely unreasonable as some of the extempore activities that developed through a desire to be free of suffocating rules, did lead to mad moments.

Dogs were always welcome in the house, as were donkeys who visited people in their rooms, never dropping anything on the carpet as if they knew it wasn't polite, while their small hooves made barely a dent or mark either. Dogs were inclined to be more boisterous, in particular one animal called Gerry who came every week with his owner Kitty to visit her sister who lived with us. Gerry was kept firmly on a lead in the day room during visits, especially if our cat, who was one of Baby's daughters was there, sitting on someone's lap, as she often was. She would eye Gerry balefully and he would eye her, until one day the cat slipped off the lap she was sitting on and stretched herself provocatively at Gerry. Unable to contain himself in the face of such saucy behaviour he launched himself at the cat who skipped off towards the open sash window and jumped through it. Gerry followed the cat, so that Kitty, still hanging onto the lead in terror of Gerry escaping, flew head-first through the window after him, landing on the grass outside, at which point she let go. The cat shot up a tree and Gerry, free at last, stood underneath barking while the cat sat overhead on a branch smirking at him. We gathered poor Kitty off the ground and dusted her off. She was unhurt but shaken, and all such incidents had to be recorded in the accident book for the inspectors to look at.

Walter had been so incensed when they stopped his races that he declared war on them, in his own way which was the invention of pranks to be played at inspections. He recruited willing volunteers from among his residents' association, most notably a mischievous Irish woman called Joyce, whom we had rescued from a home that was closing. She and Walter bonded and became conspirators plotting together. The plan was that when an inspector arrived, Walter would sidle up to this person, whoever it happened to be on that occasion, saying that room number five (Joyce's room) had a complaint. The inspector would be glad to oblige in listening to this and would go to the room. Joyce, tipped off, would lie flat on her bed covered from head to foot in a white sheet pretending to be dead, while an accomplice went to the door and opened it. When the inspector was inside, confronted by this scene, Joyce would sit up and scream. It went to plan and should have worked perfectly as a good joke, but the inspector didn't see it like that and our reputation took another hit.

The doctors were always on our side and a benefit of their fee was the weekly 'round' when one of the partners came to visit patients, review drugs and discuss any problems. It was interesting to notice that the rounds generated a sense of well-being in the household – simply seeing a doctor walking around seemed to make everyone feel better. This phenomenon was called: 'A touch of the doctor'. If for any reason one of them was unable to come due to an emergency or other call, it occurred to me that I could walk around with a life-size image of them mounted on a pole, in the same way that icons of Roman emperors were paraded among the people, with similar effect.

At about this time news came that Spindle had been transferred to Southampton Hospital with a perforated stomach and collapsed lung. He claimed to have swallowed nails but the account related to us by Muz, who had been informed as Spindle's next of kin, was so garbled that it was difficult to know quite what had happened. A barium X-ray was reported to show some kind of internal injury but that was all we knew. Muz was in no state to visit him and before anyone else was able to go, we heard that he was back in Dorchester and very ill. Ros and I hurried to his bedside where we found him in a wretched state, deathly pale and emaciated, he was lying on an iron bed in a cell-like room and was clearly dying. The nurse in charge of his care said that some kind of incident with nails was thought to have occurred, but there was no report on this from Southampton, only a discharge note stating that he had been treated for pneumonia. The nurse was attentive and kind and seemed genuinely concerned for Spindle, but it was heart wrenching to have to leave him in that bleak room with so few comforts. He didn't want us to stay, as usual feeling more comfortable with hospital staff than his own family. He was always conscious of an awkwardness, thinking that he couldn't be 'normal' like the rest of us. His hands were cold when I held them and tried to rub them warm as he looked at me and smiled the shy sweet smile which was so much his, and this time as fleeting as the thin thread of life left in his body. I knew he was ready to go and that he welcomed it after previous attempts over many years to end his life, in despair at the hopelessness of his situation. Now he would be free at last and I was glad for him, and glad that he didn't linger many days, cared for by the nurses he knew as friends at Dorchester who were with him when he died. It was a tragic end to a tragic life, and we scattered his ashes in the garden at Check House, where later Muz's ashes would join his.

Fa too was an early casualty, by strange coincidence succumbing to leukaemia, like Simon. When he could no longer work as a ship's doctor, he did locums for a local GP practice in the village until forced to concede, which he took as a signal that his time had come and, declining treatment, he died very quickly. He wanted to spare Babs the extra stress of nursing him as she already had her parents, both in their nineties, living with them. Babs never quite forgave me for what she called 'cruelly abandoning Adam', and because of this behaviour felt that Fa needed protecting from me, so we were kept apart towards the end of his life. I was sad about this but we both knew that we loved each other and that was enough, whatever Babs thought or did about it.

Elaine was in Scotland with her family, their lives very distant from ours, divided not so much by geography as religious belief that seemed to result in a sense of detachment, separating themselves from those of us who have no claim to righteousness and just ramble along as best we can.

Pete left Allhallows School with enough O and A-levels for entry to Sandhurst once he had passed RCB (the Regular Commissions Board exam), and from Sandhurst he joined the Gurkhas, which had been his ambition for many years. He was posted to Nepal almost immediately, and while there he met and married the girl he said he had been waiting all his life to meet: Rebecca (Beck) who was working for a charity based in Kathmandu. They were married at the Gurkha recruiting base in Pokhara with every member of camp staff invited from senior officers to clerks and cleaners. It was said to be the first wedding of a British officer at the British Army Pokhara Camp, and when both Pete and Beck made speeches in Nepali to their hundreds of guests all in spectacular finery, it was a crowning moment of applause and poignancy.

Louise had gone to join Adam in Tanzania where he now had a new wife and a small coffee farm at Arusha. Louise said the wife was very *kali* (strict) with him, but that he liked being kept on a tight rein and was a happy man again, so this was the best news of him that I could have hoped to hear. He had moved to Arusha on the mainland after finishing his contract with Mafia Coconuts, and later became one of the directors of a safari company, finding his niche at last. Louise's career flourished in Arusha with demand for her paintings of wildlife and landscapes, while the town's vibrant social life suited her gregarious personality. When she was commissioned by a travel company to paint safari scenes as publicity material, she met a dynamic young Dutchman, Bram, who was the safari manager, and the attraction was instant. He was twenty five and she was thirty five but that made no difference to the bond they felt, and they were married from Adam's house two years later.

By the time of the millennium more rooms were needed at Check House and we were advised by accountants to put the business into a limited company, with Charles and myself as joint directors. We had moved into the area of corporate banking and were suddenly seen as worthy clients after so many years as supplicants. This was a new experience and a revelation when we applied for a very big loan to add another wing and the loan was readily agreed. The new wing, completed in 2003, brought resident numbers to forty-nine and included facilities that had long been no more than hopes and dreams. These included a hairdressing salon, a restaurant with waiters and waitresses and a kitchen team with a pastry chef to make indulgent cakes and desserts – George still presiding. We were also able, at last, to have a bus for excursions and a full-time social organiser who was a jewel of a girl called Sue, to organise these and befriend anyone who might be lonely or bored. During this time a large group of Registered Nurses and qualified carers came to join us from the Philippines and were a complete delight: kind, conscientious and highly competent, they were a very welcome asset to the team, together with other staff who now came from further away when previously most had been local.

One of the waiters, from Liverpool, was popular with everyone for his cheeky banter, flirting with the ladies which put them in a flutter and they loved it. We served sherry before meals as an aperitif and wine with meals for those who wanted it, on the house, and the young waiter was all in favour of this, but complained one day: ‘Some of these old ladies are having triple sherries, and then they get naughty and want to have a touch of me.’

‘I don’t blame them,’ I said. ‘I will be joining them one day.’

By the time the second wing was completed, I was sixty-five and beginning to think it might be time to retire after nearly twenty years at Check House. After opening the new wing, Charles and I were in need of a holiday but too tired to go very far. We had never been to the Channel Islands only half an hour’s flying time from Exeter, so we booked a week in Guernsey and arrived to find golden beaches and French-style cuisine among other islands to explore within a short ferry ride. One of these was Sark, visible across a nine-mile slip of bouncy water, and we went for a day trip on a jaunty boat called Le Bon Marin de Serk. As we approached the island, after an initial hazy image we could see it boldly rising from the sea on cliffs of rock like a fortress, mysterious and compelling. The moment we stepped off the boat, some kind of magic folded itself around us and we knew instantly that this was where we wanted to be from now on. We had only to go back and collect our things to make a new home in Sark, and sell Check House to younger, fresher owners. That is how we came to live in Sark in the year two thousand and six, and I found that of all the places in the world where I had lived, this was the best one of all.

Printed in Great Britain
by Amazon

24218917R00190